The Body in Analysis

Edited by Nathan Schwartz-Salant and Murray Stein

CHIRON PUBLICATIONS • **Wilmette, Illinois**

The Chiron Clinical Series

ISBN: 0-933029-11-X

General Editors: Nathan Schwartz-Salant, Murray Stein
Managing Editor: Harriet Hudnut Halliday
Book Review Editor: Peter Mudd

Chiron Publications gratefully acknowledges the help of the Chicago Society of Jungian Analysts, the Inter-Regional Society of Jungian Analysts, and the International Association for Analytical Psychology in making this series possible.

Printed in the United States of America

Book design by Elaine M. Hill

Library of Congress Cataloging-in-Publication Data

The Body in analysis.

    Includes bibliographies.
    1. Mind and body.   2. Psychoanalysis.   I. Stein, Murray, 1943-   . II. Schwartz-Salant, Nathan, 1938- .
BF161.B565   1986   150.19′54   86-9728
ISBN 0-033029-11-X

Contents

The Chiron Clinical Series
Policy on capitalizing the term "Self"

Jung's understanding of the Self is significantly different from how this term is often used in other contemporary psychoanalytic literature. The difference hinges primarily on the understanding of archetypes: The Jungian conceptualization of the Self sees it as rooted in the transpersonal dimension. Hence the frequent capitalization of this term. Since the clinical concern with the Self often relates more narrowly to the sphere of ego-consciousness, however, it can be more mystifying than edifying always to allude to the archetypal level in the literature. Consequently the editors of *Chiron* have chosen to allow authors to exercise an option on the question of capitalization. They may choose to capitalize Self and thereby to emphasize its transpersonal, archetypal base; or, they may choose to employ the lower case, signifying by this that they are discussing issues that have to do principally with ego-identity and the personal relation to this central factor of psychic life, which may be less precisely articulated by reference to the archetypal substratum.

The Subjective Body in Clinical Practice

Donald F. Sandner

In giving our attention to the body, let us turn first to Nietzsche, who despised and suffered from his own body and thus came to know its power.

> What the sense feels, what the spirit knows, never has its end in itself. But sense and spirit would persuade you that they are the end of all things: that is how vain they are. . . . Behind them lies the self. . . . Always the self listens and seeks: it compares, overpowers, conquers, destroys. It controls, and it is in control of the ego too. Behind your thoughts and feelings, my brother, there stands a mighty ruler, an unknown sage—whose name is self. In your body he dwells; *he is your body*. (Nietzsche 1892, p. 34; italics added)

In commenting on this work, Jung was more cautious.

> To solve the problem you must give equal value. We cannot say the side of the spirit is twice as good as the other side, we must bring the pairs of opposites together in an altogether different way, where the rights of the body are just as much recognized as the rights of the spirit. (Jung 1934, p. 107)

Donald Sandner, M.D., is president-elect of the Northern California Society of Jungian Analysts and has a private practice in San Francisco, California. He is a graduate of the University of Illinois College of Medicine and took his psychiatric residency at Stanford University School of Medicine. He is the author of *Navaho Symbols of Healing* (1979) and many articles on Jungian analysis and symbolic healing.

With intuitive people, including most Jungians, the body is connected with the inferior sensation function. Such persons live too much in their heads, adrift in a seeming paradise of possibilities. They are in danger of losing connection not only with the life of the body, but with the substance of reality itself.

Anyone who has listened to long Jungian speeches on the meaning of symbolism will sympathize with Emperor Joseph II when, after listening to Mozart's opera, *The Abduction from the Seraglio*, he said to Mozart (in the film *Amadeus*):

> My dear fellow, don't take it too hard. There are in fact only so many notes [substitute "words"] the ear can hear in the course of an evening. . . . It's clever. It's German. It's quality work. And there are simply too many notes. Do you see?

I wish we could reply as Mozart did that there are just as many notes (words), neither more nor less, as are required. But I'm afraid neither we, nor Jung, are so impeccable.

To achieve such a balance of the body and spirit takes a long time. The process of individuation is not taken care of by one analysis in early adulthood. It is an ongoing work that involves, or rather becomes, one's whole life. The vistas opened up by knowledge and theory must be matched by the immediate experience of and in the body. Jung said:

> It is always a wise thing, when you discover a metaphysical truth, or find an answer to a metaphysical problem, to try it out for a month or so, whether it upsets your stomach or not; if it does, you can always be sure it is wrong. (Jung 1935, p. 41)

As one grows older this becomes even more serious; losing touch with the body means risking severe illness.

The body has an outer and an inner aspect. The outer aspect is what we see of ourselves and what other people see, hear, and touch. That is the *objective* body, the body that gets hot or cold, eats, eliminates, carries us about, gets sick, hurts, and dies. It is the beast of burden or, as Saint Francis called it, "brother ass." This aspect of the body is rigidly structured, substantial, and comparatively static.

Stanley Keleman describes another bodily aspect in *Your Body Speaks Its Mind*: "Our bodies are us as *process*, not as a thing. Structure is slowed-down process. As life builds structure it builds itself in." For him, body is in fact the everchanging expression of character: "My particular bodily form, my particular bodily feeling, is testimony to my particular character, my particular way of behaving, both psychologically and physically" (Keleman 1975, p. 66). This process must be mediated by an inwardly represented body, the *subjective* body. It is inwardly felt and experienced, but, of course, it affects the objective body in much the way Keleman describes.

There probably is an anatomical correlation to the subjective body, although making such a correlation is not essential to the basic concept of this paper. The most likely site is the visceral brain (limbic system) which, according to Papez's work (1958), is identified with emotional, sexual, autonomic, visceral, and olfactory mechanisms. The limbic system "seems to set the emotional background on which man functions intellectually" (Cobb 1950, p. 25), and is closely connected with the highly developed part of the brain, the neocortex. What a person *knows* is a function of the neocortex; what he *feels* may be said to be mediated by the visceral brain (Anand 1957).

According to Fordham, "the essential core that emerges from Jung's work is that an archetype is a psychosomatic entity having two aspects; the one is linked closely with physical organs, the other with unconscious and potential psychic structures" (Fordham 1969, p. 96). The archetype must integrate the two components.

The subjective body is in fact such an archetype. This *inwardly felt body*, charged with emotion and sexuality, mediates biological drive and spiritual longing. It expresses these in a *specific* inner image, which is alive with fantasy, and seeks to be lived by the whole of one's self. It is more real psychologically than the objective external body. Without its emotional stimulation the external body would be an inert lump, alive but expressionless.

Let me illustrate what this means by a clinical example. In his recently published *Visions Seminars* (1976), Jung presents the case of Christiana Morgan, a woman of about thirty when she was his patient. Jung tells us that she was a thinking, intuitive type with an inferior feeling function, but he says almost nothing about her personal life. What he does tell us and what emerges from her dreams, visionary texts, and watercolor drawings is the story of her inner passion. To reveal this story, even in symbolic form, is an exquisitely intimate disclosure. To recount how it was lived out in personal life was, for both the patient and the analyst, too painful. But from other sources we have some indications that it was emotionally lived out, both in the transference and in life.

These visions, Jung said, are

> like telegraphic communications from the unconscious, rather bloodless. Yet if you dwell on them and pour some blood into them, you can recognize their relation to important things. . . . For only through our efforts do these

things speak to us at all. We are inclined to pass on without realizing what we see. (Jung 1976, Book 2, p. 366)

The visionary material from Christiana Morgan's case is voluminous, but I want to cite just enough of the text and images to illustrate the nature of this archetypal process. In an early seminar at Polzeath, Cornwall (1923), Jung describes four main integral parts of the psyche that had been repressed and denied by modern man, oftentimes in compliance with religion. These parts are nature, animals, primitive man, and creative fantasy. They can be lumped together to characterize a natural, primitive part of the psyche that gives rise to spontaneous fantasy. It is in relation to these basic elements that the true inner life of the body is lived.

This was certainly so with Christiana Morgan. Since she lived so much in her head (thinking and intuitive functions), the whole impetus of her visionary process was to connect her ideas with her body and its natural feeling. The direction of her fantasy was earthward. In his short biographical essay on her, Henry Murray tells us that she was a favorite of her father, and often accompanied him in his intellectual pursuits. Murray says they were "bound together by a secret reciprocal understanding" that resulted in a "durable father complex with a readiness to exalt a series of passionate thinkers," among whom were Alfred North Whitehead, Morton Prince, Henry Murray himself, and of course, Jung (Jung 1976, Book 2, pp. 517–21). The course of her early life led her to the discipleship and adoration of these brilliant men. One of them, Carl Jung, led her back to reclaim her feminine being. That is what the overall vision series is about.

Very early in this series of visions, she went downward and backward in time. Her animus, in the form of an American Indian, led the way. She went down past various images until she saw the face of an animal. It was a furry, featureless face except for the prominent eyes. She spoke to it saying, "Look into my eyes that I may behold them," and then the face became dark, and "slowly I beheld what no man is meant to see, eyes full of beauty and woe and light, and I could bear it no longer" (Jung 1976, Book 1, p. 62).

Jung says: "She looks directly in the eyes of the animal . . . for they contain the truth of life, as equal sum of pain and pleasure, the capacity for joy and the capacity for suffering. . . ." He notes also that "she is positively stung; up to now she has been sightseeing, but here it gets under her skin" (Jung 1976, Book 1, p. 63). He means that this is not merely an idea; it has evoked an intense emotional response in her subjective body, and now the inner life is activated.

A little later in the visions, she saw a satyr who had green eyes and

> flames falling upon his breast. . . . He stood with the palms of his hands up-raised to me. He tore his hair from his breast and threw it upwards. As he did so the hair turned into little flames. Then it became dark. (Jung 1976, Book 1, pp. 69–70)

Jung says: "These are symbols of emotion, she is just tingling with emotion, a lot of little flames ready to burst into a big flame" (Jung 1976, Book 1, p. 70). We are justified, I think, in connecting this repressed emotion to the "secret reciprocal understanding" with her father, which has now become transferred to Jung. But because it was incestuous, it must be repressed, and nothing happens. The satyr she paints has no genitals. The satyr gives her a blue robe and a necklace of pearls with which he bestows upon her an exalted form of femininity, but that is not enough. She is ready to burst into the full flame of emotional and sexual love, but first she must descend farther into herself and into her basic feminine nature.

In another vision she drops down into the lap of the ancient mother, after which the Indian guide

> spilt some blood upon my head and my robe became scarlet. And a great swirl of blood encompassed me, vibrating with a strange and terrible throbbing. . . . I lay back in the swirl which carried me upward in spirals. . . . I passed the white face of God. I saw the sun and I saw a pool of gold. . . . Then I was in a dark forest. The swirl of a flaming red surrounded the forest, I could perceive it through the trees. . . . My robe changed to green and my feet sank into the soft earth. I lifted my hands and leaves grew from them. Then I knew that I had become a tree and lifted my face to the sun. (Jung 1976, Book 1, pp. 93–99)

Here she is no longer in the form of an observer, however moved that observer may be, nor is she in the aspect of her youthful male animus who enters the action for her. She is completely drawn into the experience as her self. After she has been baptized in blood, she goes inside the blood and becomes a living tree which is, for Jung, the symbol of slow spiritual growth. With roots in the darkness below and leaves thrust up into the sunlight, she has entered an embodiment of archetypal union, the shamanic tree, which unites heaven and earth. She has penetrated into her self.

Later, after other images of this kind, she encounters the chthonic masculine. The text says, "I beheld a Negro lying beneath a tree. In his hand were fruits. He was singing with a full throaty voice" (Jung 1976, Book 1, p. 136).

He is the black messiah, the dark god within, who has been repressed but who is now awake, offering her the fruits of his body and her own. The vision continues:

> "Must I know you?" He answered: "Whether you know me or not, I am." I asked him: "Oh Negro, what do you sing?" He answered me: "Little white child, I sing to the darkness, to flaming fields, to the children within your womb." While he sang blood poured from his heart in slow and rhythmic beats. It flowed along in a stream covering my feet. I followed the stream of blood. . . . It led down and down. At last I found myself in a rocky cavern beneath the earth. It was very dark. I saw a glowing fire. Above the fire I saw a phoenix bird which continually flew up and beat its head against the top of the cavern. The fire created small snakes which disappeared. It also created men and women. I asked the bird: "Where do they go?" The bird answered: "Away, away." The bird said: "Stand in the fire, woman." I said: "I cannot, it will burn me." Again the bird commanded me. I did so and the flames leapt up, burning my robe. At last I stood naked. (Jung 1976, Book 1, pp. 140–42)

What is this cavern to which the blood stream leads her? In Jung's commentary it is the abdomen. She has descended into her inner subjective body, visualized as a psychic location. She has entered the place from which life springs forth, the maternal womb, symbolized by the phoenix, the fire, the snakes, and the creation of men and women. Here, too, is the fount of primordial energy, the transforming fire, sometimes called kundalini. She reluctantly exposes herself to that fiery bath, and becomes her full, naked, feminine self, no longer obscured by denial and repression. She is completely in her body.

The vision goes further: "At length I heard the Negro descending. . . . He opened the door of the cavern. He laughed when he saw me. He said: 'Now you are wedded to me'" (Jung 1976, Book 1, pp. 148–49).

This inner union, filled with passion, restores the feminine inner body to its connection with the sacredness of the spirit and primordial sexuality. If her sense of this passion becomes conscious, it can become a reality in her life. The two archetypal dominants of her inner life, the ancient mother and the black fertility god, can now assert their powers. Through the contact with a powerful man (Jung), she can now seek in other men the projected passion of the dark animus. But it would seem that further contact with a strong woman, either in life or in therapy, would be necessary for her to feel within herself the fullness of the mother. Then these awakened archetypes could be lived out physically and emotionally. Perhaps the absence of the influence of the woman, and Jung's unawareness of this dimension, was the hidden factor that gave this analysis its somewhat unsatisfactory ending. Perhaps it was only half done.

Another view of the subjective body that brings the archetypal dimension into direct focus is found in Te Paske's work, *Rape and Ritual* (1982). In this book, Te Paske discusses both actual criminal rape and the intrapsychic compulsion. He shows how the body, compelled to express itself in fantasy or action, can be released by an inner sacrifice.

> The present psychological perspective views the impulse behind concrete rape and the intrapsychic fantasy of rape as the dynamic drive of the individuation process, regardless of how crude or concrete the attempt or fantasy may be. This dynamic instinctual/spiritual drive carries within it sexuality, power, and an indeterminable number of other components— including an irreducible religious instinct. (Te Paske 1982, p. 71)

The most important case in the book is that of a young man in his late twenties who demonstrates in his dreams the structure of the rapist personality. In the case, ego consciousness is strong enough to contain the fantasies and prevent the acting out of the compulsion, but the young man has a split shadow of major proportions that causes intense suffering.

I would like to describe this structure in terms of split-complex theory (Sandner and Beebe 1982). The split is always between two shadow, or ego-aligned, complexes (this refers to all complexes that are *potentially* a part of the ego), and can only be described in terms of opposite qualities. Commonly one side of the split is a sensitive, spiritual side, usually inflated, which is also weak, puerile, and closely tied to the mother. The other side (the one usually meant by the term *shadow*) contains the qualities of primitive masculinity. It is often represented by the dark man, the beast, the burglar, or the rapist, but it also contains strength, earthiness, and bodily reality. This part of the shadow complex is intimately related to the body and the instinctual longings that arise from the body. In other words, this side contains raw masculinity waiting to be initiated by the father.

In the case we are discussing, the young man is identified with the spiritual, but puerile, side, thus leaving him prey to the unconscious power of his repressed, primitive masculinity. This is expressed in a part of one of his dreams as follows:

> Dream: *I am the functionary of a Dracula-like madman, a kind of spiritual rapist, who is in my mother's bed in a totally dark room. There is a woman whom he is intent on claiming, on making insane and endlessly psychotic. His face is gore and blood and dark-*

*ness. I am taking care of the woman for him. . . . Her face is filled
with a deep and uncomprehending terror. I and the madman seek
to totally claim women's souls.* (Te Paske 1982, p. 121)

In such a case, there is the concern that this shadow complex will unconsciously possess not only the ego (as described in the dream), but also
the inner body and its autonomous sexuality.

When the shadow complex is split in this way, the anima complex is
also split. On one side is the dominant mother-related anima complex
that holds the inflated, puerile side of the shadow in thrall. Since the ego
in this case is primarily identified with that part, it is thus prevented from
identifying with the father. The other side of the anima complex is the
wounded but sensitive and tender part. It is the feminine anima that has
separated from the mother. In the structure of the rapist personality, as
Te Paske shows, this side is represented by the woman who is the victim.
In the dream previously cited, it would be "the woman whom he is intent
on claiming, on making insane and endlessly psychotic."

There is a specific development here that is unique to the personality of the rapist. The sensitive, wounded side of the anima becomes partially fused with the inflated, puerile side of the ego-aligned shadow complex. Thus part of the *potential identity* of such a man is the maiden
who is the victim. This is an essentially homosexual element in his
personality, which is loved, hated, and feared by the powerful, repressed
masculine side. It is loved because it is part of the feminine anima; it is
hated because it is also part of his puerile identity.

The hypothesis of this paper is that there is an archetypal structure
—the subjective body—that is affected by this entire psychic constellation and sums it up, so to speak, or symbolizes it in the image of the
specific sexual act of rape. By means of the subjective body archetype,
this symbolized act engenders sexual longing and readiness in the physical body for the concrete act itself.

Thus rape is the two powerfully antithetical feelings of love and hate,
felt by one part of the psyche toward another part, and fused into the one
brutal act. To break up this fusion, the maiden part of the ego-aligned
shadow complex must be freed from the inflated puerile side. If this is
not to be done brutally through actual rape, it must be done as an inward
ritual sacrifice of the maiden. This must be a fully conscious experience,
mediated by the inner subjective body with accompanying feelings of humiliation, terror, and relief. Then it will be part of the masculine initiation process, which can be accomplished only in relationship to an adequate father, or in therapy in relationship to an adequate therapist. If it is

successful, this sacrifice clears the way for further individuation. (I have not done justice here to the case as presented in the book, with its many clearly illustrative dreams. I would like to present more, but I urge you to read the book instead.)

In order to demonstrate this process more fully, I would like to present a case of my own in which similar dynamics show how the re-pressed side of a young man's primitive masculinity enters into him through the medium of the subjective body as it is represented in a dream.

The patient is a 23-year-old man who, four years prior to our first meeting, had developed lymphatic leukemia. He came from another city, but had moved to the Bay Area to get the best possible chemotherapy and to assert his independence from his family, who were trying to protect him. He found lodging in a communal setting and was proud of his abil-ity to be one of the group despite his illness.

At the time he consulted me, his illness had entered an acute phase. The chemotherapy was no longer effective. He looked thin and pale, and he felt he was going to die soon. What he hoped to gain from therapy was not to cure the disease, which he already knew was impossible, but to help him die, as he put it, "like a mensch."

He spent most of the first hour telling me of a very deep, but one-sided, love affair during his adolescence with a girl from his high school class. She liked him well enough and dated him some, but did not return his love. She rejected him as gently as she could, but nevertheless dealt him a lasting wound. It was clear to him that he had never emotionally re-covered from this disappointment, and that he connected this in some way with his illness. There was some vaguely expressed intuition that be-cause of the pain of this trauma, he no longer wished to live.

In this first hour he also told me a dream.

Dream: *I'm in a grassy field. It's dark. Twenty people are forming a round circle—as in college—a sort of dance. Suddenly there is a frenzy. A big, dark man pursues me and knocks me down. Then he stands over me with a long, pointed knife. He says some-thing to me, then lets me up. I run up in the grandstand as if it were an athletic field at college. At the top is a fence and outside the sta-dium I see an athletic ritual of some kind. It seems to be some kind of male initiation.*

We did not have time to talk much about his associations to the dream, but for me the entire session was a deeply emotional experience.

I was not just sorry for him—as one might expect—but closely tuned in to what he was really asking for.

The meaning of the dream, even without associations, seemed remarkably clear. In the first part of the dream, he was with college students of his own age who formed a circle as a collective group, but he was outside waiting to get in. The dark man was a powerful aspect of himself, an active shadow complex that threatened him with aggressive violence. Ordeal and risk of death are always a part of masculine initiatory symbolism. He ran away, but his escape was blocked. He was not only locked in, but also locked out, because the male initiation he sought was taking place beyond the fence.

In the second session about a week later he seemed quite eager to be there and immediately recounted another dream.

> Dream: *I'm in an industrial section of the city at twilight or dusk. It's reminiscent of the atmosphere of my hometown. I'm possibly with another person for a while.*
>
> *I walk into a factory setting. It is an open garage, empty except for a fork lift turned at right angles to my path, blocking the way. There are two passengers on the fork lift. I cannot see their faces, but I see the back of the man and he is wearing a thick, black, woolen stocking cap. He is reclining; his attitude is one of arrogance and defiance. With him is a woman. I hear their voices, and I assume they are black.*
>
> *I walk into another different section, a hotel lobby. It is modern and there are lots of people. A glass elevator carries people to upper floors and down again to the ground floor. It carries them between the ground floor and the 14th floor. A large line queues up; impatience hovers over the crowd. The elevator arrives unbeknownst to the crowd. A middle-aged woman (my mother) jumps in and I follow her. We press the 14th button and the thing takes off. We're the only passengers. By the time we reach the 14th floor, I've lost my wallet.*

This dream also had that special clarity that develops when therapist and patient are on the same wavelength, but he also had a few associations. The first part presented an atmosphere of depression and death. There was just such an atmosphere in the therapy room, and he and I both agreed that I was the other person.

The fork lift and the garage both made him think of the gross, mechanical aspects of living. The obstruction implied a reference to his illness. He thought of the man as an arrogant, defiant shadow figure who was also black. The woman was with him, and there was the feeling of a sexual bond between them. If they saw him, he felt they might humiliate, threaten, or attack him. He felt hopeless.

In the third section, the dreamer was prepared to go up (the spiritual direction) in the glass elevator. He again felt he would be exposed to ridicule. He pushed ahead of the crowd, out of his rightful place in line, and jumped in with his mother. When they reached the 14th floor (reference to age?) he lost his wallet. I conjectured to myself that it was really an underlying bond with his mother that made his high school love affair so tragic and led to a loss of his male identity (wallet). This session ended leaving us with a better understanding of his condition, but no sense of direction in how to approach it therapeutically.

At the last session he brought in a final dream.

> Dream: *I am lying in my bed. There is the shadow of a man over me—forceful—full of sexual energy—dark. He descends over my body. I feel vulnerable. I'm on my back and he descends over my body, drags his body over mine, and I feel the energy well up in his loins. It seems as if he is going to rape me, but then he melts into me instead. He becomes me.*

The dream was filled with energy, and the patient looked and acted more alive. It was plain to us that the dark, masculine figure was the same as in the first two dreams. Although the homosexual element in the dream made him somewhat apprehensive, he realized that the goal of the dream was not sexual, but a fusion with a powerful dream figure. I thought that the complex containing his primitive masculinity was actually integrated not only in his consciousness, but also in his inner, subjective body. The dream was archetypal and represented an initiation into manhood. I told him that he had taken on a powerful part of himself, and that this would now be available to him.

There was a sense of completion about this last dream. In any case, his deteriorating condition made it necessary for him to return home to be cared for. I learned that about six months later he died, very much as he wished, with great courage.

What emerges from these cases is the concept of the subjective body as a structural archetype of the psyche on a par with the ego, the persona, the shadow, the anima/us, and the self. By the term *subjective body* I do not mean an occult or subtle body or even a dream body (although these would be closely related phenomena), but an actual *representation and localization of bodily emotion and sexuality as an image in the psyche.* This image may not be a literal one, but a highly symbolic representation.

The subjective body is the archetype through which the psyche influences the objective body, and vice versa. Sometimes the image is very particular, involving specific areas or actions of the body.

In the first example from Jung's *Visions Seminars*, the patient followed a stream of blood down into a rocky cavern beneath the earth. As Jung points out, that is her abdomen, an image of the subjective body into which the patient's ego descended. This is a new emotional experience of the body that may then become available to her.

The subjective body may also be charged with the feeling and image of a specific sexual act. In the second example from Te Paske's book, the complex psychic structure I outlined is represented or symbolized in the subjective body as the specific sexual act of rape. The concomitant emotional charge produces a longing for acting out that is nearly irresistible. Te Paske has shown how, through analysis, changes in the image structure of the subjective body may take place to obviate the compulsion to rape.

The third example from my own case shows how the physical body can be almost literally represented in the psyche as the subjective body. Here it is entered by a powerful complex, the black man. The image is of a sexual act, but it symbolizes an abrupt change in the young man's experience of his body as a sexual and emotional entity. In this case, we can begin to make out the role of sexuality as a bridge between body and spirit. The dark man is not only a repressed, personal complex, he is also a representative of the chthonic masculine archetype that opens the way to sexuality. Mythologically speaking, he is a phallic fertility god, basically the same as the dark man who appears in the visions of Christiana Morgan. In both cases he fascinates, penetrates, and fuses. That way the subjective body (and by extension, the objective body also) is permanently changed. In therapy, this principle works in intimate association with the transference.

The role of the body in relation to the transference/countertransference has been described in a recent paper by Barbara Stevens (1984, unpublished). She makes a bridge between the alchemical symbolism found in Jung's later works and the concrete events in the therapeutic process. Regarding the transference, she says:

> And this brings me to the central technical point I want to underline about the transference experience: what is crucially important about it is that it be lived as intensely as possible. It is all right to interpret it, provided that the interpretation is not in the service of holding off a full emotional experience of it. It is that full emotional experience that is the primary healing factor. As he lives out this powerful affective drama the patient builds up his emotional

muscles and expands his capacity to have his whole emotional response in situations outside the office as well.

But this must be very concrete. As Stevens goes on to say, "If I could share her experience of life, if I could take that experience *into my body* and vicariously live it for the fifty minutes we spent together, I could reflect her wholeness back to her by embodying it" (italics added).

I would conclude then that the transference/countertransference engagement is a real, emotional experience that is reflected inwardly (consciously or not) as accompanying images much like those Jung presented in the *Psychology of the Transference* (Jung 1946). While outwardly two people sit in the therapy room, relatively quiet and inactive, inwardly there is the image of two persons in intense emotional interaction—a baby being suckled, a child being played with, two persons of the same or different sex engaged in passionate embrace. At some point in the therapy they penetrate and fuse into one another. They die in this way (that is, they lose their structure) and are reborn (or re-formed) into a new inner entity.

The images of the interactions mentioned above can be infinitely varied, but they are, as Jung pointed out, always incestuous. It is always a family relationship and never a straightforward marriage. Thus it can never be acted out without destruction of the basic therapeutic process. But at the same time, without the transference/countertransference interaction, the therapeutic process is almost impotent. We do best if the transference/countertransference process is encouraged, made conscious, fully experienced, and *contained*. It must also be real. As Wallace Stevens said:

> There is the insistence on a reality that forces itself upon our consciousness and refuses to be managed and mastered. . . . the supreme virtue here is humility, for the humble are they that move around the world with the love of the real in their hearts. (1984)

If we can emotionally embody and re-create this reality for the patient, then we fully merit our archetypal role as healer or shaman.

The subjective body can also facilitate symbolic healing. During the healing rituals in some tribal cultures, such as that of the American Indian, the physical body itself can become a symbolic representation of the inner subjective body. In the ritual, the two are symbolically united. Thus, by performing ritual symbolic acts upon the physical body, the subjective body is directly affected. Almost all tribal healing depends upon this process.

A clear illustration is found in the Navaho culture in the use of sand paintings for healing. In the ceremony, the gods and the holy beings represented in the paintings are evoked. By means of prayers and songs, their power is directed into the sand figures. When the patient sits on one of the sand figures, the power flows into him. At that moment in the ritual, his unclothed body is not only the objective body, but a symbol for the inner subjective body as well. The gods, whom we would see as archetypal components of the collective unconscious, and the subjective body are thus inwardly brought together in the psyche. The healing power flows between them.

Let me take as my final example the American Indian ritual of the sweat-lodge. Hartley Burr Alexander, an American philosopher and anthropologist, says of it:

> No rite of the Indian leads us more directly into this spirit past than does that of the sweat-lodge and bath, one of the most widespread of Indian customs. In its typical form it is a rite of purification and healing, undertaken both to restore and to maintain bodily health, but undertaken more generally as a preliminary for participation in religious exercise. (1953, p. 46)

The sweat-lodge itself is a frame of bent willow saplings in the shape of a half-dome covered by skins, blankets, or tarpaulins, and large enough to hold twelve to fifteen people seated in a circle. The covering must be tight enough to exclude all light. In the center is a fire-pit scooped out of the earth, large enough to hold six or seven fairly large rocks. Outside in front of the lodge is a large ceremonially-made fire in which the rocks are heated until they are hot and glowing. Everyone who is to attend strips down and enters the lodge on hands and knees. The leader sits inside the door and is in complete charge of all movements once the ceremony has begun. Since the rite of the sweat house has four parts, there is one person among the participants to represent each of the four directions.

When everyone is seated inside, the leader calls for the rocks; the fire assistants bring them in and place them in the central pit. The rocks are handled with deer antlers. Then the door flap is closed and the lodge is in complete darkness except for the glowing rocks. Then the songs, accompanied by the steady beat of the drum and the gourd rattles, are sung for the first round, which is dedicated to the east. They are a call to the spirits to attend the ceremony. At a certain time, the leader throws water on the rocks and the entire lodge is filled with scalding steam. The heat is almost unbearable, and the initial reaction is one of panic. Some small inner voice says, "Let's get out of here!" but the observing ego, noticing that those who have done this before do not seem frightened, decrees that one stay. There is nothing to be done but accept the fear and pain, and join in the songs welcoming the spirits. After what seems a very long time, but is probably no more than fifteen minutes, the first round is over. The tent flap is thrown open to let in the outside air, which feels like balm. After the tent flap is raised the participants may go out into the cool air, but it is better to stay inside and preserve the power.

The second round is concerned with the heart. New hot stones are shoveled in and the tent flap is again closed. Water is thrown on the rocks, and the effect is soon one of unbearable heat and suffocation. Songs are sung by the person representing the south, and anyone may express his or her deepest feelings. As the steam becomes more dense, one can feel consciousness slipping, and the discomfort begins to give way to tears and deep emotion moving imperceptibly from pain to ecstasy.

Finally the tent flap is raised again and the second quarter is over. This is the midpoint and everyone goes outside into the cold air. The feelings of relief and eagerness for more are strangely mixed.

The third quarter is devoted to healing and remembering those in need. Again new rocks are brought in, and more water produces dense steam. The person in the west starts the singing and chanting, accompanied by the drum and the rattle–two effective instruments for altering consciousness. For many, this time is the worst. There is a strong feeling of death. The steam is so hot that almost everyone must put his face down to the muddy ground in order to breathe. Now one is very much a child of the earth; one feels very much the nakedness of body and spirit with which one enters the world and leaves it. At this time of extreme vulnerability, the mind is open for healing.

The fourth and final session is for giving thanks. This belongs to the north. The same procedure is followed as for the other cardinal points. This time, however, although the rocks are just as hot and the steam is just as dense, there is a feeling of having been through the worst. There is an inner release, and a feeling of physical and mental calm.

I hope this short vignette will give you a feeling for this ceremony wherein symbolism and the body are so intimately connected. This is only one of the many forms of the sweat-lodge rite, which is a healing ceremony of great power. It produces regression or (mythologically speaking) a return to the origin. One cannot help becoming a child—if not an infant—again, awash in tears and mud. The feeling of the oneness with the earth is truly physical, and the gratitude for life is felt with one's whole body.

There is also a purification. The body is cleansed through the sweat, and the mind through the pain. Afterwards everyone jumps in the cold mountain steam without discomfort, and the bad stuff (symbolizing evil) is washed away. There is definitely a strong transference to the leader, the medicine man, who not only throws water on the stones, causing pain, but also protects and keeps each participant safe during this ordeal.

The whole process is one of death and rebirth. The ego gives up its supremacy and occupies itself with endurance. In the face of the spirit of the sweat-lodge, one loses one's petty concerns and merges into the group, the community, and the cosmos. Each time the steam fills the lodge, one dies a little; bodily participation makes this real. When one emerges at the end, to be returned to the light and the sweet coolness of the world, the feeling can only be described as deliverance.

One of the main reasons for my interest in the rituals of the American Indians is their simplicity and the use of predominantly natural substances such as earth, water, fire, wood, stone, and sand. They stay close to nature and to bodily reality. For us these rituals, however hard they are to translate into our cultural terms, contain a secret treasure that is still effective, healing, and life-giving not only for the Indians, but for all who will try to understand them. Their natural quality of bodily and emotional reality is exactly what we Jungians lack.

The cases and viewpoints I have described from Jung, Te Paske, Stevens, and myself point the way to the reintroduction of bodily and emotional reality into our analytic sessions. We cannot make sand paintings, dance with feathered wands, or chant prayers over our patients. What we can do is to stay close to the basic principle that no real change takes place unless it occurs not only in the mind, but also in the body. This is done in all cases through the activation of an archetype that integrates the physical and psychic components—the subjective body.

This archetype converts psychological conditions into bodily responses; it also converts emotional, psychic states into specific bodily sexual longings. It may also use the physical body, as in the American Indian example, to symbolize an archetypal process. In this way it ensures that the life of the mind will in some way be lived out by the body. To complete the opening quotation from Nietzsche: "There is more reason in your body than in your best wisdom. And who knows why your body needs precisely your best wisdom?" (Nietzsche 1892, p. 34).

References

Alexander, H. B. 1953. *The world's rim*. Lincoln: University of Nebraska Press.
Anand, B. K. 1957. *Indian Journal of Physiology and Pharmacology* 1:149.
Cobb, S. 1950. *Emotions and clinical medicine*. New York: Norton.

Fordham, M. 1969. *Children as individuals*. London: Hodder and Stoughton.
Jung, C. G. 1934–39. Psychological analysis of Nietzsche's Zarathustra. Unpublished seminar
    notes. Recorded and mimeographed by Mary Foote.
——————. 1946. The psychology of the transference. In *Collected works* 16:163–
    323. Princeton: Princeton University Press, 1966.
——————. 1976. *The visions seminars*, Books 1 and 2. Spring Publications: Zurich.
Keleman, S. 1975. *Your body speaks its mind*. New York: Simon and Schuster.
Nietzsche, F. 1892. *Thus spake Zarathustra*. Translated by Walter Kaufmann. Baltimore:
    Penguin Books, 1978.
Papez, J. W. 1958. In H. H. Jasper et al., *Reticular formation of the brain*, Boston: Little,
    Brown.
Sandner, D., and Beebe, J. 1982. Psychopathology and analysis. In M. Stein, ed., *Jungian
    analysis*, pp. 294–334. La Salle, Ill., and London: Open Court.
Stevens, B. 1984. Transference and countertransference: A Jungian view. Unpublished paper
    presented at second Freud-Jung symposium, San Francisco.
Stevens, W. 1984. On poetic truth. Quoted by Mark Linenthal in *American Poetry Archive
    News*, vol. 2.
Te Paske, B. 1982. *Rape and ritual: A psychological study*. Toronto: Inner City Books.

On the Subtle-Body Concept in Clinical Practice

Nathan Schwartz-Salant

There are certain experiences in the analytic setting for which interpretation or amplification plays far less a role than the direct discovery of
unconscious factors that control the analytical process. To a large degree
these experiences, which take place between myself and the analysand,
call upon our so-called adult sides, or, in other terms, the therapeutic alliance. I have come to believe that the *form* in which one searches for an
unconscious controlling factor has a good deal to do with creating and
strengthening this alliance. Here I shall be concerned with the unconscious *couple*, and generally I shall be dealing with male-female imagery.

An unconscious couple is sometimes discovered in memories related to parental interactions. Often these were tortuous events, which
became a familial way of life. A child may have tried to protect one parent
from the other, or himself or herself from both. Such experiences
formed a continual traumatic process, which then became an unconscious model for life. Frequently they become imbedded in the psyche as

Nathan Schwartz-Salant, Ph.D., University of California, Berkeley, and Diploma in
Analytical Psychology, C. G. Jung Institute, Zurich, practices as a Jungian analyst in New York
City, where he is on the faculty of the C. G. Jung Training Center. He is a past president of
the National Association for the Advancement of Psychoanalysis (NAAP) and is the author of
*Narcissism and Character Transformation: The Psychology of Narcissistic Character Disor-
ders* (1982).

images of a sado/masochistic couple. Traumatic experiences, as Levi-Strauss noted in his analysis of healing in primitive cultures, have a capacity "to induce an emotional crystallization which is molded by pre-existing structure" (1967, pp. 198–99). These structures, in this case negative, are fusion forms of the archetypal union known as the *coniunctio* in alchemy. They are "truly a-temporal" (ibid.). At times we can discover, and imaginally experience, these underlying archetypal structures and eventually regain them in positive forms.

The essence of what I want to convey here is as follows. First there is the discovery of an unconscious couple. Two people can then become aware of the fact that while they believed they were behaving in a conscious manner, their feelings and actions were to a large degree being organized by an unconscious couple, managing them as though they were obedient machines. Second, there is the crucial question—the main concern, actually—of *where* this couple exists. It can exist as internal structure in the patient or in the analyst. But there is a third possibility, which to me has unusual merit: *This couple may exist in the space between.* Exploring the qualities of this space, which is akin to but also different from Winnicott's description of transitional space, leads to the long-discarded notion of the subtle body.

The Subtle-Body Concept

"The notion that the physical body of man is as it were the exteriorization of an invisible subtle embodiment of the life of the mind is a very ancient belief." With these words written in 1919, G. R. S. Mead introduced his book *The Doctrine of the Subtle Body in Western Tradition.* His comments are still cogent:

> It is, however, the prevailing habit of sceptical rationalism of the present day to dismiss summarily all such beliefs of antiquity as the baseless dreams of a pre-scientific age. . . . I am persuaded that, the more deeply modern research penetrates into the more recondite regions of biology, psycho-physiology and psychology, the more readily will reason be inclined to welcome the notion as a fertile working hypothesis to co-ordinate a considerable number of the mental, vital and physical phenomena of human personality which otherwise remain on our hands as a confused and inexplicable conglomerate. (1919, pp. 1–2)

The subtle body can be experienced imaginally as a kind of energy field that extends outwards from our physical being. It is invisible to ordinary perceptions, but can be seen imaginally. Through clinical material, I shall show how it appears in the context of two people in analysis. Their subtle bodies can interact and manifest in states of fusion, or (the extreme opposite) in a state of separation that can become extremely afflicted and persecutory in its soullessness. They may also interact in the *coniunctio*, that mysterious state described by Winnicott in which separation is not a separation but a form of union (1971, pp. 97–98).

Before further explaining why I find it important to consider the subtle-body concept as clinically useful, I wish to take note of A. Mindell's book *Dreambody* (1982). Mindell has shown how phenomena that we normally consider to be psychic and relate to as affect-toned images can also be approached from a more embodied point of view. In a sense, Mindell took up a distinction that Jung made between the psychic and somatic unconscious in his unpublished *Seminars* on Nietzsche's *Thus Spake Zarathustra* (1934–39), where he carefully showed how psychic imagery could be reflected through the somatic unconscious.

It is not the existence of the subtle body that should be at issue. We are at that stage in our development, as predicted by Mead and exemplified, for example, by Mindell's work, at which we can be relatively comfortable with an attitude that is rooted in the reality of the imagination. When we deal with the subtle body, we are concerned not with ordinary perceptions, but with imaginal ones. Those who can *see* will do so; others will remain skeptical. There are clinicians, however, who are quite aware of the existence of such subtle body phenomena but who also question the suitability of the concept for clinical practice. That is a far more important issue. Is the notion of the subtle body deleterious in that it may shift attention away from the importance of the physical body, especially of body energies and associated sexual states of mind in analysis? Is the subtle body so impossible to explain in terms that are communicable as to run the danger of our clinical efforts becoming mired in confusion that is passed off as mystery?

The phenomena I shall be considering do not require any change of the normal analytical attitude or setting. In fact, they are enhanced and properly controlled by it. There is a great deal of wisdom in the analytical attitude, especially in its concern with dreams and with transference material. But I think we are at that stage that Ferenzci spoke of when he said we must return to animism on a new level, after we have integrated psychoanalytic understanding (Brown 1959, p. 315).

Two people can become aware of a state in which their subtle bodies are interacting. This is often felt as a change in the quality of space between them; it is experienced as energized and more material in nature. They are then at the threshold of an awareness of archetypal processes, a *mundus imaginalis*, as it was designated by Henry Corbin (1972, pp. 1–19). Recently, Andrew Samuels (1985, pp. 58–59) has pursuasively argued that "there is a two-person or shared *mundus imaginalis* which is constellated in analysis." This imaginal realm is what Jung, following tradition, called the *Unus Mundus* (1963, par. 759), and what David Bohm in physics, devising his own terminology, has called the *implicate order* (1980, pp. 172–73).

By this Bohm means a primary level of reality, with its own laws, not yet fully understood, and out of which the world as we know it, the separate events in a space-time framework, manifests as the *explicate order*. The *implicate order* is characterized by Oneness, whose essence is carried throughout the implicate order. It has a holographic structure, through which any part contains the whole. Events in the *explicate order* enter the implicate order and are, in Bohm's terms, *enfolded* there so that they spread over the entire *implicate order* (1980, pp. 177–79). As these appear in time-space, they separate out again as discrete events. Bohm's position is that we must reorient our thinking back toward such notions of order and away from our Cartesian models if we are to ever make sense of the physical universe. So far as I can tell, his position is a restatement of the ancient notion of a *Unus Mundus* structured by archetypes, but with attention to the interaction between this unitary world and space-time events. As his ideas develop we may find more and more importance in them for psychological models. His special contribution, for our purposes, lies in his fresh view of the subject and in his critique of the limits of Newtonian and Cartesian approaches that still, I may add, dominate most thinking in psychoanalysis, especially in object relations theory.

Whether we deal with complexes, or with developmental stages such as the depressive position, Mahler's separation-individuation process with its rapprochement crises, oedipal levels, and so forth, we are dealing with what can be observed or inferred in time-space considerations. But these are only fragments that stem from a vastly larger process of the *Unus Mundus*. This, to paraphrase Bohm, is a "vast energy sea" (1980, p. 191–92). Its processes can be imaginally grasped and known through mutual subtle-body experience.

The central structure of the background realm that can be encountered by two people through subtle-body experience is the *coniunctio*, an archetypal form of union. This is often an event and an ensuing process felt to occur in a space that is at least partially created by their subtle bodies. When the *coniunctio* is an active, imaginal experience, both people will feel a sense of alternately being pulled together towards fusion, and then pulled apart towards separation, while in the realm between them there is a continual sense of unity. The *coniunctio* experience has this rhythmic quality, which is characteristic of archetypal processes. It is a form of union characteristic of this level of reality, and it can be known and experienced in the kind of subtle-body interactions I am here concerned with.

Experiencing the *coniunctio* is a source of healing for developmental failures in those key phases in personality development in which opposites combine, for example, the depressive position and the rapprochement subphase of the separation-individuation process. Such subtle-body encounters strengthen psychic structure and build a firmer mind-body unity, one which is less afflicted by splitting and defensive projective identification.

The Subtle Body as an Intermediate Realm

Jungians have given attention to the body in the past (Whitmont 1972, pp. 5–16), and this interest has lately increased (Green 1984, pp. 2–24; Woodman 1984, pp. 25–37; Chodorow 1984, pp. 39–48). Clinical material can often be approached with reference to either body or psyche. For example, a 23-year-old male, suffering from occasional impotence, complaining of extreme inertia, masturbatory compulsions, and an inability to control his use of marijuana, recalled the following childhood experience. At the age of seven he became frightened by the Popeye character called Alice the Goon. At night he would imagine her in his bedroom. She would be immense, and this terrified him. The only way he could protect himself against her was by pulling the covers tightly up to his chin, so that only his head showed. This ritual occurred for the next seven years, and it only stopped when he discovered masturbation and marijuana and used them compulsively to block his anxiety attacks.

His body posture had the look of someone "with the covers pulled up." As he would breathe in and then hold his breath for what seemed like an interminable time, his body from the chest down would pull inward towards the back of the chair and somewhat recede from view, as if it were covered up. Holding his breath seemed to reduce him to a head, with his body stiffly cut off from any signs of life. He would then spasmodically release his breath. Then "the covers would be pulled up" again, his body would become rigid, and the sudden and forceful release of his breath would eventually follow.

The treatment only marginally addressed his breathing patterns and character armoring. Instead, it focused upon his parental complexes, and was especially fruitful when his hatred of sexuality could be explored. This intense reaction took the form of a revulsion toward foreplay. As a result of this brief, one-year treatment, his masturbatory compulsion ceased, he entered into a relationship with a woman his age, and his addiction to marijuana diminished. His breathing pattern improved, but he still retained that quality of "pulling up the covers."

This brief vignette shows how an intense negative mother complex manifested itself through body and psyche. As a result of my particular training, I chose to work with psychic complexes. Someone else might have approached this young man's problems through his body armoring and breathing patterns. My approach was moderately successful; a body-oriented therapy would also have been at least as fruitful.

The patient employed splitting defenses against the threat of being overwhelmed by psychotic anxieties. Mind-body splitting was his major defense. Whether pulling up the covers in actuality—*just to his chin*—as in his childhood ritual, or as this later became a metaphor for his body structure, he was splitting off body-awareness. Clearly, his intense anxieties lived, so to speak, in his body, and could be hidden there as long as his splitting defenses worked.

While his anxiety level was high, untempered by drug use, his body and breathing pattern was gripped in the kind of rigidity I have described. *This is a general pattern: Any time a complex is constellated and threatens to assimilate ego functions, the body-ego takes on a pattern associated with the complex.* In relationship to a complex constellation, there is not only an array of physiological responses such as changes in respiration, heart rate, and galvanic skin response, demonstrated by Jung in his word-association experiments, but there is a change in the overall body structure. Psychically, this is experienced as a body image. When the man I described was threatened by his negative mother complex, his body image was of being in pieces, ugly, and filled with repulsive desires. His physical body also took on the characteristic form of hiding, "pulling the covers up to his chin."

One way of synthesizing these observations is as follows: *Every complex has a body.* The *body of the complex* is neither the physical body nor a purely mental structure, but an in-between phenomenon. In Mead's words, it is an "invisible subtle embodiment of the life of the mind" (1919, p. 1). The subtle body can manifest itself psychically in terms of dream, fantasy, and body images, and it can manifest physically in terms of body structure. It is both spiritual and physical, and rather than studying one or the other of these opposites, I shall show, through clinical material, that there is much to be gained by attending instead to that often obscure middle realm of which they both partake.

This intermediate realm of subtle bodies was the major concern of alchemy. When in Paracelsus we read his common refrain "destroy the bodies," he is speaking, I believe, about transforming *the body of the complex*. In bioenergetic work one attempts to break down body armoring. That is an approach on the physical body level, but not on the subtle-body level. The latter requires the imagination—the key, as Jung has said, to the entire alchemical opus (1953, par. 396). If one can successfully work through the subtle-body realm, there is often a chance to transform not only psychic structure but physical structure as well. Mind-body splitting can mend when the subtle-body realm is successfully encountered.

While Jung gives a survey of the alchemist's use of the subtle-body idea in *Psychology and Alchemy* (1944, pars. 394ff.), in his unpublished "Seminars on Nietzsche's *Thus Spake Zarathustra*," he develops the subtle-body idea more fully than anywhere in his *Collected Works*. He tells us that the psyche has real effects that are performed through the *medium* called the subtle body (1934–39, vol. 3, p. 139). Projections are transmitted through this medium and manifest in physical and psychic effects from one person to another (1934–39, vol. 10, p. 144). To this I would like to add that the medium, the subtle body, may be projected and imaginally perceived as operating between people. Furthermore, the intermediate, subtle-body realm can be a conjoined body, made up of the individual subtle bodies of two people in analysis. This particular form of the subtle-body experience is our main interest. It is this kind of imagery that we meet in the alchemical treatise the *Rosarium Philosophorum*,[1] which Jung took as an Ariadne thread through the complexities of the transference (1946, par. 538).

Winnicott's discovery of transitional space and phenomena stems, I believe, from subtle-body perceptions, something Samuels has noted (Samuels 1985). Winnicott says:

> My claim is that [there is] an intermediate area of *experiencing*, to which inner reality and external life both contribute. It is an area that is not challenged, because no claim is made on its behalf except that it shall exist as a resting-place for the individual engaged in the perpetual human task of keeping inner and outer reality separate yet interrelated. . . .
>
> I am here staking a claim for an intermediate state between a baby's inability and his growing ability to recognize and accept reality. I am therefore studying the substance of *illusion*, that which is allowed to the infant, and which in adult life is inherent in art and religion, and yet becomes the hallmark of madness when an adult puts too powerful a claim on the credulity of others, forcing them to acknowledge a sharing of illusion that is not their own. We can share a respect for *illusory experience*, and if we wish we may collect together and form a group on the basis of similarity of our illusory experiences. . . . (1971, pp. 2–3)

We need something of Winnicott's courage when attempting to describe subtle-body phenomena. For we are dealing with *illusions,* and while a good deal can be said about the reality of the imagination, or about its potential for perceiving "the intermediate area between the subjective and that which is objectively perceived" (1971, p. 3), we are nevertheless confronted with an exceptionally difficult task of communicating our imagination in some understandable form.

The Subtle Body in Clinical Practice

For many reasons I think we need to introduce the subtle-body concept into actual clinical practice. The most immediate reason is that actively engaging its dynamics often works where all other approaches, whether they be purely interpretive, interactive field concepts, gestalt enactments, or body work of various kinds, have little effect. But there is a larger issue at stake. As mentioned already, it is likely, I believe, that much of the phenomenology we tend to take as the primary date of the analytical endeavor may be secondary to an underlying process that is outside of our normal sense of time and space. They are possibly secondary in the same way that Bohm finds the quarks and profusion of particles in physics to be secondary manifestations of a usually unknown, larger process (1982, pp. 48–49). In Jung's terminology, which has roots in his cultural predecessors, we deal with manifestations of processes in the *Unus Mundus* that synchronistically manifest in time (von Franz 1974, p. 261). Once there, these processes may be understood causally and structured developmentally. But it is an open issue whether that is the best way to understand and set right their pathology.

Major developmental processes can be seen as reflections of aspects of the process of union in the *Unus Mundus.* The experience of union through the medium of the subtle body is one in which the conjoining and separation of opposites rhythmically alternate in a frequency pattern, while a sense of Oneness permeates. But in observations set in a space-time framework, these processes appear to be separated and are not conceived of as various stages or aspects of an underlying Oneness of existence. Key developmental issues, such as those that Melanie Klein called the paranoid-schizoid and the depressive positions (Segal 1979, pp. 113–24), and what Margaret Mahler (1980, p. 9) called the rapprochement subphase of the separation-individuation process, can be seen as processes in space-time that reflect the event of the *coniunctio,* and other processes that attend it, in the *Unus Mundus.* But these events can readily lose contact with their source, the vast energy sea of the *Unus Mundus,* and especially so when they are further cast into a developmental framework. This is not to criticize the value of developmental models, but to fully partake of their value, the archetypal source of the events they sequentially structure as stages in development must not drift into a dim metapsychological background. Furthermore, developmental theories themselves need to be related to their sources in archetypal patterns.

The paranoid-schizoid position can be seen to accord with picture 7 of the *Rosarium,* "the ascent of the soul," which Jung likens to a schizophrenic dissociation (1946, par. 476). It is a state in which all linking (Bion 1967, pp. 93–109) is attacked, something the alchemists speak of as a loss of the *vinculum,* the connecting function of the soul (Jung 1946, par. 504). Seen from the perspective of an ego entering time-space, this state can represent intense anxiety that must be sufficiently neutralized by "good enough mothering" (Winnicott, 1971 p. 10ff.). But what is the function of this intense, persecutory anxiety? Since it is sometimes linked to abandonment anxiety, it is often considered to instigate the dissolution of omnipotence. Persecutory anxiety of the paranoid-schizoid position is linked by Klein to the "death instinct," and in Freud's view the "death instinct" drives the ego towards an *eros* relationship to objects, and thus desires to love and be loved (Freud 1923, p. 56). In Bion's view the paranoid-schizoid state can dissolve psychic structure or containers so that new structures and new thoughts can develop (Eigen 1985, pp. 321–22). This gets closer to what we can learn from imagery such as that in the *Rosarium.* There, the purpose of this extremely disorienting state is to transform personality structure, and especially body armoring, to allow a new embodiment of union.

That is, the pictures of the *Rosarium* depict the soul's experience of union, the *coniunctio* of King and Queen (which is an event largely outside of time-space, ever occurring in the *Unus Mundus,* and occasionally experienced by the human soul), which is in the process of incarnating. This cannot happen if body armoring and early personal-shadow material are rigidly organized. In terms of the *Rosarium,* which is to say of processes in the *Unus Mundus* as apprehended through the subtle-body experience, the stage of "the ascent of the soul," the intense persecutory energy field that attacks all connections with oneself and others, must be seen as a vital and important state. It prepares for and allows the eventual embodiment of the Self as a union of opposites.

There is a great difference if one can experience these "death-dealing" affects with a viewpoint that they have a purpose that is genuinely mysterious. Winnicott's brilliant observation that the self is created through the continuous destruction of fantasy objects that somehow survive (Eigen 1981, p. 418) certainly helps. One can at times experience these devastating interactive fields with an awareness or faith in a basic Oneness of which they partake. As this intense anxiety is part of a process of embodiment, one task of the analyst is to become faithfully embodied amidst them. This is extremely difficult, since his or her survival as a self is uncertain. This is thinking along alchemical lines, and it corresponds with Bion's notion of faith in "O" (Eigen 1981, p. 426).

The depressive position is one in which opposites such as "good" and "bad" breast combine into a whole object, with depression or pining often taken to be a result of the child's awareness of harm it may now *also* do to the "good breast." Klein suggested that in the depressive position, the omnipotence of the "good" and "bad" mother is lost, and with it the child's sense of omnipotence. This loss is also taken to be responsible for the depressive position. Other explanations have been given as well. Elkin suggests, "It is not the question of impotence or omnipotence . . . that gets to the core of the depressive position, but rather *the infant's new capacity to distinguish physical omnipotence from mental omniscience*" (1972, pp. 404–405). These are all ways of apprehending, in space-time considerations, a process that follows the *coniunctio* in the *Unus Mundus*. This process is called the *nigredo,* represented by picture 6 of the *Rosarium.*

The depressive position looks very different when viewed from a vantage point of an ego seeking outer objects, from that of a soul experiencing inner and outer union. The set-up is not dissimilar from how incest can be viewed, with Freud's emphasis upon the taboo, which leads to separation, and Jung's on incest as the drive to union. From the point of view of subtle-body experiences of the *coniunctio,* what we understand as the depressive position is a stage of mourning for a loss of fusion with archetypal dominants in union, the King and Queen of the *Rosarium.* The depressive position would be understood, as such, as a result of a union of opposites and of a loss of omnipotence (Klein) and as the result of distinguishing physical omnipotence from mental omniscience (Elkin). But more: It would be seen as a stage of mourning, not primarily to repair injury inflicted on a single good-and-bad object by unconscious destructive fantasy life, but mourning for a loss of direct contact with the archetypal sphere, a loss of the beauty and numinous quality of union. This cannot be cast, with any sufficiency, into a loss of a primal scene fantasy, unless the latter is taken to be a projection of the archetypal drama of the union of King and Queen.

In the paranoid-schizoid position, the soul is beset with a separation from its union with God, the *unio mystica*. In the depressive position, the soul must separate from the experience of union as a *hieros gamos,* the sacred marriage of opposites. These are different experiences of union, one more concerned with *Logos* and Light, the other with *Eros*. The developing or incarnating soul must separate from both in order that the product of union may eventually incarnate.

The rapprochement subphase of the separation-individuation process also can be seen as a space-time fragment of the *coniunctio*. The child's separation and return, the latter so filled with energy, may again —as in the depressive position—represent the *coniunctio* process and its effects as they fall, with much diminished energy-value, into space-time. In the depressive position, the opposites unite in the background of the child's psyche while the child is still in fusion with this sacred event. In the rapprochement subphase, the child is more an actor in the drama of union. But it is an attempt at union that falls into discrete parts, a separation and a return, opposites that attempt to harmonize but lack the "glue" of unity, as it can be known in the archetypal rhythmical quality of the *coniunctio*. Instead, mother and child must sufficiently, but always incompletely, create it. Seeking unity, the archetypal root of rapprochement, may underpin this phase being seen as something that is a lifelong endeavor. But experiencing the prototype of this process, the *coniunctio* in the subtle-body realm, can often both reveal and heal separation and rapprochement wounds, the major focus of borderline disorders.

The oedipal stage represents yet another pattern of the joining of opposites and their separation, again the opposites contained by the *coniunctio* in the *Unus Mundus*. In the oedipal level, the ego is getting close to the culmination of its sacrifice of fusion with the numinous energy of union, libido now cast under the control of the incest taboo. From Layard and Jung (Jung 1946, par. 438) we have learned that this sacrifice allows for the development of inner structure, especially in the sphere of a differentiated relationship to the feminine and to culture. All of this reflects the *coniunctio* in the subtle-body experience, in which kinship libido is created and inner structures, especially anima and animus, are transformed. It is the danger of fusion with the archetypal sphere that necessitates the incest taboo and the oedipal transit. Yet its rewards are very indirect and fragmentary relative to the imaginal experience of its prototype, the *coniunctio*.

When the subtle-body experience is constellated between two people, both people begin to gain access to knowing experientially the kind of phenomenology that Jung discusses in his work on the *Rosarium*. These images are an example of a process that structures the subtle-body experience. And the central event in that process, which organizes all the others, is the *coniunctio*. That is why nearly all of my clinical material will revolve about this state.

Healing and the *Coniunctio*

Experiencing the *coniunctio* as a here and now, imaginal reality can contribute to healing the mad parts of psyche, parts in which mindlessness dominates, thinking is broken, a sense of personal continuity is lost (Winnicott 1971, p. 97). A mother may cure or mend such ruptures in psychic structure and "reestablish the baby's capacity to use a symbol of union" (ibid.). The *coniunctio* may have this potential, when it is imaginally experienced in the analytic setting.

It should be noted that a good deal of healing in analysis can occur without *explicit* experience of the *coniunctio,* without imaginal *sight.* In "The Psychology of the Transference," Jung says that this event often passes off in the unconscious (1946, par. 461), its occurrence unknown at the time. Healing, as Judith Hubback (1983, pp. 313–27) has shown with reference to depressed patients, can often be understood as the patient's introjection of the analyst's conscious-unconscious union. This process may underlie healing in numerous other instances. Any time an interpretation has value, it is not likely that its value stems from an increase in the the patient's cognitive mastery of conflict. Nor is it a result of the affective experience that a good interpretation may facilitate. These are phenomena that are relatively visible and tangible. The primary source of healing lies in the process the analyst and patient have lived through, the process whereby the analyst has been able to maintain a self, to recover an imagination and capacity to think, while bombarded by projective and introjective processes whose goal is to attack linking (Meltzer 1978, pp. 30–31) and imagination. Imagination or thoughts that the analyst or patient may have amidst such destructive "field phenomena" are rarely the result of a discursive thinking process. They are created, the "child" of a union, in Meltzer's phrase, of a "combined object" (1979, p. 138; 1973, p. 85). The imaginal, archetypal couple, the *coniunctio,* is the source of healing that can be introjected by the patient and, it should be added, by the therapist as well.

The *coniunctio* may be a more or less unconscious phenomenon, whose existence we sense or intuit on the edges of consciousness, much like the unconscious dyad that André Green finds so crucial to analytic work (1975, p. 12). It is likely that the *coniunctio* underpins the "secured space" that is central to the theory of Langs. Considerable therapeutic value can accrue from the *coniunctio* as a more or less unconscious phenomenon between analyst and patient.

Strong sexual feelings often emerge with the stirring of the *coniunctio,* and a person may fear being overwhelmed, or fear/sense that the analytical process cannot contain such affects. In these situations, a good deal of preliminary effort through interpretive or body work is first necessary. The imaginal process may be ill-advised when, to use Masud Kahn's terminology, symbiotic omnipotence (1974, pp. 82–92) is a dominant factor. Generally, when a patient uses fusion to hide and control a psychotic kernel, the imaginal activity that goes into the discovery/creation of the *coniunctio* can unleash an unmanageable psychotic transference. Raising the *coniunctio* to an imaginal here and now awareness is a process, like the alchemical elixir, that can be a poison or a cure. It can be so destructive that, if I did not believe, based on a good deal of clinical evidence, that the imaginal experience of the *coniunctio* and its associated process has a value often not readily achieved by interpretive-analytical, spiritual, or body techniques, including the more unconscious occurrence of the *coniunctio,* I would not suggest that we seriously re-examine its manifestation as a viable clinical factor.

The Somatic Unconscious and the Subtle Body

In his *Nietzsche Seminars,* Jung makes an extremely clear statement about the subtle body. He tells us that the subtle body refers to that part of the unconscious that becomes more and more identical with the functioning of the body, growing darker and darker and ending in the utter darkness of matter. For this reason, he explains, the subtle body is exceedingly incomprehensible. But Jung must bring it into his analysis of *Zarathustra* because, he tells us, Nietzsche's concept of the Self includes the body, *and this cannot be reduced to the psychological shadow.* The latter forms part of the psychological or psychic unconscious, while the subtle body represents the somatic unconscious, the unconscious as it is experienced as we descend into the body. Having stated his wariness of employing the subtle-body concept, Jung goes on to display a mastery of the subject! He tells us that the subtle body must be beyond space and time, that it must be a body that does not fill space. When he sufficiently deals with the intellectual difficulties of the subject, he then tells us that the subtle body is a very important concept.

It is marvelous to encounter it in a text which naively comes from the wholeness of man. . . . *Zarathustra* is one of those books that is written with blood, and anything written with blood contains the notion of the subtle body, the equivalent of the somatic unconscious. (1934–39, vol. 3, pp. 151–52)

Jung goes on to raise key issues: The subtle body is extremely important, but can it be made comprehensible? The grasp of these phenomena depends upon speaking in images, and hence upon imagination. Jung's concern with being scientific (ibid.) led him to deal rarely with the subtle-body concept in his *Collected Works* (except to explain its significance in alchemy, in the process of which he revealed a mine of information on the subject). A few notable exceptions can be found. For example, in his essay "Psychology and Religion," he writes:

> Our usual materialistic conception of the psyche is, I am afraid, not particularly helpful in cases of neurosis. If only the soul were endowed with a subtle-body, then one could at least say that this breath—or vapour— body was suffering from a real though somewhat ethereal cancer, in the same way that the gross material body can succumb to a cancerous disease. (1940, par. 13)

He went on to say, "I have often felt tempted to advise my patients to think of the psyche as a subtle body in which subtle tumours can grow" (1940, par. 36).

Jung's concern was with the comprehensibility of the subtle-body concept. Can we employ it without degenerating into a vague kind of primary process thinking? I think it can be made sufficiently comprehensible; clinical examples will portray the imaginal processes that come into play.

At times, a couple may simply find themselves in a subtle-body encounter. At other times, an imaginal technique must be employed. Alchemy, with its concern for the *imaginatio,* conceived to be "half spiritual, half physical" and the "most important key to the understanding of the *opus*" (Jung 1953, par. 396), has at times cast the imaginal process into an obscure saying (Jung 1963, par. 68), the so-called *Axiom of Maria.* The qualitative logic of the enigmatic *Axiom* runs as follows: *Out of the One comes the Two, out of the Two comes the Three, and from the Third comes the One as the Fourth* (von Franz 1974, p. 65). This axiom is a way of apprehending processes in the Unus Mundus as they intersect with space-time perceptions. The path that the axiom sets out is one that can lead into an awareness of the subtle body and into its central, ordering structure, the *coniunctio.*

A Clinical Vignette: An Example of the Axiom of Maria

Kate

Kate sits down and says, "Everything is okay. Life was never better." As she continues talking I feel both uncontacted and *tend* not to make any contact myself. I *tend* to withdraw, straining to respond in some mirroring way and feeling false if I try too much. Yet this is all inadequate; it feels very uncomfortable. I think of changing the subject, and almost say, "How are you doing in your business?" But that, I quickly recognize, would only be a way of trying to create some contact. Instead, I just feel depressed, and with that resolve to stay put and just wait it out.

I then begin to make some effort to sort out what opposites are at play. She seems manic, and I feel depressed and abandoned. It gradually becomes clear that a pair of split opposites is functioning through projective identification, with her depression put into me. Or is it my mania put into her? Thus a state of "Twoness" is differentiating out of the "Oneness" of fusion that had dominated.

As Kate continues, I reflect upon my depressed state. At the same time that I begin to wonder about its manic opposite in Kate, and about fusion fears and desires, my experience changes. Now, I begin to feel both opposites, a manic component and a depressive one. In von Franz's terms, I begin to grasp "the Two aspect of the One," by "hypostacizing the Two" (1974, p. 64) into the qualities I have called "mania" and "depression." In other words, a field quality of "Twoness" has become clear. The process of thinking in terms of "her mania" and "my depression," along with splitting mechanisms, is largely a convenience, a way of grasping a quality of Twoness in an interactive field.

Now I have a choice. What do I do with the "Twoness?" Several possibilities emerge. Having contained the opposites, I can choose to interpret the projective identification. It would be possible to tell Kate that she has been splitting off from depressive anxiety, having me contain it, and further relate this to her abandonment fears that arise when she is on the verge of success. In this instance, an emerging business issue was a source of joy that in turn terrified her, as did her emerging independence from me. If I proceed in this way, the stage of "Twoness" would lead to "Threeness" in the form of an interpretation.

Thus, holding the opposites together in consciousness, I could choose to interpret, and hence to concretize, the "Two" aspect of the field. Instead, I choose to *see*. Metaphorically, I attempt to make imaginal contact with her by seeing, in William Blake's sense, *through* my eyes (Damrosch 1980, p. 16) rather than *with* them. This process involves a sacrifice of clarity, an act of lowering the consciousness gained in differentiating the field into the opposites manic/depressive, or of giving up some of the high-grade energy produced in this process. This is a process of becoming less conscious and less active, in a sense dumb. It is an introverted act in which psychic energy—attention and consciousness—is given over to the unconscious, and therein to a symbolic sense of Oneness, the One Continuum (von Franz).

This imaginal act is a background issue, something that is dimly perceived along with the act of *seeing,* of looking and waiting for something to appear, for some kind of *sight* to emerge. In a sense, during this activity I am looking at Kate as if she were a dream image or a process of active imagination (Jung 1960, par. 167). This can also be understood as a form of "object usage" in Winnicott's sense, which depends upon the transformation of a defensive projective-identification field into a capacity for play (Eigen 1981, p. 415).

I begin to *see* her differently. I *see* that she is terrified. While the opposites were split, imagination was blocked. I could not *see* this nor could I infer it from countertransference reactions.

Once again, interpretation can now come forth as "the Third": I can interpret how Kate's splitting is hiding her terror of being *seen.* But there is another, imaginal alternative. As I focus more energy on the unconscious and a sense of the One Continuum, this energy can be felt to flow upwards and back towards the One, *and then in a circuit that returns through my heart toward Kate.* This focus is an effort, for the affects of the "Dyad" that had preceded the potential of "Threeness" include inertia. A fundamental quality of "Threeness" is having overcome the sense of being stuck and leaden, the condition of inertia (Jung 1946, par. 404). It is out of this kind of heart-centered act that the field of projective identification is finally transformed and changed into the vision of the heart.

An unmistakable quality of this experience is an aesthetic element. This has been explored by James Hillman in his paper "The Thought of the Heart" (1979, pp. 156–57). A perception of beauty lingers, a beauty of wholeness and its mystery that would have been destroyed by "making the unconscious conscious."

When I perceived Kate's terror and said nothing, but just *saw* it, she said: "I've been avoiding you; I have been terrified of making contact. I am scared of sexual feelings and the vulnerability they bring." And now, still experiencing my imagination as heart-centered, something new begins to emerge. This time it is a vague image, a sense of the energy field or the space between us changing, becoming more textured and alive. It is neither "in her" nor "in me." We both *see* and *experience* it.

This is a subtle body experience. The *coniunctio* had emerged "out of the Two." In the *Axiom of Maria,* "Out of the Two came the Three as the One." The appearance of the *coniunctio* can be recognized as a synchronistic event because of the simultaneous meaning it has for both of

us. It represents a sacred event, a moment of grace, and perhaps also a result of faith in a background sense of Oneness.

Due to the sexual anxieties that were awakened in Kate, the opposites, held together by the *coniunctio,* did fall apart. The *coniunctio* disappeared into a *nigredo,* and left us eventually in a soulless state, a lack of
contact that was the complete opposite of the sense of union afforded
through the *coniunctio.* These are typical stages after the *coniunctio* experience. They correspond to pictures 6 and 7 of the *Rosarium* (1946,
pars. 467–82). But, as usual, the *coniunctio* experience did not vanish.
Rather, experience proves that in a series of unions and deaths, a pool of
kinship libido slowly builds up (Jung 1946, par. 445).

Generally one does not explicitly go through the logic of the *axiom.*
But I believe that it represents the process of dealing with opposites, especially in projective identification, that is more or less consciously carried out if any heart-centered act of vision or empathy is created. Further
examples will deal more fully with the *coniunctio.* Here I have emphasized transformative possibilities in the subtle-body field, which have an
inherent logic and through which the *coniunctio*'s appearance, while
aways an act of grace, can also be facilitated. In a sense, analysis is the art
of moving from "the Two to the Three." In the next section, I shall explore a very important form of "Twoness," the unconscious couple that
often underlies the behavior and activity of ego consciousness and
relationships.

The Unconscious Couple

In "The Psychology of the Transference," Jung presented a model of
transference/countertransference phenomena. He proposed that the
connection between analyst and analysand be understood as an interaction between four factors, two being the conscious attitudes of the participants, the other two being the anima and animus, the unconscious personalities of the male and female partners, respectively (1946 par. 423).

Jung described the various connections between these elements, the
most unconscious and determinative link being between the man's anima and the woman's animus. He found this couple portrayed in the alchemical pictures from the *Rosarium Philosophorum.* "Everything that
the doctor discovers and experiences when analyzing the unconscious of
his patient coincides in the most remarkable way with the content of
these pictures" (1946, par. 401).

Concluding his study, Jung says:

To give any description of the transference phenomena is a very difficult and
delicate task, and I did not know how to set about it except by drawing upon
the symbolism of the alchemical opus. The theoria of alchemy, as I think I
have shown, is for the most part a projection of unconscious contents, of
those archetypal forms which are the characteristic features of all pure
fantasy-products, such as are to be met with in myths and fairy tales, or in the
dreams, visions, and the manias of individual men and women. The important part played in the history of alchemy by the hieros gamos and the mysti-
cal marriage, and also by the coniunctio, corresponds to the central
significance of the transference in psychotherapy on the one hand and in the
field of human relationships on the other. (1946, par. 538)

The picture series from the *Rosarium* centers upon a couple, with
the *coniunctio* (as in picture 5) being the central mystery. Others in the
series do not necessarily have *its* quality. For example, picture 2 represents a fusion state in which incestuous energies play a major role, and
picture 7 represents a state of total loss of relatedness. In psychotherapy
we generally find at first an image of an unconscious couple that is far
from the desirable state of union. This couple can often be a representation of the patient's own parents, usually a portrayal of this couple as the
patient actually *saw* them, but an image that was too difficult to accept.
(*See* the following case material of Nora.) It can also be a composite form,
complicated by the analyst's unconscious dyad. This is the type of image
for which anima/animus interaction is a special case. A host of unconscious components can actually form the couple. At times of disturbance
due to a severe countertransference, the couple may be largely the analyst's own.

Awareness of the patient's unconscious couple is often a starting
point, a *prima materia*. Identifying it, and eventually—as the following
clinical material will show—*seeing* it in the intermediate region of subtle
bodies, can have a potent transformative action. This is probably only understandable in terms of the archetypal image of the *coniunctio* and its
symbolic link to the "energy sea" of the *Unus Mundus*. It would seem
that the very awareness of an inner couple opens the way to that mystery.

Examples of Unconscious Couples

Nora

Nora began her session with a yawn and handed me a check. I noted
that it was in error, less one week's fee. In her usual playful manner she
said:

N: Don't make too much of slips like that, I'm just tired. And besides, I have wonderful news about my favorite subject, my su-

pervisor. I finally stopped being a wimp and stood up to her. Her evaluation of my work was awful, filled with envy, and I confronted her on each point and got her to totally change it.

This was an important event, a landmark in terms of her behavior with authority figures. To Nora it was a culmination of months of analytic work oriented toward owning her own authority.

Throughout these months, there had been a constant theme: her contempt for other people. Most everyone in her past and present, especially her supervisor, had been a prime target. Refrains such as "their lack of strength," or "their cowardice," or "their refusal to be honest about what they believe" were common. In this session, there was a just-so-ness about her story; there was no recognizable contempt for her supervisor.

As she spoke, I still wondered about her initial yawn and slip about the check. But I could make little of it. Her outer success was very important, and I acknowledged that, but clearly more was happening than the manifest material.

As in the technique of active imagination, I allowed my consciousness to lower and began to look at Nora "*through* my eyes." In the imaginal process that occurred, I was aware of *being in my body*. Through this lowered consciousness, a kind of perceptual haziness existed through which my body surface seemed to expand, as if its energy field reached outward. Another way to describe this is to say that an experience of a new field between us slowly developed, a sense that the space that separated us gained a quality, became more material, and seemed to have its own autonomy in the form of a flickering of imagery.

It is difficult to distinguish whether this experience is of the body or of the psyche. Both seem to participate, and imagination seems to arise out of this body-psyche field. As in the above example of Kate, at times this vision seemed to be of Nora's intrapsychic process, at other times of contents in a shared, subtle-body field.

Throughout this subtle body or somatic unconscious experience, I remembered her initial "slip." What was it about? A dual vision is often essential to the imaginal process, as this and the following example will demonstrate. The imaginal act often can be structured by history—here by the initial data and its meaning in our process and as it could relate to her past, but of which I could make no sense—and by an acausal process, a spontaneous appearance of imagery through the somatic unconscious. This dual awareness into timebound and atemporal forms has always structured imaginal activity and attempts to sort out "true" from "false," or "fantastic," imagination. One finds this duality central in mantic procedures (von Franz 1974, p. 198), in Blake's structuring of vision through particularity and the Divine Jesus (Damrosch 1980, pp. 151–52), in alchemy (Jung 1953, par. 360), and in Bion's "binocular vision" (Meltzer 1978, pp. 49–50).

In the hour I have been describing, I initially saw Nora in her new state of feeling effective. This was a separation from internal, persecutory images. I experienced her subject-object clarity, a sense that she was contained and was her own person. But in the more vague, trance-like state that I descended into, I began to *see* a pocket of contempt in her. There was a sense of glee, quite split off from the separate and mature person she also was, glee at the way her supervisor squirmed under her confrontation.

The subtle-body experience is often a background, a subliminal field of imagery, against which we form interpretations and other cognitive acts. In psychoanalytic terms, it would be reduced to so-called primary process. In the kind of analytical activity that I am describing, this is reversed: The clarity of contents and process, especially developmental considerations, become a background issue; the more hazy and imaginal processes become the foreground. (This may have some relationship to switching from left-hemisphere to right-hemisphere dominance.)

While her contempt was strong in the past, it was now (imaginally) perceptible, but weaker and less intrusive. This, of course, is something one would expect. In such developments there is always repression and some splitting. One could say that she was able to separate from the shadow (of contempt), which was now in her unconscious as an inferior quality. But here I am stressing something different. It was not that more "shadow integration" was necessary, nor was any interpretation of the transference or countertransference useful. Rather, what proved to be important was an imaginal process.

Here is how this came about. Having *seen* her contempt, I again returned to her initial behavior in the session, saying:

M: I think the contempt you have had, especially over the last few months, needs also to be seen as a contempt of me. Perhaps your yawn and underpayment is a sign of this contempt.

N: I don't think so. I can follow with my head, but it doesn't feel right.

M: You have spoken about how limited our time is together. That could be a link to your father, who spent so little time with you, and for whom you have great contempt. Also, we have been spending a lot of time on outer, manifest levels, such as talking about your supervisor. I wonder if you experienced that, in part,

as a message that I didn't want to directly relate to you. That
could engender contempt.

N: I'll think about it, but I don't think so. I think we had to deal on
the outer level. Look what's happened in the process! I'm finally
standing up for myself.

Throughout these interpretive attempts, which soon felt feeble, I
maintained an "imaginal eye" on her contempt, allowing it to become
more background for the time being. I then felt more deeply into my
body and waited for some image to emerge.

Nora was now talking about her supervisor's physical size. She
noted being much taller, overpowering her. She was belittling her size,
"putting her down," dismissing her. She mentioned enjoying making her
supervisor cry during their confrontation.

In several minutes something began to appear vaguely to me, a combination of a hazy thought mixed in with what I was *seeing* in her and between us. I said:

M: Perhaps what is going on now is that you and I are like your
mother, I mean father . . . talking about your mother.

I stumbled, felt confused and was surprised at my lack of clarity. I thought
I knew what I was going to say, but was tongue-tied, and "mother" and
"father" got all tangled up. While I was trying to sort this out, she said:

N: Wait, maybe we are mother and father talking about Nora.

With that she was very reflective, immersed in thought, and looked
away. She was experiencing something; I was more an onlooker at this
point than a participant. With a suddenness, as if awaking from a dream,
she said:

N: That's it! I always felt they were contemptuous of me and I completely blocked it out. It seems they were *always* talking about
me in the way I just talked about her.

Her experience had a clear ring of truth to it. She had contacted a
painful experience of her parental couple, their contempt for her, and
her lifelong need to deny this awareness. She *saw* their contempt.

In the next session I learned that when she turned away she felt she
was in a place that was not fully in time. It had a strange quality she had
never known before, a sense of mystery that was out of the ordinary. She
saw her parent's contempt while in this trance-like state. This has all the
qualities of an entrance into the somatic unconscious. It also bears simi-

larities to liminal processes, rituals that occur in the subtle-body state of awareness.

Here are elements of the dream she had the night following her vision of her parental couple.

> *I am walking along a street. . . . In the gutters are layers of dried eucalyptus or bay leaves and a rich, pure, finely-textured topsoil washed there by spring rains. The soil and leaves are light and layered. I look down and see a manhole cover, which is actually a grille. It is black wrought iron and octagonal. The design is a Hapsburg* Zweiadler, *a double-headed, crowned eagle with one body. In its claws are a bundle of arrows. I lift it and look down and across the tunnel. . . . It is well constructed, solid and safe. The other end is about ten yards away. I can see the opening. Outside it is golden and glowing-warm, sunny and earthy.*

She associated the topsoil to her initial dream in analysis of *an Olympic-sized swimming pool filled with shit.* Now it was transformed into the rich, aerated topsoil. One understanding we now gained of that remarkable initial dream was that it represented her psyche filled up by other people's projections. For example, she was a vessel for the contempt of her surroundings. As a result of her tendency towards idealization and fusion, she could not process these affects; they created a psychic (and also physical) constipation.

Her psyche swallowed projections and could not expel them. This also explains her contemptuous attitudes towards others. It was an attempt to expel introjects, a life-long process beginning with her parents' contempt for her and her splitting defenses.

With her *vision* and ensuing dream, a change took place. The descent and light at the end of the tunnel was the potential for a birth of a self, an anal birth, a capacity to trust her spontaneity and especially her creativity. That proved to be the long-range process, an individuation thread and goal. But the remarkable immediate gain was ushered in by the double-headed eagle, the hermaphrodite that is a central image of the *Rosarium*—for example, picture 10. *It represents, among other things, overcoming splitting.* There is no question that her splitting defenses sharply diminished after this dream. Her need for idealization and her terror at seeing how contempt ruled her life was faced and changed. And her chronic mind-body splitting was on the way to being healed. For example, she dreamed of a young girl, around nine years old, who was recovering from an operation for a spinal cord injury. She had a crescent-shaped scar on the back of her neck. The operation had been a success.

She had been in a full body cast from early childhood. She was now out of the cast, fragile but recovering.

Unfortunately, much more space is necessary to do justice to this process and its ramifications. One that merits mention here is the *use* of the contemptuous couple in the analysis that followed. When projective identification mechanisms would return, which happened mildly, but at times when she was afraid of embracing some creative task, I could recall the couple, often just to myself, at times also to her. This would have the effect of imaginally creating the couple as a "third thing" between us, which in turn cleared the projective-identification from a defensive to an empathic field.

Paula

Paula is a forty-year-old woman who entered analysis after many years of psychoanalysis from a developmental and Freudian point of view. Her stated reason for seeing me, a Jungian, was a desire for a spiritual vantage point, but with someone who was also aware of these other disciplines. Sexual energies played a large role in Paula's life, and they also proved to be crucial to our analytical work. This became clear only after two years of treatment, the time of the following verbatim.

P: I want to be here and stay here today, not wandering in outer thoughts. I need your help.

M: How can I help you?

P: I don't know, I just know I want to stay here. I want to feel the excitement, be with it, not run away.

M: You are beginning to split now. [I infer this from the intensity with which I find myself fragmenting at this moment.] Your attention is wandering. Try to stay with the excitement. What fantasy arises?

P: [After a long pause.] It's difficult to just stay here and not split. The word naughty comes to me—I shouldn't feel this way with father.

At this point, with her and my sexual excitement rising, the atmosphere or space between us begins to feel alive, vibrant. Both of us recognize this change; it is an example of an emerging awareness of the somatic unconscious or the subtle body, a kind of texturing of space in which we both seem to be inside something that is also between us. This flickering awareness of the subtle body is not of a *thing* that is localized in space. It is sensed as a change in the feel of space (and time) as perceived during the previous moments. It is insufficient to reduce this to regression. We were inside this experience and also outside, both aware of its autonomy and of our oneness with it.

Our mutually implicit reference point in this dialogue is her father's spanking her from the ages of approximately six to thirteen, and her recollections of fantasies of his sexual arousal. She had described the events as having an entrance phase set by her being nasty to her mother, then her father's telling her to go to her room and wait for him, the spanking in prescribed fashion, and then his exit as if nothing had happened. This all has a sadomasochistic tone that elicited a transitional, or in ritual terms a *liminal,* experience.

This had been the material of the previous sessions, a reconstruction that had been made during the prior two months. With it a link was made with her chronic history of sexually acting out with nearly all of her previous male analysts. She had also begun to feel sexual desires with me during the analytical hour. Her splitting was interpreted as a defense against these desires. She feared they would overwhelm her, override any control she might have, and lead to yet another episode of sexual acting out.

As a result of her father's sexual abuse, and what she had now recognized as her oedipal victory, which was a part of their ritual, she had been left with no recourse but schizoid splitting defenses. It was with these defenses that she entered analysis. Years of work from an object-relations, interpretive point of view, gestalt work, and group therapy had failed to make a dent in her schizoid character structure. As I mentioned, nearly all her previous work with male analysts had led to sexual acting out, always with her fantasies being ones of impersonal, intense penetration. The men were generally either impotent or sadistic in their behavior, either during or after the sexual act.

At the time of the session I am describing, we had had several weeks of sessions in which a rather stable erotic field existed between us. This was a new development, but had always been attacked by splitting defenses that resulted in her typically schizoid "in and out program" (Guntrip 1969, p. 36), whereby it was very difficult to maintain attention on her, as if she would fade in and out of focus during the hour. I may also add that her need to defend against these feelings was reinforced during the first year of analysis through various sexual affairs. Splitting off her oedipal victory and the associated sexual and aggressive drives were analyzed, but Paula needed this defense. Acting out prevented an awareness of the sexual abuse by her father and dissipated her sexual feelings and anxiety in the analytical hour.

In the context of her desire to not dissociate and withdraw from me, I recalled this previous work, especially as it related to the recurrent childhood event of her father's spankings and his sexual arousal. This work had led to an awareness that her father's sexual abuse of her created an unconscious transference couple. It was our unconscious dyad. In the session being described, I began to *see* this couple for the first time. As described in the previous example, this imaginal act is akin to active imagination, but instead of attention focusing on the unconscious as an inner reality, focus is on the unconscious "out there," in the subtle body or somatic unconscious that had begun to constellate. My next remark stemmed from this perception of the imaginal couple composed of Paula and her father in their spanking ritual.

> M: Can you sense a kind of energy field between us, as if there is an imaginary couple here, you and your father?
> P: I'm not sure. I talked to my father recently. He was so forgetful. I sensed his impotence. I guess that's a loss of the oedipal father. I feel your potency. What a relief! I guess I need both for the existence of these fantasies and feelings. I can sense the couple now, me and my father.
> M: I'm not sure how you and I and the couple connect. I don't sense the fantasy clearly.
> P: I am over your legs on my bed. You are spanking me, I'm feeling the tightness/tautness of your arm hitting me, the tightness/tautness of your thighs and penis, it all blended, the excitement in your body—I can't tell whose excitement it is, mine or yours.

My attention is on the imaginal couple between us and also on her. The structure of this is essential to grasp. (I also discussed it in Nora's case.) There are two "objects": a couple made up of me and the patient, and the imaginal couple whose presence can be sensed and their form imaginally *seen* in the space between us. My attention is on both couples at once, oscillating or hovering between both of them. In response to her question, I do feel excited. I choose to tell her:

> M: I am excited.

But then I am surprised to find that I also want to—and do—say:

> M: What do you want to do?

This last question is a result of imaginally focusing on the transference couple, the drives and fantasies of the dyad. I feel slightly on the edge of losing boundaries, but also that *not* saying what I do would lead to breaking the field between us. It feels honest to ask this seemingly seductive question. At the same time, I have a stabilizing reference point through the triangle of the patient, the couple, and myself.

P: I want to *see* your excitement. I want to undress you, to *see* it.

At this point the field intensity rises and I begin to feel somewhat identified with the activity of the male in the couple. I am surprised to have the following fantasy emerge, and I tell it to her:

M: I want to penetrate you from the rear.
P: Then do it! I want it too! Don't hide it!

Engaged in my own feelings and *vision* of the couple, waiting to see what might emerge, the following thought forcefully occurs to me:

M: What about mother?
P: Fuck her—she doesn't matter. All that matters is us!
M: I'm scared.
P: I don't believe it. It's incredible. You'd leave me in it all alone because you're scared. Well, I'm not! She doesn't count. It doesn't matter what she thinks.
M: But I'm scared.
P: I feel hate, rage, awe. Disbelief. You're a fucking bastard—you *can't* leave me in it alone. I feel a fury, chaos, a splitting in my mind. Oh God, I don't believe it. I feel like a tornado inside, fragmented, like my insides were just taken out of me, sucked out of me. You are denying your feelings and desires, and since we are merged I have to deny mine, or split them off. I can't trust.
M: I think that is just what happened to you with your father.

I say this partly because some clarity seems useful, but also to partially dampen what seems to me to be a rising level of unconscious processes that could be overwhelming. After several silent minutes, reflecting in a new, uncharacteristic way, she says:

P: So all his other denials (of my sore throats, anger, etc.) were just a screen for this primary denial. The only way I could then ever remain integrated was to be engaged in a mutually acknowledged sexual relationship. This is powerful. No wonder I've acted it all out—mentors with unresolved mother complexes and unresolved father complexes. I remember one analyst with whom I couldn't collude and I rationalized that he was incompetent. I continued to experience anxiety in the sessions because there was no mutually acknowledged desire. With my fiance I feel intact when I'm with him, and then when alone, during the middle of the week, my anxiety begins to rise. The only way to maintain cohesion is to be in a mutually desired sexual relationship. Otherwise I lose cognitive skills. I can't think. I only regain them when I have a relationship. I've always thought that I had a learning disorder or, worse, some brain damage.

It is important to underscore the features of our analytic work that accounted for the capacity for containment of the erotic energy field. I especially engaged this field, after a considerable amount of psychic integration had occurred in the analytical process, when I asked the question "What do you want to do?" In the *Rosarium* imagery, one finds containment centering upon the image of the descending dove in pictures 2, 3, and 4. This spiritual factor forms a tension with the lower, aggressive and erotic energies (known in alchemy as the lion and the unicorn) that would tend to concretize the human relationship by identifying it with the unconscious couple. This is a constant hazard in the alchemical process. It results in a series of unions and deaths, aimed at purifying away the concretizing tendency, the drive that obscures not only inner and outer, but also the awareness of the centrality of the in-between, the subtle-body realm. This transformation process cannot occur without erotic energies, yet a spiritual reference point is critical (Schwartz-Salant 1984, pp. 13–14).

The descending dove represents not only the result of a transcendent vision, the *unio mystica,* nor only ecclesiastical wisdom. It is the carrier of a previous process that was known as the *unio mentalis* (Jung 1955, par. 664). In alchemy this unites with the dead body, leading to the body's renewal. This *unio mentalis* was accomplished by collecting parts of the personality (psychic complexes), both through their analysis and also by engaging them with the imagination. But illumination, awareness of a transcendent Light, was also necessary. Only then could the attempt be made to embody the product into the mind-body unity of the *lapis*.

In Paula's case, there had already been considerable work done toward establishing mental unity through self knowledge. Paula also had a spiritual level of awareness. While the *unio mentalis* could not be said to have been complete, it was sufficiently established to allow the kind of dialogue we engaged in. The difficulty one often faces, however, is that the fullness of mental unity that is desired is itself only substantially achieved *after* the kind of subtle-body experiences we engaged in.

There is always an element of risk and judgment involved. The concerns of the alchemical process for the existence of the *unio mentalis* are a good guide. This would also mean that considerable working through of the transference and countertransference had occurred.

Anyone treating schizoid personality disorders knows how resistant certain psychic parts are to integration, and at the same time how much of the true self they contain. I think that the procedure I am exploring is a possible aid to a treatment that employs a model of regression into early childhood. But I emphasize that a considerable amount of analysis on the level of mental consolidation, especially through transference analysis of projective identification and splitting, is essential before such erotic-imaginal realms can be approached successfully.

The expression of erotic desires in the analytical process has long been recognized to be extremely dangerous. Consequently, I have allowed the verbatim material in Paula's case to be published with some reticence. It certainly will be shocking to many people, and not universally welcomed! It also will inevitably draw projections onto me, and that is an uncomfortable prospect. But it would be dishonest to withhold the material, especially since it was vital to the successful outcome of the treatment.

I must again stress that the last thing I am suggesting in subtle-body experiences is the free expression of the analyst's erotic thoughts. That is dangerous and unethical. These ideas may, however, spontaneously appear within an imaginal *structure,* as I have carefully explained in this paper. One part of this structure is historical and the other part is mythical, one determined by developmental considerations and the other by imagery. When erotic imagery and affects appear within a proper structure, they can further an entrance into a deeper level of transformation.

As a result of our imaginal, subtle-body encounter, Paula discovered, for the first time, the root of her severe anxieties and tendencies to withdraw, especially of her painful and chronic fear of having an organic brain disorder that she believed was responsible for the occasional loss of her capacity to think. The intense rage and despair she experienced in response to her father's denial were employed to attack any linking processes, especially in her thinking. Through re-experiencing her trauma as we did, she finally understood and eventually gained mastery over her dissociative processes.

In this case, what had been accomplished, up to now, was an awareness of the unconscious couple that had been dominating our sessions and all of her relationships, and the activation of that couple in the imaginal here and now. I would like to emphasize the difference between this event and gestalt-like enactment: I actually felt the desires I spoke of. I was totally in it, but *my attention was in two places at once, with one "lens" on the transference couple and another on me and the patient.* Both were complete in their own right, yet the simultaneous awareness of the two couples, the unconscious dyad representing an imaginal or mythical couple and the patient and myself representing a present-day, historical pair, led our statements to have a clear quality of truth. Previously we had reconstructed the past, but we had not nearly succeeded in revealing the depths of her despair and dissociation. *The reconstruction alone left us at an oedipal level; the imaginal replay plunged into the schizoid world of mindlessness that had plagued her throughout her entire adult life.*

There is no question but that the drama we entered into was enacted in a transitional realm; it was a subtle-body experience. With this enactment, the intensity of her sexual and aggressive drives was revealed, but we had not gone very far in their transformation. What could aid this? She still tended to be overwhelmed by the sexual energies, and her only way to control them was still to find someone with whom to enact them. She now did have a suitable partner, and she was far more conscious of her history and psychological process than ever before. In the sessions that followed, there was less splitting, but still some fragmenting and a sense that she was not yet fully embodied. The "in and out" dynamic was still present, but at reduced intensity. She recognized its persistence, and wondered how it might change. Her tendency was to believe that her present fiancé was the answer. I noted the defensive nature of this approach, saying that it actually solved very little and was probably fated to lead to a dead end in which her father and her husband-to-be were more and more fused.

In the session I shall now describe, the transformative possibilities that reside in the *coniunctio* are clear. Up to now, we had been aware of a transference couple, an unconscious dyad that was raised to consciousness. But this dyad was made up of personal images, and it may be said to stem from the personal unconscious. In the session I shall now describe, which came four weeks later, the dyad took archetypal expression—a couple in tantric union. I especially want to describe the transformative effects of this shared vision in the subtle body.

There had been a development of particular importance. While alone, Paula began to do active imagination. In fantasy, she would attempt to return to her childhood bedroom and re-experience what had occurred there. That often proved to be very anxiety provoking, and she had to insert a different male figure in her father's place. Along with this imaginal activity, an insight emerged. Paula recognized that when she was hungry, she felt sexually aroused. She then wanted a penis to fill her void, any penis, which she recognized always meant her father's. At such times she would usually eat; now she gained the courage to not eat and instead experienced her feelings and intense anxieties. This proved to be an important experiment. Through it—feeling hungry and a sense of being empty, at times succumbing to eating but usually standing her ground and experiencing her desires—Paula became more and more capable of entering into her severe anxieties and sexual/aggressive arousal with her father as an inner image. These same affects could then also be experienced with me during our analytical hours.

In this session, she had felt hungry about an hour prior to her appointment. In the past, she had tended to eat before sessions. When she arrived, there was a mild "in-and-out" pattern. I noted this to her and we spoke about it as a sign that sexual desires were present and that she feared they could overwhelm not only her, but both of us. Now that she had not acted-out through eating, these desires were especially intense and palpable in the room. We knew them in the session I previously described; there they had existed in the unconscious couple made up of Paula and her father. Now they were even stronger.

As we felt their power, a new quality emerged: Paula was very embarrassed. She felt a sense of an inner void, and she wanted to fill it with my penis. Not with me, but just with my penis. What was most embarrassing to her was the intensity of her desire and its amoral quality. She had great difficulty containing the tide of impulse and desire. What was needed was that we both stay in this intensely charged erotic atmosphere and simply experience it.

This stage is depicted in "The Psychology of the Transference" and the *Rosarium* as "Immersion in the Bath," picture 4. We were experiencing the sexual energies that can dominate the subtle-body field. They are generally highly impersonal, and often have a strongly compulsive nature. The purpose of this libido is to effect an immersion in the unconscious, *not*—it must be emphasized—of the egos of both people, but of their unconscious dyad. Jung says:

> In [the Bath] the immersion is effected by the rising up of the fiery, chthonic Mercurius, presumably the sexual libido which engulfs the pair and is the obvious counterpart to the heavenly dove. . . . Thus the pair are united *above* by the symbol of the Holy Ghost, and it looks as if the immersion in the bath were uniting them from *below*, i.e., in the water which is the counterpart of the spirit. . . . Opposition and identity at once. . . . (1946, par. 455)

The sexuality we were experiencing may have held out this possibility, the emergence of the *coniunctio,* "opposition and identity at once," and hence it was vital to not interpret it away as acting out or as some defense mechanism.

This was an afterthought, not a conscious reflection at the time. While we were in "The Bath" together I recalled little of what had previously occurred. The main focus was on our experience and not, for example, on the unconscious couple we had previously worked with. In a sense, the session felt as if it could have been our first. Only gradually did our past process begin to filter into our awareness. She then began to speak.

> P: What can I do about this? What does one do with these feelings?
>   They seem so cut off from anything human. Do they change?
> M: You can talk about them. You can feel them, feel how they link to
>   your father. They can't be solved by acting on them.

I soon realized that what I was saying made sense, and was somewhat calming to her. But I also recognized that I was repeating something like Freud's recipe of sublimation and repression. What I had been saying took me away from the experience of "The Bath" and from affective contact. My approach had been a superego ploy, a shallow escape from her question "Do they change?" Consequently, I stopped "problem solving," and waited instead. Only now did I begin to remember the session in which we experienced her and her father as an imaginal couple. I recalled this to Paula.

Soon something new began to occur. We could both imaginally *see* and *experience* a couple, but it was very different from the previous one. The couple seemed to hover in the space between us, engaged in a tantric-like sexual embrace that determined the energy field we experienced.

This field, which can be said to now have changed from the image of "The Bath" to the "Conjunction," picture 5 of the *Rosarium,* had its own rhythmic energy. Through it our subtle bodies were pulled toward, but not into, fusion, and then rhythmically separated.

Previous to the manifestation of the *coniunctio,* the energies we had felt were primarily sexual. Now a change occurred. The *coniunctio* experience brought us a sense of closeness, the I–Thou state of "kinship," in Jung's term (1946, par. 445), or *communitas* in Turner's (1974). And sexuality no longer dominated our contact, but it was as if the libido rose upward and opened our hearts. Our contact now was primarily heart-centered.

In "The Psychology of the Transference," Jung discusses a case that illustrates the appearance of the transference. Working with a woman's dream of a very special six-month-old child, Jung asked what happened six months prior to the dream. He found that another archetypal dream had occurred, and further, that upon writing it down the woman had had a vision of a golden child lying at the foot of a tree. This indicated how a "child" was being formed in the unconscious, and this led to the next question: What happened nine months before that vision?

> She had painted a picture showing, on the left, a heap of coloured and polished (precious) stones surmounted by a silver serpent, winged and crowned. In the middle of the picture there stands a naked female figure *from whose genital region the same serpent rears up towards the heart,* where it bursts into a five-pointed, gorgeously flashing golden star. . . .

And, Jung adds: "The serpent represents the hissing ascent of Kundalini, and in the corresponding yoga this marks the first moment in a process which ends with the deification of the divine Self, the syzygy of Shiva and Shakti." A footnote is added here: "This is not a metaphysical statement, but a psychological fact" (1954, pars. 376–80 & n.31).

In a sense, the heart is the central issue of the transformation process. Often people are afraid of sexual energies in their intense, impersonal form *because* acting on them destroys the process of opening the heart. It is often quite wrong to think that a fear of these energies is based upon flooding concerns, such as the threat of narcissistic injuries that are based upon loss of control. This is often a manifest issue, but the far deeper one is a fear of destroying a sacred process that can lead to the *coniunctio* and the opening of the heart.

It was clear that an answer had been given to her question: "How do the energies change?" They change by working their own transformation, by opening the heart. As always in the *coniunctio* experience, but especially in a heart-centered vision, both people feel a kind of linking of their bodies. Flesh and blood feels exchanged in this subtle-body experience.

I must add that Paula's experience was also one of all the chakras opening, while her (and my) heart was the major and most energized of these imaginal centers. She spoke of the sense of a column of energy rising up her back and also through her. This is the well-known imagery, in mild form, of the rising Kundalini.

From a clinical point of view one must of course now ask about the effects of such subtle-body experiences. The fact that they occur is not news. The fact that people know they have been through something unique, something different from any previous experience, is also common. But these testimonies alone tell us very little; we often hear similar things about drug experiences, which then have little effect upon behavior and one's sense of self following the return to a more normal consciousness. We know something about whether subtle-body experiences truly matter from observing the person's behavior, in analytical sessions, for example, and also what we are told about other changes in life. But it is especially the dreams that follow the subtle-body interaction which are diagnostic. Without dreams that register inner, structural change, we have nothing truly solid to go on.

I would like to record the entire dream series that followed, but space will not allow it. Instead, I shall recount the last dream of a series of four, all on the same theme of *a change in her inner relationship to a male figure*. Subsequent dreams also continue this theme of a fundamental change in her relationship to her animus.

Paula's dream

> *I am in a boat, steering it. I don't know how it is propelled, but it moves slowly and gently in water that is aqua blue. Beauty and stillness is all around. I can see no land, just water; I feel safe, moving slowly ahead. I look to my left and I see a man is swimming in the water next to me. He seems like a composite of my father and fiancé, but his eyes are different from anyone's I know. He swims gently, carefully with me. He seems like my father at times, and when he does, he is about 40, my age. I see land ahead and continue steering. I think to myself that when we get to land he probably won't go with me but will keep on his way. This feels okay. As we approach land, I ask him about this and he says, "I'll come with you." It feels safe, like he is a partner. I awake to the jolt of the boat hitting up against the shore.*

This dream came after I told her about wanting to use her material for publication, and in the process I explained about the *coniunctio*. I had not used this term previously, and after the dream Paula said, "You gave what happened a cognitive quality. That was an addition, and I felt it somehow changed things." It is important to note that her dream figure is not only a sum of present-day figures, but something new as well: he has unknown eyes.

Thus, the result of the *coniunctio* experience culminated in the integration of an inner figure, the animus, neither purely a synthesis of introjects, nor an autonomous image of the objective psyche, but a combination of both. As a consequence of this dream, when her fiancé left her for several days, or when she left analytical sessions, she had no strong loss experiences, no feeling of "a hole in [her] stomach" accompanied by frantic wanderings or the need to sleep. These reactions had been diminishing all along, especially after the imaginal experience of her father and herself as an unconscious dyad; but they sharply diminished after the *coniunctio,* the archetypal level of union. Also, after this her attention was even more fully in the treatment, and fears of sexual flooding were no longer an issue. Furthermore, a newly won sense of being embodied was firm. Prior to her subtle-body experiences, the only time she knew embodiment was during sexual intercourse. Now she also knew it when she was alone doing everyday things. After the dream of the animus, for the first time she had an inner companion and very little depressive or persecutory anxiety.

The dream I cited is the culmination of a series of dreams in which Paula's relationship to her animus developed. There had been dreams of stabilizing each other on an icy path, and of his leaving on a bus yet throwing his wallet and money for her to follow, with no panic of loss on her part. Through the many years of earlier analytical work, she had never had dreams of inner, supportive figures.

After the *coniunctio* experience through the subtle body, dreams and ego-integration often change in a radical way. At times one *coniunctio* experience is a key event, at other times a series of such experiences occurs over several years, eventually with transformative results.

Notes

1. The first ten pictures of the series of twenty that comprise the woodcuts of the *Rosarium Philosophorum* are included at the end of this paper. The series shown here are taken from Jung's "Psychology of the Transference" (1946).

References

Bion, W. R. 1967. *Second thoughts.* London: Heinemann.
Bohm, D. 1980. *Wholeness and the implicate order.* London: Routledge & Kegan Paul.
Brown, N. O. 1959. *Life against death.* Middletown: Wesleyan.
Chodorow, J. 1984. To move and be moved. *Quadrant* 17:2.
Corbin, H. 1969. *Creative imagination in the Sufism of Ibn Arabi.* Translated by Ralph Manheim. Princeton: Princeton University Press.
————. 1972. *Mundus Imaginalis, or the imaginary and the imaginal.* Dallas: Spring Publications.
Damrosch, L. 1980. *Symbol and truth in Blake's myth.* Princeton: Princeton University Press.
Eigen, M. 1981. The area of faith in Winnicott, Lacan and Bion. *International Journal of Psycho-Analysis* 62:413.
————. 1983. Dual union or undifferentiation? A critique of Marion Milner's view of the sense of psychic creativeness. *International Review of Psycho-Analysis* 10:415.
Elkin, H. 1972. On selfhood and the development of ego structures in infancy. *Psychoanalytic Review* 59:3.
Fabricius, J. 1971. The individuation process as reflected by 'The rosary of the philosophers' (1550). *Journal of Analytical Psychology* 16:1.
Franz, M.-L. von. 1974. *Number and time.* Evanston: Northwestern University Press.

Freud, S. 1923. The ego and the id. *Standard edition of the complete psychological works of Sigmund Freud.* Vol. XIX. 1961. London: Hogarth Press.

Green, Andre. 1975. The analyst, symbolization and absence in the analytic setting (On changes in analytic practice and experience). *International Journal of Psycho-Analysis* 56:1.

Green, Anita. 1984. Giving the body its due. *Quadrant* 17:2.

Guntrip, H. 1969. *Schizoid phenomena, object relations and the self.* New York: International Universities Press.

Hillman, J. 1979. The thought of the heart. *Eranos Yearbook* 48. Insel Verlag.

Hubback, J. 1983. Depressed patients and the coniunctio. *Journal of Analytical Psychology* 28:4.

Jung, C. G. 1916. The transcendent function. In *Collected works* 8:67–91. Princeton: Princeton University Press, 1960.

————. 1934–39. Psychological analysis of Nietzsche's Zarathustra. Unpublished seminar notes. Recorded and mimeographed by Mary Foote.

————. 1940. Psychology and religion. *Psychology and religion: West and east.* Second ed. In *Collected works,* vol. 11. Princeton: Princeton University Press, 1969.

————. 1946. The psychology of the transference. In *Collected works* 16: 163–323. Princeton: Princeton University Press, 1966.

————. 1953. *Psychology and alchemy.* In *Collected works,* vol. 12. Princeton: Princeton University Press, 1968.

————. 1955. *Mysterium coniunctionis.* In *Collected works,* vol. 14. Princeton: Princeton University Press, 1970.

Kahn, M. Masud R. 1974. *The privacy of the self.* London: Hogarth.

Levi-Strauss, C. 1967. *Structural anthropology.* New York: Doubleday.

Mahler, M. 1980. Rapprochement subphase of the separation-individuation process. In R. Lax et al., eds., *Rapprochement.* New York: Jason Aronson.

McLean, A. ed. 1980. *The rosary of the philosophers.* Edinburgh: Magnum Opus Hermetic Sourceworks Number 6.

Mead, G. R. S. 1919. *The doctrine of the subtle body in Western tradition.* London: Stuart & Watkins.

Meltzer, D. 1973. *Sexual states of mind.* Perthshire, England: Clunie.

————. 1978. The clinical significance of the work of Bion. In *The Kleinian Development,* part III. Perthshire England: Clunie Press.

Mindell, A. 1982. *Dreambody.* Santa Monica: Sigo Press.

Samuels, A. 1985. Countertransference, the mundus imaginalis, and a research project. *Journal of Analytical Psychology* 30:1.

Segal, H. 1979. *Melanie Klein.* New York: Viking Press.

Schwartz-Salant, N. 1982. *Narcissism and character transformation.* Toronto: Inner City Books.

————. 1984. Archetypal factors underlying sexual acting-out in the transference/countertransference process. *Chiron: A Review of Jungian Analysis* 1984:1–32.

Turner, V. 1974. *Dramas, fields, and metaphors.* Ithaca, N.Y.: Cornell University Press.

Whitmont, E. C. 1972. Body experience and psychological awareness. *Quadrant* 12: 5–16.

Winnicott, D. W. 1971. *Playing and reality.* London: Tavistock.

Woodman, M. 1984. Psyche/soma awareness. *Quadrant* 17:2.

Figure 1. The Mercurial Fountain. (This appears as Figure 1 in the *Rosarium Philosophorum*; see Jung 1946, p. 205.)

Figure 2. King and Queen. (This appears as Figure 2 in the *Rosarium Philosophorum*; see Jung 1946, p. 213.)

Figure 3. The Naked Truth. (This appears as Figure 3 in the *Rosarium Philosophorum*; see Jung 1946, p. 237.)

Figure 4. Immersion in the Bath. (This appears as Figure 4 in the *Rosarium Philosophorum*; see Jung 1946, p. 243.)

Figure 5. The Conjunction.   (This appears as Figure 5 in the *Rosarium Philosophorum*; see Jung 1946, p. 249.)

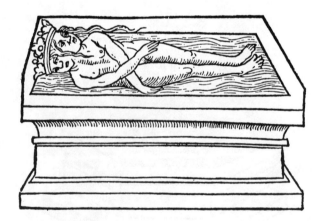

Figure 6. Death. (This appears as Figure 6 in the *Rosarium Philosophorum*; see Jung 1946, p. 259.)

Figure 7. The Ascent of the Soul. (This appears as Figure 7 in the *Rosarium Philosophorum*; see Jung 1946, p. 269.)

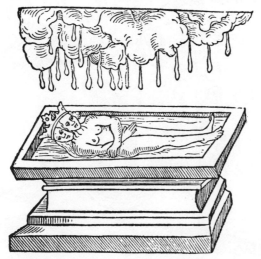

Figure 8. Purification. (This appears as Figure 8 in the *Rosarium Philosophorum*; see Jung 1946, p. 275.)

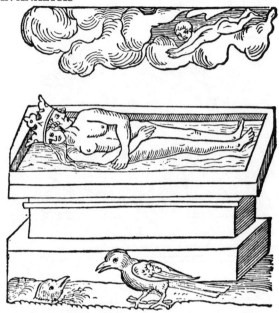

Figure 9. The Return of the Soul. (This appears as Figure 9 in the *Rosarium Philosophorum*; see Jung 1946, p. 285.)

Figure 10. The New Birth. (This appears as Figure 10 in the *Rosarium Philosophorum*; see Jung 1946, p. 307.)

Ceremonies of the Emerging Ego in Psychotherapy

Sylvia Brinton Perera

The ritual is the upward movement of the archetypal world toward mankind which is taken up by man and answered in his act. This means that the activity first arises from the archetypal background which seizes on a man.   (Neumann 1976, p. 19)

In the beginning there was action, and only afterwards did people invent . . . a dogma, an explanation for what they were doing.   (Jung 1984, p. 331)

Way below the conscious level, the beat opens doors.   (May Sarton 1980, p. 112)

In regressive mood, magical gestures [are the] . . . only idiom of communication.   (M. M. R. Khan 1974, p. 173)

If you haven't had some experience, you can't know it.   (Analysand)

All the taboo places are where the Goddess is most incarnate. They carry a new order, where earth and spirit meet. My body knows them, but the rest of me knows nothing until later, so I have to let my body lead.   (Analysand)

Sylvia Brinton Perera, M.A., is on the faculty of the C. G. Jung Institute of New York and has a private practice in New York. She holds graduate degrees from Harvard in Art History and the New School for Social Research in Psychology. Her analytic training was completed at the C. G. Jung Institute of New York. She is the author of *Descent to the Goddess: A Way of Initiation for Women* (1981), and *Scapegoat Complex: Toward a Mythology of Shadow and Guilt (1986).*

My first conscious experience with individually created ceremony occurred when my children were in the "magic years" and developed their own rituals against the night forces that came to them as fears. Sometimes they warded off demons apotropaically with an object to guard the window and bed. Sometimes they called on beneficent forces by naming with a "good night" all the objects and beings in the garden and house; sometimes by invoking the names of all remembered relatives and friends to embed them in a strong and loving community. They had to make up their own incantations in lieu of the conventional prayers that have for millenia created beds of comfort in which to pass through the darkness.

Then I remembered my own childhood ceremonies: prayers taught by my beloved grandmother that linked me to her and her god even when we were apart. I remembered the private good-bye parties to my old year the night before each birthday, starting at age four when my third sibling came almost as a birthday present for my envied younger brother. I remembered the worlds created each day in the blanket folds during illnesses, and a curious game of drawing with my brother on the doll house roof with soggy tissues that I think now must have been related to toilet-training issues.

Later a numinous ceremonial moment in my own therapy gave me an experience that has stayed with me. It occurred in a session when I felt both disoriented and suddenly thirsty. I asked if I could get a drink of water. My therapist brought me a filled cup and seemed to stand before me offering it as if he were serving communion. Swallowing that water slaked much more than my body's thirst. It gave me a sense of the transpersonal suddenly immediate and alive in the room, and it opened into an area of oral and spiritual deprivation that I could not have consciously known was there to be worked on.

On the other hand, a colleague told me recently that one of the regrets of her long therapy occurred at a time when she was in a very regressed state, feeling in her body like a three-year-old child. She found herself compelled to ask her therapist to sing with her. He was silent, allowing her to re-experience the grief of her father's abrupt dismissal of an important early childhood connection to him when he had seemed to feel she was too old for such things. The analyst interpreted her grief empathically, but the experience of rejection had been repeated, and she felt the old wound had been dug again. Again she swallowed her anger in the despair of abandonment, and the child and the musical voice went back into hiding along with it (cf. Schwartz-Salant 1982, p. 161).

* * * *

Ceremony means *rite of veneration, sanctity.* The word comes from a Sanskrit root meaning *to do.* Thus, ceremony implies action originating from and in service to the transpersonal, while its action implies the body and the world of incarnate, material reality in which the body acts. Ceremony includes specific body action and transpersonal, psychic pattern. It has meaning on more than one plane of existence, partaking of both sides of what our rationality perceives as duality. It encloses and bridges this duality with a paradox, plunging the participants into a healing and creative descent, into the unifying matrix that underlies both matter and spirit. We find in ceremonial action that the "soul and body are not two things . . . they are one" (Jung 1935, Part 3, p. 41–42). We find our beginnings again, through return to the matrix of psychic life in the "sympathetic system [where] . . . psychic contents . . . are not yet conscious [and] express themselves only in symbolic actions" (Jung 1984, p. 334). Here "the self of the body as a transpersonal entity superior to the ego and transcending ordinary consciousness" acts (Neumann 1976, p. 11). The "heaven enclosed within man's skin" (Paracelsus' phrase quoted by Jung) guides the ceremony from the psychoid level, from the interface of what we later separate into instinct and meaningful symbol. Here at the interface there is no gap between object in itself and object as perceived—no gap in which the vision of the symbolic image could occur. For

> a psychic entity can be a conscious content, that is, it can be represented only if it has the quality of an image that is *representable*. . . . [In] the processes that lie beneath the mind [as reflex arcs] the response is automatic and is not registered consciously until afterwards. (Jung 1926, pars. 607, 608)

Here the psyche cannot be directly perceived or represented. It can only be presented. And here concrete, embodied "magical" action is "the only idiom of communication." Thus at the interface of body and soul, between instinct and image, the Self creates ceremonies through which it emerges into consciousness.

The ceremonies I discuss here are different from those deliberately staged in psychodramatic enactments (Whitmont 1982, pp. 235–57) and in active imagination. They do not operate as a technique nor by conscious stage management of the repressed, fearful/fascinating affects. Indeed, they are not yet able to be discussed nor even elaborated in fantasy and image, for they are still embedded in magic consciousness and the spontaneous urges and anxieties of the preverbal, pre-symbolic body-ego in the extremes of the therapeutic regression. Thus the therapist is used as witness and partner; meaningful symbolic images can emerge only as the raw, compulsive energy moves safely within the therapeutic ceremonial container to crystallize and join image to emerging consciousness. This is the opposite direction of the formula of Eleusis, wherein the initiate's experience proceeded in terms of: I saw, I said, I did. Conversely, in the ceremonies of the emergent body-Self, the direction comes from the developmentally earlier and equally valid: I moved, I sounded, I saw (or found the image).

In therapy, the use of enacted ceremony permits the interactional field to be expanded and intruded into by the body of the patient and by the compulsions of the patient's psyche, and the responding somatic and intuitive reactions of the therapist (Chodorow 1982). What is enabled by not inhibiting such action is the "pure nature" of the prima materia, the "left-hand (sinister) side (which is) . . . dark, . . . unconscious, . . . inauspicious and awkward, . . . the side of the heart" (Jung 1954, par. 410). This needs a ceremony as a transitional object until it can become conscious enough to become speakable, for the dark, compelling, instinctive and tabooed emotions and behaviors threaten to overwhelm the emerging ego, even as they are necessary for its development.

In standing at the very border where the archetypal content seizes the body, the ceremonies provide a safe container for its threatening dynamic. This counters the fear of disintegration and permits shared, relatively safe play with the energies that need to be integrated. In the space between the no longer viable old gestalt of identity and the new, the ceremony is analogous to the maternal function supporting the emergent ego. It thus allows the therapeutic alliance to survive relatively intact, while giving the overwhelming affects of the regressive transference their own creative space within the larger frame of the analysis.[1] This often permits the working through of "psychotic" pockets in weekly (but preferably tri- or bi-weekly) analysis.

While the use of ceremonial enactment does open the analytic space beyond the safe holding frame that permits only verbal interchange, it does not violate therapeutic neutrality. For that is an attitude of nonjudgmental, witnessing, empathic reflectiveness that stands, as consciously as possible, disidentified from the therapist's own complexes to serve the patient's process.

* * * *

There is a legend from the Cree people of the northern Great Plains that provides an account of the origin of a ceremony, and illuminates the analogous developments of ceremonies that I have found created in individual psychotherapy.

The myth recounts the origins of the Young Dog Dance, a ceremony much like the Sun Dance of the more southerly Plains Indians. In the story, a young Cree brave sets out to catch an eagle in order to get its sacred feathers for his headdress. Following the custom of the tribe, he prepares a covered pit on the hilltop frequented by the eagles. Then he waits, ritually naked, praying for a bird of the Great Spirit to descend for the bait of meat he has set on the grass-concealed poles above him. He expects to catch and kill the bird. Into his vigil comes the sound of distant drumming, but not the expected bird. After two nights of the sound, he climbs from his pit and sets off to find its origins. Before dawn he comes to a lake from which the sound emerges. It stops at daybreak and resumes again at nightfall, when animals and birds appear and swim in the lake. Here the Indian maintains his fast and prayerful vigil for four days until he falls, exhausted, into sleep. He awakes to find himself in a lodge surrounded by people wearing animal skins. Some of them are dancing. They are the animals he has seen in the lake, who have changed themselves into human forms. Their chief introduces himself:

> My friend, we have heard your prayers, and our desire is to help you . . . .
> These people represent the animals. I am the Dog. The Great Spirit is very
> fond of dogs. I have much power, and my power I shall give to you, so that
> you may be like me and my spirit shall always protect you. Take this dance
> home to your people.

And he "imparts the nature of the rite to the Indian by action" (Spence, p. 192). Then the Dog asks his brother animals to take pity on the brave. After some time, the other animals give objects embodying their powers. The owl gives feathers for night vision; the buffalo gives tanned leather for strength; the porcupine, quills for weakening enemies and making them take flight. The eagle promises to be constantly with him, and hands the brave some feathers to give killing prowess in war. The crane gives a wing bone to cause fear in enemies. Other animals also bestow their gifts. After receiving all they wanted to give, the Indian falls asleep again and awakens at the lake shore. "Returning home, he taught the Crees the Young Dog Dance . . . and showed them the articles he had received. So the young men formed a Society of Young Dogs, which practiced the dance and obtained its benefits" (ibid., p. 193).

This tale tells us that the discovery/creation of the ceremony is not the original motivation of the individual's quest. Rather, a personal need leads the young man to seek the animal powers to claim by assault what he needs. The collective initiation provides him with the initial steps required. At the place where the spirit birds alight, away from ordinary interactions, he must prepare an individual pit, a temenos in the earth. He must be ritually naked and bait the pit to lure the great bird down.

So individuals come into therapy out of personal need, seeking a safe space to gain the blessing/healing they think they need from the archetypal powers: a relief of symptoms. But by working initially through defenses and resistances, like the Cree brave, the analysand goes further. She or he returns to her or his naked beginnings, going beyond what could have been expected. By offering as bait the sacrifice of established habitual adaptations, the analysand opens to the source. Like the shaman's flesh, this sacrifice attracts the powers. But unlike the shaman, this seeker and hopefully those entering therapy are not forced to total dismemberment; willing sacrifice may stave it off (cf. Perera 1981, pp. 56–62).

Going down into the womb-like earth vessel suggests the sacrifice of light and movement. It is the beginning of altering consciousness, lowering down into the dark, manmade pit to contact the spirit bird of the heights. Here, in the pit, the still-existing separation of the opposites is made conscious and opens awareness of the deeper layers of the psyche, where they are still split apart and felt sequentially. Only thereby does the brave open his awareness to ecstatic and extramundane penetrations. It is a ritual-religious analogy to what we would term regression, for the purpose of bringing about the ultimate healing of the split opposites (reconnecting spirit and matter, sky and earth, in a new pattern). In therapy, when we deal with these levels of consciousness in the regressed or not yet coherently-ambivalent ego, a holding environment must be constructed to provide opportunity for the relatively safe experience of the archetypal powers.

Our first step takes us into the depths to which our dis-eased needs have brought us, shorn of our defenses and confronting the habits of life that are no longer in tune with the Self's intent. But the myth tells us that we also need to have access to the healing patterns that can permit "corrective emotional experiences." Out of the lowered consciousness of night comes the resonance of another rhythm. It is the "upward movement of the archetypal world" rising toward manifestation. It comes in its own time, at the Kairos. All the seeker can do is to allow for a change of his or her consciousness through accepting the stresses of deprivation and pain that take him or her from accustomed modes of processing reality. Then his or her senses become attuned to the deeper levels that are heralded in the myth by the throbbing drum rhythm. This calls to the instinctive rhythms within the seeker's body. Its beat "opens doors." It evokes the primitive pulsings of the animal brain within man and invites

the seeker to the deep psychoid space where he or she is called to encounter the gods as animal powers.

These are to be met in water, not earth—in the pre-birth fluid matrix analogous to the uroboric or symbiotic field, what we call the magic
dimension of consciousness that prevails in "participation mystique."
They are beyond and below the opposites of the pit. Here the modalities
of the older, precortical brain prevail with their survival-based instinct
patterns and their raw, limbic emotionality. Here energy and emotions
and even thought patterns can be exchanged or induced, for there is no
separation of individuals, just as there is no separation of opposites. In
the fluid water of the lake world boundaries open to permit the exchanges that can possess and compel, but that can also heal. The contents
of this realm are transpersonal, collective. They have a "cosmic character"
relating to "the whole history of mankind, including animals" (Jung 1984,
p. 335).

We connect to these animal powers as they rise toward consciousness. In the myth they temporarily adopt human forms to communicate
with the Indian. In experience they make themselves known through the
body-Self, which they cause to use sounds, gestures, silences, motions, all
the senses and muscles and breath to express what feels like emotionally-
toned compulsions. This knowing by the body is virtually impossible to
articulate verbally, for it is an invisible energic attunement with archetypal intent at its instinctual pole. It has integrity and precise accuracy, mirroring the form patterns with the repertoire of the preverbal body-Self,
enabling the body to express archetypal events directly.

There is no need for symbolic image as mediator of this knowing,
for the unconscious speaks directly. And just as a dream image may affect
the dreamer without his or her knowing its meaning, so these somatic
events affect, reverberate, and change the actor. They can sear into the
soul to enforce their own modes of awareness. Thus the hands of the shaman or healer receive preconscious messages and react with them to
change the energy patterns of the patient's body. Thus the perceptions
and actions of the body-Self enacting a ceremony affect the subject who is
the object of their messages. They may help to crystallize symbolic images and further ego consciousness, but they may also by-pass ego and
still have profound healing effects, changing energy in the psychic field.
Such body knowing is comparable to that of animals, and makes them
into god forms in many mythologies. It is the object of special training for
shamans, druids, yogis, and therapists. It pervades the world of the young
child, and can be recovered through various body/ spirit disciplines.

Such altered consciousness is mediated through meditative or hypnotic trance, through body awareness, and/or through affect-laden passions. To work at the transpersonal core of our complexes where the animal powers give their gifts, we need to be able to bring these modes into psychotherapy. Free association and reverie are means of inducing mild trance. Individual patients find other modes such as gazing, automatic drawing, sounding in chant or the tones elicited by body tensions and emotion, moving the body rhythmically, or using deep breathing.

Attending to body sensations and the multi-sensory images they constellate in both patient and therapist is one way of opening lower brain consciousness. Large and subtle body motions, as well as breathing placement and depth, reveal the messages of the body-Self. Abreaction and the affects of the transference/countertransference evoke the passions of the archaic brain and its instinctive nurturant, attachment, territorial, aggressive, defensive, and erotic patterns. What grips or moves us in concrete object or person is like the animal gifts; it shows us where the powers are potent and need to be reverenced. By opening our attention and working to intensify awareness of these levels, we can learn to communicate with them.

When these magic-level states are honored in the forms given by the instinctual energies themselves—the ceremonial dance or power-embued object—the emerging ego can begin to meet the transpersonal energy in ways that can hold, tame, and mediate it into personal life (Whitmont 235). The forms of the ceremony are given by the various animal powers. Each aspect represents the incarnating archetypal intent in the here and now. In the myth the leader dog, mediator between man and other animals in northern tribes, gives the overall dance form. Then each animal gives that portion of its power from the vast reservoir of potential that fits the theme. Instead of repression or splitting, there is balancing within the larger pattern. Together the gifts provide a mixture of relevant, focused manifestations of libido that harmonize organically, summed up and rendered coherent in the created, sacred dance. Thus the ceremony, discovered/created in the "transitional space" of the animal powers, gives acceptable form to transpersonal energies and permits them to enter the personal life of the returning individual seeker to enrich consciousness.

Backlash

This legend, however, does not go far enough when it comes to modern analysands. It is only relevant to cultures that welcome visions and ceremonies and have means of testing and adapting them as sacred elements protected by the elders. In psychotherapy, the behavior that becomes the basis of the ceremonies is taboo by the collective standards of the individual. Because it has not been acceptable to the parental complexes that were the first carriers of the Self projection, it has not been mediated into conscious, personal life. It has remained in a primary state, not yet deintegrated. It has remained on the magic levels, unspeakable. When in therapy such behaviors begin to enter the life of the body-Self, they are vigorously attacked by backlashes from the negative parental complexes.

Indian culture has collective means of integrating individual ceremony and vision, for it acknowledges their sacrality. Psychoanalysis seeks to promote such integration by the inner figures of the analysand's psyche, by warding off envying destructiveness that can turn against the emerging ego or the therapist as carrier of the new energy, against the therapy, or against the energy itself as source of new life patterns.

Because the human mind becomes conscious through differences, this dialogue between the old, closed, primarily negative-to-life system and the latent patterns made accessible in therapy is a vital part of the integration of the true ego. It helps to strengthen the emerging-ego's relation to the instinct for self-assertion, as well as his or her capacity to discriminate.[2]

Individual Ceremonies

The ceremonies that arise in therapy within the regressive phase of analysis need to be individually created/discovered. Although there are many spiritual disciplines, including psychoanalysis, and it helps for the therapist to know techniques from many of them, those who develop ceremonies in therapy need to find their own. This avoids a subtle form of infantilizing that can impede individuation (Kaminer 1978, p. 241) and it circumvents resistance and/or empty compliance. Generally the individuals who create their own ceremonies in therapy have been forced into collective adaptation too early, to their own peril, and have a fierce integrity preventing submission to borrowed techniques (even sandtray or bioenergetic and gestalt activities). They are passionate about reaching through their own fears to invent rites that express their individual Self's necessity in the specific concrete forms and at the particular times in which that necessity compels their bodies to enactment.

The Animal Gifts in Psychotherapy

In psychotherapy the gifts of the animals are revealed in the themes of the most common ceremonies. All of these themes are related to basic survival patterns. Roughly grouped, they fall into nine (sometimes over-lapping) categories:

Perceiving—including the various modes of altered consciousness, mild trance and hypnotic trance when self-induced, as well as the role exchanges of the transference/countertransference that permit discovery of disabling complexes and of healing archetypal constellations.

Affirming of existence—including the use of mirror and mirroring, the leaving of objects in the therapy space as tokens of the individual's continued existence for the therapist, and the naming and affirming of the body and its perceptions.

Nurturing—including the use of blanket, food; and the acquisition of life skills such as the care of the body.

Holding—including touch and staring in session, and the use of concrete objects, drawing, writing, and the telephone and answering machine to contain affects that threaten fragmentation of the fragile pre-ego.

Orienting—including gazing to assemble the parts of the therapist's body and face images, as well as projected emotional states; the use of concrete objects, drawing, and gestalt enactments that manifest current psychic states.

Guarding—including ceremonies of protection and warding off that might use song or gesture, incantation, or mana-endowed objects.

Identifying with the powerful and protective therapist—including wearing similar clothes, rings, using similar body language.

Constancy of connecting—including objects passed back and forth, letters, telephone sessions between meetings, as well as objects, pictures, songs taken home as transitional objects.

Binding and mastering of still raw energies—including the re-peated enactment of fearful/fascinating aggressive and nurturant and attachment behaviors.

All of these use the material world and the body, the first vessel of identity for humans. Since they operate from and with the patient's body, they make the treatment of very deep regressions possible in weekly and bi-weekly therapy. They begin to build a sense of the body itself as a transitional object between the healing temenos of therapy and everyday life. Thus states of panic and disorientation and the felt loss of identity that accompany such states can sometimes be assuaged, contained, and reoriented through awareness of breath and body. Like the talismans and ceremonial actions linking patient and the therapy and therapist on which are projected the Self, the body ultimately becomes a link to the Self, regaining the sacrality it has lost in our culture (Woodman 1980, 1982; A. Greene 1984; Chodorow 1982). Care of the body, its messages, pleasures, and needs, becomes an individuating necessity when it is seen as the vessel of incarnation.

A Nurturance Ceremony

The patient was a 41-year-old single professional woman with a history of depressions and victimizations and a sadistic-critical animus derived from her negative mother complex. After several years of peeling away persona defenses that guarded her traumatized Self child, she brought me the gift of a comb, a replica of one she had bought for herself. Because of the open boundaries in the regressive transference, gifts for the therapist may also be concrete messages from the animal powers. They may be ceremonial tokens for the emerging part of the patient projected into the symbiosis. I wondered about that, since the comb was a replica of her own. But first I checked the transference messages carefully as a flood of comb images entered my mind: Was something messy? Did I need to straighten my thoughts or straiten them? Was I being warded off like Baba Yaga? Was there some Snow White-smothery witchiness around inducing unconsciousness? Was there a Lorelei seductiveness present? Did I need more awareness, so she could temporarily have less? Did she feel I was not sufficiently mirroring her thought?

I sat with my musings as she tried to evade focusing on the gift, and I brought her attention back to it, wondering silently if she needed to take care of me as an expression of her own habitual role as caretaker. She began to talk about her memories of childhood care, of her hair being scrubbed and scraped like the kitchen floor, of her feeling and body sensitivities being ignored. I began dimly to sense her longing, like a distant drumming, for something she could not express, for it was unthinkable. I asked if she had brought the comb so she could begin to wonder about the feel of her hair combed a different way. Savoring that thought, she slowly and at the very end of the hour asked if I could possibly imagine or bear to comb her hair. It felt clear that the gift to me was a message about her valid compulsion to seek the care she had always before felt she was unworthy to receive.

At the next hour I had the comb on the table, and she was frightened and excited to have it/herself remembered. I knew we were at the level of the animal lake, for she magically identified the comb with herself. She talked about the craving that had grown in her to have me answer what she had asked. She found herself obsessed with the idea of my combing her hair, but she felt ashamed of the "ridiculous dependency." She told me a dream that had convinced her that her question was "a gross overstepping of boundaries." In the dream she is in session and I ask if she would like to try some freshly baked bread. I also show her paintings by a "very interesting patient" whose session she, the dreamer, thought had been a violation of the office because she had painted in session. Working on the dream, she described nauseous feelings that she had violated our work with her gift. How could I imagine combing her hair or feeding her fresh bread? Anyway, she was not interesting like the other patient who could paint vivid, free-form colors. Slowly we began to sort out her assumptions, based on her experience of her mother's self-care and care of her daughter. The mother's room was inviolate; it was taboo to enter; there was no tenderness of child care. Child care was a nuisance. Dirt was everywhere and cleanliness was the supreme virtue.

Her gift had opened into the core of her negative mother complex and her learned fears of intimacy. But again, near the end of the hour, she reflected, "If you haven't had some experience, you can't know it. Somewhere in my body I sense there is something here I need. Something like a comb ceremony. Would you do it?"

I decided, feeling some resonance of its rightness for her, that I must not keep her in the withdrawn space of her childhood, not force her again to have to imagine her world instead of experiencing it, as she had learned so well to do. So I picked up the comb. She sat with her eyes closed and her sense of touch vibrantly alive. When I finished combing every hair carefully in the manner that came through to me as I tuned into the animal powers, she said very reverently, after silence, "Thank you. That was like receiving a benediction."

At the next session the comb was available on the table, but she had to process "the backlash"—her guilt for what she felt was a theft, and her fears of the negative mother projected into me, of being called dirty, and of her certainty that she had disgusted me. She brought a compensatory dream in which an officious woman accuses her of stealing meat from a store when she is only comparing two packages of it. After we talked about the sadistic shadow figure and its misperceptions, she told me how she had experienced the combing. It was soft, different from what she had known. It opened up comparisons between the ways she had lived and cared for her body and another style of living. She said she was scared to see the comb again, but would have felt rejected not to. Now that she had had the experience, however, I could put it away. I commented that that sounded like her mother's "once is all you get," and she smiled wryly and thought she would like another combing. Again I complied, for I knew repetition aided the new learning.

I stood for a moment gathering myself and opening to the ritual space and time. I felt the aura of energy around her head as my hand approached it, and sensed our mutual submission to the impersonal process unfolding within the limits of our capacities. Then after this *rite d'entrée* I began gently to comb her hair. Almost immediately I was hit with a deep revulsion and a sadistic wish to pull and scratch with the comb. I paused, trying to stay open to the ceremony, aware that it had been invaded. I knew I was projectively identified with the mother, who could not metabolize raw affect. I felt an image of snakes rise from the pit of my stomach's revulsion. I knew I was facing hair turned to snakes, some immense envy that had turned the once beautiful Medusa into a petrifying monster.

I breathed deeply and tried to orient. I had some choice as to whether to stop, accepting the petrification, or to try to contain it and continue the ceremony of nurturance. This was her hair, fine as a baby's, and this was a ceremony that we had consciously entered. As I struggled to keep the toxins away from the hand that held the comb, I held my consciousness vigilantly focused on the comb as vessel of the healing energy she had felt before. It was like a meditation exercise for me. As I held off the toxic envy, an image of Shiva, with his long hair that let the Ganges fall softly to earth and his face blue from holding the world's poison in his throat, came into my mind. I found I could then relax from the tension of my inner conflict, knowing there was a transpersonal container of the toxins and a deep purpose to the combing.

The woman before me sat comfortably secure, sensing with her skin every touch of the comb. She was awed this time, she said, that she could feel so much with her body, and that the ceremony could be so powerful even a second time. I was quite shaken and tired, but I knew I had to work on what had happened to me.

That evening when I had time, I decided to return to the ceremonial space to meditate on the revulsion in my stomach, with my notebook beside me to try and witness the backlash that had invaded me. In session before the combing, we had explored the backlash for her. She had confronted the sadistic shadow figure and been freed to enter the ceremony. For her the spoiling and creating came sequentially. The opposites were separate and split. But the two ends of the value had hit me simultaneously. Fortunately, while she was open only to the sensory/ spiritual levels of the presymbolic experience, I was operating with consciousness that also made associative personal and archetypal images available. I opened to them again to find orientation as I sat intensifying the sense of revulsion and the sadism. I knew I had got caught in the induced spoiling reactions of her negative parental complexes that resonated through some complexes of my own, and I had to process the poisons as part of the necessary ritual cleansing of the countertransference. I knew that later I could use some of the differentiated material with the analysand interpretively.

My body reactions led me into affects and memories showing me where my negative mother complex intersected with hers, and I saw where I needed to do some work there. Meditation on the image of Medusa, underworld goddess and rival of Athena, led me to my fear and my power complex. I realized I had some anxiety about encouraging "gross acting-out" as I experienced an inner image of an animus figure accusing me of violating the father's daughter's rules for analytic behavior. That was my fear. Then there was the dark Goddess's fury, my own envy of the good care I was giving away. It made me look for where I needed better to honor my own body. And as I felt the Medusa as "ruleress" and Goddess of the Sea (Kerenyi, p. 49), I found a transpersonal orientation for power issues. It showed that the flickers of sadistic power I had felt at the woman's total dependency on me, and the power against me in her potential demandingness, were aspects of the Abysmal Goddess. They were not to be taken personally, but were part of Her power over us to enforce the ceremony and the analysis as it took us both into areas of the great matrix, the underworld.

I realized there were aspects of the ceremony between us that had nothing to do with the nurturance she experienced. There were profound meanings related to redeeming the underworld feminine from the collective animus's derogation. For me these meanings had to do with the ethics that value conscience as the voice of the transpersonal Self above the superego animus. They had to do with honoring the body as a sacred duty, reverencing the spirit in the concrete, literal world. They had to do with making the sacrifices of personal power and ego consciousness necessary to go where the process leads us. And they had to do with my connecting to a new kind of animus, imaged in the ceremony as Shiva. Like the Dog of the Cree legend, he creates the dance in which all the parts find their ordered balance, and he serves the energy of the whole, the Goddess as Shakti.

I awaited the woman's next session with a sense of the depths moving us, and I thought about the deep relevance of the symbols, Medusa and Shiva, for her psychology. She came looking very attractive, bringing material about her idealizing transference and memories of her personal mother complex. We proceded with the work. After several weeks she asked for the comb ceremony once again, and in the next weeks reported that she was treating her own body with a different touch and a different attitude. The enabling space and action of the ceremony had released the healing process latent in the transpersonal pattern that could emerge when that nurturant pattern found its own structure matched in the environment (Bowlby, quoted in Stevens 1982, p. 53). Thus the ceremony matched the Self's intent and served as a bridge for bringing the gift of the animal powers into the analysand's personal life. She said she had learned an alternative attitude to being "alive and female," which would have been beyond her ken without the ceremony. "My body feels sacred when I touch it that way," she commented. Repetition of the hair combing was no longer needed, and I began to forget to put the comb out on the table when she came. She had internalized the nurturant and healing touch that reverences body as manifestation of the Self and the Goddess, and the use of the ceremony as "transition object" lapsed.

A Multi-theme Ceremony

The patient was a 30-year-old woman, married but separated, struggling to complete her second year of law school. She had had two previous therapies, each of about two to three years' duration. She came into analysis in crisis over fear of exams and living alone. Her intellectual personal defenses had collapsed. Her initial dream presented an accurate picture of her state. In it there was a small fish darting about wildly in an old wreck, chased by sharks. I felt her to be flooded with anxiety, her sense of identity wrecked and largely unconscious, her psyche overwhelmed and darting about, unable to focus.

Sitting with her rapid changes of subject and her desperation was hard. When I tried to follow, my effort seemed to feel like the sharks to her. Any interpretation was experienced either as devouring criticism or as a potential threat that she had to chase off with a barrage of words. I fell silent and began to attend to my breathing and body reactions, to hold the anxiety that her state engendered in me. The effect of the stillness and very rare empathic comments about her fear eventually had an effect. In contrast to the stillness, she began to recognize her own propulsion and her own shallow breathing.

As we began to name her fears, she began to hold some degree of disidentified witnessing of them in session. She found she could model on my therapeutic attitude in the biweekly sessions, which were all that were possible, and it soon became clear that she needed the same relative clarity outside the consulting room. Musing on the problem, she found her attention drawn to a wooden box on my desk. It compelled her. She found it fascinating, magical. She asked if she could borrow it. She wanted to try writing the names of her "sharks" on pieces of paper to store them in the box until she could dump them out in session. I thought of the way Moslems write the names of blessings onto a plate and then water and drink the ink to assimilate the beneficence. Here she would name to bind and eject the malevolences.

The wooden vessel became an extension of the holding environment of the therapy, a transition object. It functioned as a portable guardian of the toxins that her fragile sense of identity could not yet tolerate. As vessel, it had archetypal connections to the maternal embrace, the infant's first experience of mediating boundary between inside and outside. And unlike the old wreck in her dream and her experience of an alcoholic and depressed mother, what she both projected onto and discovered and recognized in the box's objective, literal form shored up her capacity to survive fragmenting anxiety. It served as a constantly available, concrete manifestation of the new experience of safety and holding that she experienced in therapy and of which she had no previous experience. Because the wound to her positive maternal complex reached back to the time before object memory was stabilized, she had developed precocious intellectual defenses and a caretaking persona, but had no opportunity to develop the relatively continuous experience of identity from within.

The box became a surrogate membrane of protection, and naming her fears gave her a modicum of control over them. After some weeks, she no longer brought in the box with its torn and scribbled strips of paper. The ceremony lost its energy, which is the fate of transition objects. But she did not return the box. I realized it still filled a magic need and did not speak about it.

Her fears resurfaced some weeks before my vacation, and she began to bring the box filled with small crackers for us to share. Again it seemed important not to analyze the communion snacks, simply to accept them. At the last session before the holiday, she asked me to refill the box from the store container of crackers she knew I had. At the leave-taking meal, there was a sense of "the last supper" as she talked about her fears of the separation. Again, however, the ceremony she created held her. When I returned from vacation, she told me she had eaten those "special crackers" from the box whenever she felt lonely or anxious.

The box with its good filling had now acquired a sense of the breast from which she could have nourishment and solace. The wheat crackers had for me symbolic analogies with the loaves baked in honor of the Goddess and Her connection to grain. They ensured the analysand's communion with the Great Mother, projected onto the therapist, and she followed the Christian enjoinder, "Do this in memory of me," albeit without conscious connection to the great collective ceremonies. For the small, personal rite had the same source. I steered by the symbolic images to corroborate instinct, but since she was not interested, and they would have been experienced as spoiling her personal discovery, I held them silently.

The analysis proceeded. The woman took a leave from law school and began to explore her painful childhood in dream images and memories, and in the transference. By taking me into carefully defended areas and opening to new experiences, her sense of identity as she knew herself began to fall away. She found herself consciously in a deep regression.

During this time she used the wooden box again in a ceremony. One session, she brought it to the table beside my chair and opened it with obvious fear, yet was compelled to show me its contents. Inside the box was a small figure drawn as if the artist were four years old—a round torso with stick limbs and a round head with huge eyes and no mouth. I could feel that she was asking me to relate to an unfed, unspeaking proxy of a part of herself about which she had deep shame. I felt she was pushing me to react, to help her to find an attitude on which to model her own reactions. I was aware of a mix of tenderness toward the child part of her, of admiration for the woman's courageous confession of the state of her "true" ego behind her schizoid and intellectual defenses, and of dismay. I could sense the burden of what would be demanded: hourly feedings with an eyedropper—an accurate intimation of what the work was to be like during phases of the regressive transference when she telephoned frequently to be reassured that the bond between us held. I could also feel her expectation that I react to the drawn figure as if it were real, for on the magic level of her consciousness at that moment, there was no distance between object and percept in which to react symbolically.

We were on the level of the animal powers, and they had not yet assumed human form to speak verbally to us. Appropriate gesture and act were required, for when I made a verbal comment about the child part of her, she was miserably silent, as if I had betrayed her. I could feel the intentionality in her wordlessness, and realized that not only was it a clue to the level of her regression, but also it was a fierce test from her guarding defenses to discover whether I could react differently from the manner in which her earliest caretakers had behaved. I felt challenged, and I felt the induced reaction to reject the moment with some glib remark, as she felt her mother had often rejected her.

I commented that the child had been alone a long time. She remained silent. I looked at her clenched lips and silent face and at the box on the table. In the impersonality of the two forms presented as a terrible display—wood box madonna and paper child—there was a starkness that confirmed the exclusion of empathic care. I found myself thinking, "This box is not good enough." But I also sensed that my "being present at the process [which] brings about an effect of grace" (Jung 1951, par. 205) was going to demand my own sacrifices, which I would need to process as I went. I did not know where we would go, and I would be forced to levels of trust alongside her.

I thought about what to do. The response elicited at such moments must vary according to the field constellated between analysand and analyst and the Powers that guide the process of the therapy. I realized I was there with my own set of complexes, inhibitions, routines, and experiences. But thinking, and even feeling, was too rational for the moment. I fell back on instinct, the "right way" (Neumann 1976, p. 15), through memories of playing with my children; thereby I could contact the animal powers.

Silently and very slowly, sensing her intensity at every move, I took a tissue, folded it, and put it under the paper figure. The woman hovering beside me sobbed with what I felt was both relief and terror that she, too, was now committed to something about which she could have no conscious knowledge nor intention. After a period of silent tears, she responded. She took another tissue and made a blanket for the figure. Then she pulled herself together, took the box with its mutually accepted and therefore precious contents, and departed. We had ceremonially entered a new level of the analytic dialogue.

We were playing like a mother and child playing dolls (cf. Grolnick 1984, p. 261), but the tone was solemn and ceremonial. Thus every action, although using simple objects, seemed to have reverberations through time and the deepest layers of the psyche. This sense of sacred play underlies the old rituals of chess, whereby the movements on the gameboard have magical effects on the battlefield (cf. the Welsh tale of "The Dream of Rhonabwy" in the *Mabinogion*).

The woman brought a dream to the next session that oriented us about the play's relationship to the healing of infant-mother bonding issues. She dreamt that "we are sitting side by side; no, maybe I am on your lap on a kind of throne seat, almost like another lap. We are looking out in the same direction. I'm safe." This level of holding is antecedent to mirroring (Nelson & Smith 1984, p. 38). It expresses the basic support that confirms that the body of the child is safe and that its perceptions can be shared and affirmed, stood under. It is a particularly poignant form of support for an analysand whose view of reality was often disconfirmed in childhood. The dream image also reassured me that the process by which the ego was emerging was appropriately supported by the therapist as carrier of the projected mother/Self, and both were supported by the Goddess as throne (Isis, or here the ancient earth Goddess Anu—St. Anne, whom the Celts infiltrated into medieval Christian iconography).

Our shared sense of the seriousness of the play guided the analytic process for the next years. The box and its paper contents were temporarily left in my office for care when she dreamt that the child was "sickly and autistic." Then she found a box of her own in which she as "healthy child" carried back and forth tokens and revelations: things that gripped her interest and compelled her to take them. "This wanted to come," she often said, operating magically where things seem to have life of their own. She brought a photo of herself at six months, already anxious and precocious, sea shells, burrs, pins, mementoes of her walks around the city and of her life and feelings. They were concrete expressions of tenderness, rage, need, disgust—the whole gamut. Each demanded to be received and acknowledged in its place in her daily life and in the transference. She began to learn about symbolic consciousness.

Looking back now at that moment when we began to play, I see that the use of the box and drawing was not only to soothe the separation/individuation process as transitional objects evolve in infancy, but also served as a bridge from her defended, autistic part toward the possibility of a therapeutic symbiosis. It created/discovered the possibility, in ceremonial form, of repairing very early—even fetal—bonding wounds through return to the transpersonal matrix that was rising up to compel the actions. And it enabled the creation of the healthy child.

The deepest part of the regression was analogous to gestation in a womb vessel, and she expressed that sense of it much later when she felt able to be more directly and verbally intimate in the transference relationship. I learned then that there were several motives behind her compulsion to use a ceremonial object in the depths of the regression. One derived from the magic mode of substituting box for mother. The young child *has* to use a concrete vehicle for preverbal communication. It is not yet able to function symbolically. But another motive lay in her fear of invading the therapist's body to gain it as a sheltering womb. Since image and object are not separate on this level of consciousness, she feared that her need to enter the therapist's body would do actual damage to her person; thus she created the use of the box as a transitional object, and it was magically analogous to the body. Thirdly, her "relatedness to a non-human object (was a) substitute for an (as yet) unattainable relatedness . . . toward another human being" (Searles 1960, p. 303).

In patients with extreme early maternal deprivation, there is inter-nalized a taboo against relatedness that involves use of another's body. As this woman expressed it, "It's not legitimate to use you. I need to invade your body, and that's not legitimate, even to think." On the level of magic, a thought is equivalent to action, and her need for shelter endangered the source of shelter. The degree of intimacy implied by touch and hold-ing or by imaging bathing, nursing, and feeding is hard enough for pa-tients with this damaged early dyadic relation. But the intimacy implied in entering another's body, "being received into your womb, so I can find a home on earth," as she put it, was unbearable and terrifying, albeit necessary.

By the time she was able to verbalize the "invasion," the deepest part of the regression was over and she had successfully sorted out the nega-tive parental complexes from current transferential reality. She had some capacity to separate from the magic-omnipotent level of the transference, to realize that the therapist did not need her as her parents had. Their misuse of her care-taking capacities and their failure to respect valid lim-its, exploiting the child she had been, had overstimulated her omnipo-tence in service to their needs. When in the transference she had created a standpoint outside that corrupted omnipotence, had accepted her own realistic dependency needs and limitations, and had found she was ac-ceptable "just simple and me," only then did she find a perspective sufficiently outside the old system's exacerbated magic and malforma-tions. This perspective enabled symbolic thinking and an intimacy that could be felt as valid, since it grew from within her own subjectivity. Until that time, unable to "think" her needs because thought was too potent and her needs were taboo, the child part of her had had to use concrete objects and actions as substitutes for thought.

Interpretations

The forward motion of the psyche with its creative, healing ceremo-nies comes spontaneously from the animal powers, the Self, through the magic level. It moves us and reveals itself through body action and concrete objects. It is primitive, primary, elementary, and original. It requires new modes of expression to be conveyed accurately. It is too new to speak in conceptual language, because the concepts we would use necessarily belong to old patterns. Like the sprouting tip of green, the new patterns arrive through action and cannot yet be categorized because they are insufficiently visible. Yet they are already fully alive and specific.

Conceptual interpretation has little value at this point. It may be useful earlier, and again later. Not only has it little effect on the child part of the analysand, with his or her magic consciousness, but it makes that part feel ignored, since thinking interpretation comes from a different level of consciousness.[3] It may also threaten the pre-ego, since much verbal interpretation makes it feel looked *at,* distanced from, in ways that seem to reduce the analysand's sense of subjective being. Thus it may reinforce the schizoid defenses and experience of alienation, and actively threaten the organic growth of the emergent ego in the transferential relationship. Silence is the usual response that analysts offer to this problem when a patient protests, "You're putting things into words before they're ready, like taking bulbs out of darkness before they are rooted;" or, as another said, "This is a female mystery; we can only speak after we have lost speech."

While "subjectivity needs to be experienced, not interpreted" (Ujhely, personal communication), interpretations, when accurately timed, are the best tool for dealing with the fixed, negative complexes of the backlashes. They serve to foster objective discrimination, and thus distance and separation (Grunes 1984, p. 140). They help to establish an emptied and protected psychic space into which new patterns of libido can grow, but they do not nourish the new.

In the space between silence and concept there are many empathic sounds and statements, gestures and facial expressions, to mirror affect and to nurture the emerging ego. There are also simile and metaphor. A very wide range of therapeutic interventions can be presented in metaphor. They do not threaten the emergent libido patterns, and they do not reinstate old complexes by naming new wine with old labels. Instead they playfully find and activate new energy because they come creatively from the subjectivity of the analyst sharing the mutual field. They come from below, from proprioceptive intuitions, from the level of the animal power. And they point toward, but they do not define or pin down, what needs emerging space. They suggest and circumambulate the new in a feminine, receptive, musing manner. They dig up the possibility of a sensed fit, but give initiative back to the analysand to play with the connection and to make or create a precisely valid fit. Thus they do not rob the analysand of his or her own creativity. The metaphoric image is not symbolic for the analysand until this fit between the preverbal libido pattern and the verbal image form is recognized or created. By playing and experimenting here, the emergent ego opens to symbolic and mythic capacities.

This form of verbal playing leaves open the gap between subjective and objective perceptions in the transition space (Winnicott 1971, p. 151). Thus it is a linguistic analogy to the ceremony. It operates with the paradox that the individual is both actor/speaker and spectator/receiver in his or her own communication, moved and moving from within, sharing and supported from without.

There are other modes of ceremonial play to enable the perceiving and creating of bridges between levels of consciousness, as well as between the individuals engaged in the ceremony. One example of such a perceiving ceremony occurred in therapy with a deeply defended man who had a history of abuse in childhood and a period of visual hallucinations during adolescence. After five years of analysis, he developed what he called the "gazing ceremony." To enter this, he anchored himself by staring into my eyes in a way that I came to feel was like that of a nursing infant. Then he let his preverbal, body-sense imagination be free in trance. After shared silence he moved to a verbal level, and needed us to share the visual, auditory, and kinesthetic images that had arisen separately in each of us. When he realized, over time, that our perceptions were usually very similar or centered around a similar body-affect experience of the silent field between us, he could begin to trust his own processing of sensory data. He could begin to let his fear of an hallucinatory recurrence dissipate. We called the experience *matrix vision.* Since it gave him a safe and shared view of the potency of the unconscious to bond with another, it offset his schizoid loneliness and confirmed his capacity to see medially and to move between levels of consciousness in a shared world.

A Mastering Ceremony: Issues of Management

The therapist needs to decide whether the enactments are safe and acceptable. Usually the taboo against action is excessive, and the analysand operates fearfully within the field of the therapist's acceptance, testing and intuiting permission to release.

One woman was compelled to buy a set of wooden blocks on the way to session. She used them for some minutes, building on the floor. When I found myself wondering whether she had read about Jung's stones, I knew that her energy was absent. She began to knock the blocks down and asked me to join her in playing. Soon she began to grip a small piece of wood with determined fervor. I could sense that she began to feel it as a missile, and waited silently as the energy built in her. She began to look around the room. I nodded toward the couch, risking that her aim would be good enough. She tossed the block rather hesitantly, and looked at my face. I nodded again, and she began to throw one block after another. Her energy built to a fierce pressure, then it dwindled until she had had enough. The action both bound and mastered an opening phase of her aggression, providing a revelation of strength and a capacity for focus that were altogether new. It also brought a flood of deeply buried somatic memories of rage and abuse that provided material for verbal analysis.

In general, I try not to allow action if I cannot feel the situation is safe for both the analysand and myself. I then say, "Wait a minute," and process the intention verbally, insisting on imaging and feeling through the intended act. Not until I have a clear sense of the individual's trust in my witnessing presence and responsibility, and of his or her connection to the therapeutic vessel as valued space, would I concur to the release of such aggressive actions. The block-thrower did not throw at me or the lights and windows, because she had included me in her play and because I suggested an alternative within the ceremonial frame.

Problems

There can be problems, deflections, impasses, and even failures in the use of ceremonial enactments in the regressive transference. From the therapist's perspective, these occur mainly out of fear, both instinctive and animus-based. There can also be dread of the intensification of the transference to symbiotic fusion levels, but in my experience, working through near-psychotic pockets is facilitated and contained through the use of created ceremonies. There can also be occasions where the analytic persona may seem threatened, or we think we lack the skill to relate to the emerging-ego's need and reject the essential requirement to have all levels of experience gathered then into one container. Dissipation of this primary focus may occur when we are tempted to send the analysand off to other caretakers during critical phases of the regressive transference. But it is equally important for the analyst to have personally experienced and studied the modalities used in ceremony, especially sensory awareness and body work.

There are also potential problems relating to the psychic hygiene required to monitor the induced reactions and the personal complexes and archetypal levels touched in the therapist's psyche. There are all the potential permutations of the power shadow of the analyst. There may be too little or too much fear of the numinosum, and the lack of personal integrity that accompanies such disrespect. There is also the danger of the analyst's need for self-gratification and the attendant encouragement of merger and acting-out by the analysand, rather than supporting his or her Self needs. It is always important to question whether the ceremonial action deflects rage, which could be verbally expressed toward the analyst, or encourages personal bonding or fixation in relation to the person of the therapist, rather than facilitating the bond to his or her individual Self.[4]

There are also problems relating to the analysand's psychology. Ceremonies have autonomy, and can transform the participants and themselves, but they can also "stay and become mere habits which do not transform—i.e., do not bring about any change in the psyche" (Plaut 1975, p. 12). They then become addictive sources of gratification. This is especially true with borderline patients who lack a coherent body/Self sense or image in which to contain and assimilate experience. When identity is based on stolen moments of symbiotic fusion with which they seek to ward off the omnipresent fear of fragmentation, the ceremonial mode is counterproductive. Fixation at the level of uroboric bliss and its delusion of omnipotent merger with the parent/ Self may result from originally alienating connections with the parent that the analysand attempts to repeat, trying to redeem them. Acting out such compulsions reinforces the addiction to the traumatizing parental complex and remains a sterile habit. Such behaviors need to be confronted verbally and analysed, to release the rage and despair on which they are based.

Besides addictive compulsions aimed at illusory gratification, there may also be habitual defenses aimed at destroying the analytic vessel itself—attacks on the illusory negative and withholding therapist. The extreme forms of the negative transference, "attacks on linking," may be seen as compulsive defenses. They are stereotypic, quasi-ceremonial attempts by the analysand to control his or her fear of dependency on an assumed abuser. But they are based on identification with the aggressor, and serve to spoil the possibility of a transformational space both between analyst and patient and between Self and fear-struck, potential ego. When such defenses occur, the therapist needs simply to survive without retaliation, and to analyze the impasse.

In these cases, where there is an excess of fear and an inadequate sense of holding environment and inner core, the ceremony becomes a stopgap fetish. Dream images and the therapist's felt sense of the situation bring this to consciousness and can be used in the interpretations of the transference/countertransference to create, eventually, a trusted vessel.

Since the use of ceremony always alternates with working through the backlash, there is the possibility that the ceremony can become co-opted into this resistance to its transformational possibilities, by making the therapist into the directive authority. This is especially true in the early stages of the creation of a ceremony, and it requires subtlety of perception for the therapist to sense the projective identification of himself or herself with old complexes or an animus that the analysand obeys in order to avoid the sacrifices of individual descent. Here the therapist needs to reframe issues so they are centered between analysand and Self—to learn to be dumb and patient, fostering the initiative that comes from the animal powers, if they are waited upon. This is especially a problem for the narcissistic sectors of the analyst, where identification with the mana-filled omniscient or omnipotent authority robs the analysand of creativity.

In some cases there may be empty ceremonies, attempts by the analysand to reach the depths by rote affect release or intellectual means. They feel hollow and lacking in libido, and it is important to analyze the collective dependency they reveal. Whenever the act feels facile, or the ceremony verges on hysterical play, whenever there is no fear, then the actions are probably a resistance to the transpersonal and need to be dealt with as if they were backlashes.

The Instinct for Ceremony

The analysands who create ceremonies have a special talent for it—a profound aesthetic-religious core, what Jung has called the instinct for the transpersonal. It has been with them throughout life, erupting unconsciously and otherwise dormant, often buried too deeply for the analysand to find it. This confirms that the hidden, true ego of the dis-eased personality lives close to magic-ceremonial roots, close to the transpersonal and the Self. That hidden ego does not incarnate to develop in the untrusted outer world, but maintains a secret, defended link to the center that is as fresh and as overwhelmingly raw as a child's. When recovered, accepted for itself, and allowed to awaken and play in the safe, mediating ceremonies of psychotherapy, it discovers again the animal powers and relates to them openly from the body-Self that creates profound and awesome forms. These forms provide attunement to transpersonal energy patterns that can then be "practiced" to "obtain . . . the benefits" that enrich personal and collective life.

Notes

1. The analytic frame is not the same as the transpersonal, ceremonial vessel. The two exist in a necessary therapeutic tension, the maintaining of which is an important aspect of the therapeutic art (Wyler Greene, comments in response to this paper at Ghost Ranch, 1985). Thus, although it posits the risk of controlled acting-out, ceremonial enactment does not merely gratify and thereby diffuse consciousness. Rather it is a form of experiential learning, of "corrective emotional experience" to dose and form the hitherto tabooed energies that the Self and Self-child require, and guide by means of the newly created, spontaneous forms of the ceremony.

2. The new learning, one in resonance with archetypal intent, comes out of the preverbal, magic-level matrix of consciousness. It alternates in analysis with backlashes from the fixed, inertial, and debilitating complexes that would spoil the new. This happens in an organic, even necessary, rhythm, analogous to the dialogue between Moses and Pharoah in the Old Testament. Every time Moses succeeded with God's help in getting permission to leave the place of enslavement, God also hardened Pharoah's heart. Over and over the process repeated in a numinous, miserable alternation. Similarly, the emerging ego suffers the rhythm that brings consciousness and increasing will and strength.

3. The levels I am here discriminating—by no means all the possible ones—are: a) the preverbal, concrete-literal, magic level of consciousness, with its embodied and affectual perceptions and expressions; b) the level of the metaphor, symbolic image, and mythologem; and c) the rational, conceptual, explanatory level. The development of these levels of capacity correlates roughly with child development, and may be roughly analogous to the lower and right and left brain functions. While any of these levels can open toward spiritual and transpersonal experience, and while each of them is structured by archetypal form patterns, each functions with its own modalities and demands its own kinds of imagination and relationships (Ujhely 1980; Whitmont 1982, pp. 41–75). Each level has its own integrity and is not reducible to another; however, as adults, we can optimally move back and forth among them.

4. Such personal bonding may be a necessary interim stage, but the therapist needs to know that it is not the end point. Cf. Kohut's discussion of Schweniger's indispensible role in Bismark's life as an "idealized selfobject" (Kohut 1984, pp. 19–20).

References

Chodorow, J. 1982. Dance/Movement and body experience in analysis. In *Jungian Analysis*, M. Stein, ed., pp. 192–203. La Salle, Ill., and London: Open Court.
———. 1984. To move and be moved. *Quadrant* 17/2:39–48.
Corbin, H. 1972. *Mundus imaginalis* or the imaginary and the imaginal. *Spring* 1972: 1–19.
Finley, P. 1975. Dialogue drawing: An image-evoking communication between analyst and analysand. *Arts Psychotherapy* 2:87–99.
Greene, A. 1984. Giving the body its due. *Quadrant* 17/2:9–24.
Grunes, M. 1984. The therapeutic object relationship. *Psychoanalytic Review* 71/1: 123–24.
Harrell, M. 1983. The hidden self: A study in the development of the feminine psyche. Diploma thesis, C. G. Jung Institute, New York.
Jung, C. G. 1926. Spirit and life. In *Collected works,* vol. 8, pp. 319–37. Princeton: Princeton University Press.
———. 1935. Psychological analysis of Nietzsche's Zarathustra. Unpublished seminar notes. Recorded and mimeographed by Mary Foote.

_____. 1946. On the nature of the psyche. In *Collected works*, vol. 8, pp. 159–234. Princeton: Princeton University Press.

_____. 1952. Synchronicity: An acausal connecting principle. In *Collected works*, vol. 8, pp. 417–519. Princeton: Princeton University Press.

_____. 1954. The practice of psychotherapy. In *Collected works*, vol. 16. Princeton: Princeton University Press.

_____. 1959. *Aion: Researches into the phenomenology of the self.* In *Collected works*, vol. 9/i. Princeton: Princeton University Press.

_____. 1963. *Mysterium coniunctionis.* In *Collected works*, vol. 14. Princeton: Princeton University Press.

_____. 1984. *Dream analysis: Notes on the seminar given in 1928–30 by C. G. Jung,* W. McGuire, ed. Bollingen Series XCIX. New York: Pantheon.

Kaminer, H. 1978. Transitional object components in self and object relations. In *Between reality and fantasy: Transitional objects and phenomena,* S. Grolnick and L. Barkin, eds., pp. 223–43. New York: Jason Aronson.

Kerenyi, C. 1951. *The gods of the Greeks.* London and New York: Thames and Hudson.

Khan, M. M. R. 1974. *The privacy of the self: Papers on psychoanalytic theory and technique.* New York: International Universities Press.

_____. 1983. *Hidden selves: Between theory and practice in psychoanalysis.* New York: International Universities Press.

Kohut, H. 1984. *How does analysis cure?* A. Goldberg, ed. Chicago: University of Chicago Press.

Machtiger, H. G. 1982. Countertransference/Transference. In *Jungian analysis,* M. Stein, ed., pp. 86–110. La Salle, Ill. and London: Open Court.

Nelson, L., and Smith, N. S. 1984. Perceiving in action: Interview with Bonnie Bainbridge Cohen on the developmental process underlying perceptual-motor integration. *Contact Quarterly,* Spring/Summer, pp. 24–29.

Neumann, E. 1976. On the psychological meaning of ritual. *Quadrant* 9/2:5–34.

Perera, S. 1981. *Descent to the goddess: A way of initiation for women.* Toronto: Inner City Books.

Plaut, A. 1975. Where have all the rituals gone? Observations on the transforming function of rituals and the proliferation of psychotherapies. *The Journal of Analytic Psychology* 20:3–17.

Sarton, M. 1980. *Recovering: A journal, 1978–79.* New York: W. W. Norton.

Schwartz-Salant, N. 1982. *Narcissism and character transformation: The psychology of narcissistic character disorders.* Toronto: Inner City Books.

Searles, H. 1960. *The nonhuman environment in normal development and in schizophrenia.* New York: International Universities Press.

Spence, L. (n.d.) *The myths of the North American Indians.* New York: Farrar and Rinehart.

Stevens, A. 1982. *Archetypes: A natural history of the self.* New York: Wm. Morrow and Co.

Ujhely, G. 1980. Thoughts concerning the *causa finalis* of the cognitive mode inherent in pre-oedipal psychopathology. Diploma thesis, C. G. Jung Institute, New York.

Whitmont, E. 1982. *Return of the goddess.* New York: Crossroad Publishing Co.

Winnicott, D. W. 1965. *The maturational processes and the facilitating environment: Studies in the theory of emotional development.* New York: International Universities Press.

_____. 1971. *Playing and reality.* New York: Basic Books.

Woodman, M. 1980. *The owl was a baker's daughter: Obesity, anorexia nervosa, and the repressed feminine.* Toronto: Inner City Books.

_____. 1982. *Addiction to perfection: The still unravished bride.* Toronto: Inner City Books.

Zimmer, H. 1960. On the significance of the Indian tantric yoga. In *Spiritual disciplines: Papers from the Eranos yearbooks.* Bollingen Series XXX. New York: Pantheon Press.

The Body as Symbol:
Dance/Movement in Analysis

Joan Chodorow

The dance is the mother of the arts. Music and poetry exist in time; paint-
ing and architecture in space. But the dance lives at once in time and
space. The creator and the thing created . . . are still one and the same
thing. (Sachs 1937, p. 3)

This paper will discuss the use of dance/movement as a form of active imagination in analysis. The history of this work emerges out of two
traditions: depth psychology and dance therapy. The roots of both can be
traced to earliest human history, when disease was seen as a loss of soul
and dance was an intrinsic part of the healing ritual.

The importance of bodily experience in depth psychology has not
been fully recognized, despite Jung's interest in and experience of the
body and his understanding of its relationship to the creative process. I
will take up some of this material; look at the early development of dance
movement therapy, with attention to Mary Starks Whitehouse and her
contribution to the development of active imagination through move-

Joan Chodorow, M.A., is a Jungian analyst practicing in California's Bay Area. She is a
graduate of the C. G. Jung Institute of Los Angeles and a member of the C. G. Jung Institute
of San Francisco. Her dance therapy training was with Trudi Schoop and Mary Whitehouse.
She is a member and former president of the American Dance Therapy Association. She and
Louis H. Stewart teach an annual summer course for professionals on dance/movement as
active imagination.

ment; and explore the process of using dance/movement in analysis. This will lead to discussion of dance/movement as a bridge to early, preverbal stages of development.

Depth Psychology

Throughout his life, C. G. Jung seemed to listen to the experience of his own body: "I hated gymnastics. I could not endure having others tell me how to move" (1961, p. 29). "My heart suddenly began to pound. I had to stand up and draw a deep breath" (ibid., p. 108). "I had a curious sensation. It was as if my diaphragm were made of iron and were becoming red-hot—a glowing vault" (ibid., p. 155). His visions, too, were clearly experienced in his body:

> Suddenly it was as though the ground literally gave way beneath my feet, and I plunged down into dark depths. I could not fend off a feeling of panic. But then, abruptly, at not too great a depth, I landed on my feet in a soft sticky mass. I felt great relief. (Ibid., p. 179)

From his boyhood realization that he had two "personalities,"[1] Jung was interested in questions about the relationship of body and psyche. His earliest psychological study included observations of unconscious motor phenomena (1902, par. 82). His work with some of the severely regressed patients at Burgholzli led him to question and eventually discover the meaning of their peculiar, perseverative, symptomatic actions (1907, par. 358). His word association studies involved measurement of physiological changes that occur when a psychological complex is touched. His later speculations about the existence of a psychoid level and his alchemical studies continued to explore the relationship between instinct and archetype, matter and spirit. In an evocative paper entitled "Giving the Body Its Due," Anita Greene (1984) writes: "For Jung, matter and spirit, body and psyche, the intangible and the concrete were not split or disconnected but always remained interfused with each other" (p. 12).

Adela Wharton, an English woman physician, told Joseph Henderson that during one of her analytic hours, Jung "encouraged her to dance her mandala-like designs for him when she could not draw them satisfactorily." The room was not large, but a small clear space was sufficient (Henderson 1985a, p. 9; 1985b). We know very little about the details of her dance, or what it stirred in each of them, or how they came together afterwards. But in his "Commentary on 'The Secret of the Golden Flower,'" Jung wrote:

Among my patients I have come across cases of women who did not draw mandalas but danced them instead. In India there is a special name for this: *mandala nrithya*, the mandala dance. The dance figures express the same meanings as the drawings. My patients can say very little about the meaning of the symbols but are fascinated by them and find that they somehow express and have an effect on their subjective psychic state. (1929, par. 32)

Jung touched on this theme again in his 1929 seminar on dreams:

A patient once brought me a drawing of a mandala, telling me that it was a sketch for certain movements along lines in space. She danced it for me, but most of us are too self conscious and not brave enough to do it. It was a conjuration or incantation to the sacred pool or flame in the middle, the final goal, to be approached not directly but by the stations of the cardinal points. (1938, p. 304)

As early as 1916, Jung suggested that expressive body movement is one of numerous ways to give form to the unconscious (1916, par. 171). In a description of active imagination, he wrote that it could be done in any number of ways: "according to individual taste and talent . . . dramatic, dialectic, visual, acoustic, or in the form of dancing, painting, drawing, or modelling" (1946, par. 400). As with so many aspects of his work, he was far ahead of his time. The idea of using the arts as part of a psychotherapeutic process must have been startling in 1916. The original paper was circulated privately among some of Jung's students, and remained unpublished until 1957. Still more time had to pass before the creative art therapies could emerge and be recognized by the mental health community.

Dance Movement Therapy

Dance therapy became a profession in 1966, with the formation of the American Dance Therapy Association. The pioneer dance therapists were all women: dancers, choreographers, and teachers of dance, they shared a common passion and deep respect for the therapeutic value of their art. At first, they were without any kind of clinical training and they lacked a theoretical framework. But each of them knew the transformative power of dance from personal experience. Although isolated from each other, they taught in private studios and made their way into psychiatric hospitals and other clinical settings throughout the 1940s and '50s. Some of them started as volunteers; part-time or full-time jobs were created for them after they established themselves. Dancers, psychotherapists, and others came to study and apprentice with the early practitioners, who began to develop theories to support their keen observations.

The need to develop a theoretical framework led most of them to psychological and other related studies (Chaiklin and Gantt, 1979).

Mary Starks Whitehouse was one of the early movement therapy pioneers. She received her diploma from the Wigman School in Germany and also was a student of Martha Graham. Her personal analysis with Hilde Kirsch in Los Angeles and studies at the Jung Institute in Zurich resulted in the development of an approach that is sometimes called *authentic movement* or *movement-in-depth*. In a paper entitled "Reflections on a Metamorphosis" (1968), she told the story of this transition:

> It was an important day when I recognized that I did not teach Dance, I taught People. . . . It indicated a possibility that my primary interest might have to do with process, not results, that it might not be art I was after but another kind of human development. (p. 273)

Her work has many aspects. She was the first to describe movement from different sources in the psyche:

> "I move" is the clear knowledge that I, personally, am moving. The opposite of this is the sudden and astonishing moment when "I am moved." It is a moment when the ego gives up control, stops choosing, stops exerting demands, allowing the Self to take over moving the physical body as it will. It is a moment of unpremeditated surrender that cannot be explained, repeated exactly, sought for, or tried out. (1979, p. 57)

> The core of the movement experience is the sensation of moving and being moved. Ideally, both are present in the same instant. It is a moment of total awareness, the coming together of what I am doing and what is happening to me. (1958)

As she developed her approach to movement, she taught her students to become aware of a specific inner impulse that has the quality of a bodily felt sensation:

> Following the inner sensation, allowing the impulse to take the form of physical action, is active imagination in movement, just as following the visual image is active imagination in fantasy. It is here that the most dramatic psychophysical connections are made available to consciousness. (1963, p. 3)

She was also interested in visual images that come out of the movement experience, as well as images from memories, dreams, and fantasies. Whether the images were God-like, human, animal, vegetable, or mineral, she encouraged her students to remain in their own bodies and interact with the interior landscapes and personified beings that appeared. There were times when the images themselves seemed to want to be embodied, as if the image could make itself better known by entering the body of the mover. Then her students would experience not only *dancing with,* but they would allow themselves at times to *be danced by* a compelling inner image.

She developed much of her work through an extremely simple structure. It involves two people: a mover and a witness. Whitehouse was primarily concerned with exploring and understanding the inner experience of the mover. Some of her students, other dance therapists, and analysts have been developing the work further, toward a deeper understanding of the inner experience of the witness and the relationship between mover and witness. When this work is brought into the analytic *temenos,* many questions arise about how the dance/movement process weaves into the larger context of a Jungian analysis.

Dance/Movement in Analysis

The use of dance movement in analysis is similar in many ways to the use of sandplay. Both are a nonverbal, symbolic process that usually takes place within the analytic hour. The analyst serves as participant/witness. It is the quality of the analyst's attentive presence that can create the "free and sheltered space" that has been so beautifully described by Dora Kalff.

As with other forms of active imagination, the use of dance/movement relies on a sense of inner timing—inner readiness. Sometimes the timing is wrong. For example, when tension or discomfort is building in the verbal work, the idea of moving may be an unconscious form of avoidance. But most people are able to sense when it's time to imagine an inner dialogue, when to move, when to build a sandworld, or use art materials, or write, or bring in a guitar to sing their own song of lamentation or celebration.

The various forms affect each other. For example, when sandplay and movement are both part of the analytic process, analysands may sometimes experience themselves moving as if they were inside one of their own sandworlds, interacting with some of the tiny figures. When this happens, it tends to evoke in the mover an Alice-in-Wonderland quality, as she or he meets the imaginal world with intensified interest and curiosity. Whether the mover has grown smaller, or the sandworld larger, things are getting "curiouser and curiouser." The mover usually meets such a novel situation by becoming even more alert and attentive, learning all she or he can about this strange, yet familiar, landscape and its inhabitants.

Alice may be a particularly useful model of a strong, young feminine ego who is learning how to follow her curiosity (down the rabbit hole, or through the looking glass) into an unknown realm—the unconscious. She is wide awake, questioning everyone and everything. The story offers a helpful image for any form of active imagination, that of the ongoing, interwoven relationship between Alice (curiosity) and Wonderland (imagination).

Another similarity between dance/movement and sandplay is that specific themes emerge that seem to follow stages of development in early childhood. More about this later.

Analysts and analysands find individual ways to introduce dance/movement into the analysis. When initiated by the analysand, it may be as spontaneous as the mandala dance described above. Or, there may be much previous discussion and exploration of feelings and fantasies about moving.

When initiated by the analyst, movement may be as spontaneous as a moment of playful, nonverbal interaction. Or it may be as subtle as the mirroring and synchronous breathing that naturally occurs when we open ourselves to a state of "participation mystique." An analyst may invite the analysand to enact a specific dream image (Whitmont 1972, pp. 13–14), or psychosomatic symptom (Mindell 1982, pp. 175–97; 1985). Analytic work on a body level may be grounded in a specific approach that includes the use of gentle touch techniques (Greene 1984). Or, dance and movement may be introduced through a series of workshops and continued in the individual analytic hours that follow (Woodman 1982, 1983).

When the analyst is familiar with and interested in dance/movement as active imagination, his or her analysands are likely to want to move at some point in their work. But there are also analysands who are fully committed to work with the unconscious, yet never or rarely feel the need to leave their chairs. Some people move every hour, some a few times a year. Some get involved with a particular body level theme and work on it intensely for weeks or months, and then continue on a verbal level.

The movement itself may take no more than ten minutes—or it can go on for an hour or more. Sometimes it is helpful to decide in advance on a time period, perhaps twenty minutes, and have the analyst serve as timekeeper, letting the mover know when to (gradually) bring the movement process to an end.

Physical safety issues need to be discussed. The mover closes his or her eyes in order to listen for the inner sensations and images. But if he or she begins any kind of large swinging, spinning, leaping movements, any kind of momentum that could lead to a collision with windows, furniture, or what have you, it is essential that the eyes be open. Even when the quality of movement is smaller and slower, movers have to learn to open their eyes from time to time to keep an orientation to the room. It is difficult to do this without losing the inner-directed focus. But if the work involves a true meeting of conscious and unconscious, maintaining a sense of where one is in a room becomes part of the conscious standpoint. This is easy to say, but often extremely difficult to do. When one is moving in this way, the eyes usually *want* to stay closed. To open the eyes (even a tiny slit) takes a major effort. At times, one's eyes feel as if they are glued shut.

A photograph of a Siberian shaman depicts him in a garment that has ropes hanging from his waist. Heavy metal weights are tied to the end of each rope. The shaman enters an ecstatic state as he begins to dance, whirling around. The ropes with their heavy weights fly out around him; a person could be badly injured, if hit by even one of them. The shaman is in a trance, but at the same time, remains conscious and restricts his dancing to an area that is safe. No one gets hurt (Henderson 1985b).

This aspect of the shamanic tradition is similar to the process of active imagination. The essence of both processes requires the capacity to bear the tension of the opposites, i.e., to open fully to the unconscious, while at the same time maintaining a strong conscious standpoint.

The Mover and the Witness

Dance/movement usually needs a brief warm-up period. A time to stretch, relax, and attend to the depth and rhythm of one's breathing helps to prepare the physical body for inner-directed movement. It may also serve as a rite d'entrée into the experience—a time when both mover and witness may become more fully present. After the warm-up, the mover/analysand closes his or her eyes, attends inwardly, and waits for an impulse to move, while the witness/analyst finds a corner in the studio where she or he can sit and watch. Movers are encouraged to give themselves over to whatever the body wants to do, to let themselves be moved by the stream of unconscious impulses and images. At the beginning, the witness/analyst carries a larger responsibility for consciousness while the mover/analysand is simply invited to immerse in his or her own fluctuating rhythms of movement and stillness. In time, the mover will begin to internalize the reflective function of the witness, and develop the capacity to allow the body to yield to the unconscious stream of impulses and images, while at the same time bringing the experience into conscious awareness.

In movement, the unconscious seems to manifest in two recognizable ways: in images and in bodily felt sensations. Some movers experience the unconscious predominantly through a stream of inner visual images. Others may experience it primarily through the body. The initial preference seems related to typology. But the movement process tends to develop an increasingly balanced relationship to both realms. As we learn to listen and respond, our attention usually fluctuates back and forth. Each realm may constellate and enrich the other. A woman describes a movement experience that has the quality of such a dialectic:

> My left hand became hard fisted. It was like a phallus. I moved through all levels with this strong, hard, left forearm and fist. Then, the fist opened. It opened so slowly that it was like a reversal from numbness. As my hand relaxed slowly into openness, a large diamond appeared in my palm. It was heavy. I began to move my left arm in slow spirals around myself. I was aware of feeling the sequential, overlapping rotations of shoulder, elbow, wrist, and even fingers. Both arms came to stillness together, joined behind my back. The left hand continued to hold the diamond. Then, the image of the diamond came in front of my eyes. It grew larger, until I could see through it with both eyes. It showed me a vision of everything broken up by its facets. The diamond grew larger, until I was inside it looking out. The light was bright—almost golden. I bathed in it and felt that it was a healing kind of light. Now, my body shape took on the diamond's many facets. I was myself, my own shape, but each part of me had many cut surfaces. It was as if I could "see" through the myriad facets of all of me. There was a sense of wonder and suspension and peacefulness.

This mover describes a fluctuation and constant interchange between two sources of movement, the world of the body and the world of the imagination.

The experience of the analyst/witness ranges along a continuum that has at its poles two modes of consciousness. They are sometimes described as Logos or directed consciousness, and Eros or fantasy consciousness (Jung 1912; Stewart 1986, pp. 190–94). They are known by many names. The alchemists spoke of a mysterious marriage between Sol and Luna.

Let us take a moment and imagine how the same landscape might be affected by sunlight and by moonlight. Sunlight, or a solar attitude, offers us clarity. It enables us to divide what we see into its separate parts. But when it gets too bright, everything becomes harsh, glaring, dry. When the sun is at its peak, we live in a world without shadow. The moon, on the other hand, reflects a mild light. It reveals a moist, shimmering landscape. Everything merges. In the darkness we find an unsuspected unity (Jung 1963, par. 223).

What does this have to do with witnessing movement? The witness fluctuates between a solar, differentiated, objective, definitive way of seeing, to a lunar, merging, subjective, imaginative way of seeing. The same movement event may be seen and described in many ways:

> As I watch, I see the mover crouch low with her face hidden. Only her arms reach forward, with wide-spread hands pressing flat on the ground. With an increasingly deep cycle of breathing, she slowly drops forward onto her knees and elbows, and finally slides flat onto her stomach, stretched full length on the ground. Her arms draw together in a long narrow shape, slipping between her body and the floor. She rests, breathing deeply.

> As I watch, I let myself imagine and remember what it is like to go deeply inside. I know that this woman was largely ignored during the early years of her life, due to a series of illnesses in her family. As I watch, I feel an ache in my throat and my heart goes out to her. I now see her as if she were a very young infant. I imagine holding her close to my body, we rock back and forth with merging rhythms. As I imagine holding and rocking her, I slowly become aware that I am actually rocking slightly. Later on, I realize that our breathing has become synchronous.

> As she presses her hands into the ground, I experience mounting tension and for a moment, I'm fearful that she'll press harder and harder and suddenly explode. But instead, she slides forward and lies on her stomach. She has now withdrawn so much that there is very little movement. My mind wanders. I pick at a hangnail. I feel irritated with her, then guilty and irritated with myself. I imagine she is sitting on a volcano. In any case, it feels as if I am: my shoulder muscles are contracted, my jaw is tight, I'm not breathing very much. My mind dimly wonders whether I might be picking up something about her father's cycle of violent outbursts and subsequent remorse. Or is her withdrawal too close to my own way of avoiding anger?

As she kneels low, the shape of her body reminds me of the Moslem prayer ritual. Another image comes: one of the paintings Jung did for his Red Book shows a little figure that bows low, while covering its face. An enormous fire spout is erupting out of the earth in front of the little person. It fills the upper half of the painting with intricately formed red, orange, and yellow flames.

We know from ancient tradition that the Feminine Mysteries are not to be spoken. Yet consciousness demands that we reflect on and at some point name our experience. When and how do we speak about the experience of dance/movement? How do we understand the meaning of the symbolic action? Do we interpret it from the perspective of transference and countertransference? When and how do we allow the symbolic process to speak for itself? When and how do we respond to it in its own language?

Dancers know instinctively that there is danger in "talking away" an experience that is not ready to be put into words. Isadora Duncan was asked to explain the meaning of a particular dance. Her reply: "If I could tell you what it meant, there would be no point in dancing it."

Analysis offers a different perspective, but analysts, too, know the danger of making premature interpretations that would analyze feelings away (Greene 1984, p. 14, pp. 20–21; Machtiger 1984, p. 136; Ulanov 1982, p. 78).

There are three aspects of dance/movement in analysis that we gradually learn to remember: 1) What was the body doing? 2) What was the associated image? 3) What was the associated affect or emotional tone? There are heightened moments when all three are clearly known and remembered by both mover and witness. When we're aware of both physical action and inner image, we are likely to be conscious of the emotion as well. But there are times, just as with dreams, that we remember very little. When the mover is conscious of his or her experience, it can be told. Telling it to the analyst is not unlike telling a dream. But a dream is different from active imagination. Active imagination is closer to consciousness. Also, in dance/movement as active imagination, the analyst is literally present and able to witness the experience as it unfolds. The analyst/witness may be unaware of what the motivating images are until after the movement, when the two participants sit together and talk. Or, the analyst/witness may be so familiar with the mover's previous dream and fantasy images that he or she can sense and imagine the nature of the images while watching. Sometimes, the movement comes from such depths that mover and witness experience a state of participation mystique.

When an untransformed primal affect is touched, the mover may "space out," or feel dazed, or stuck, or in some other way become numb to it. Or, if the mover goes with it—if she or he merges with the affect/archetypal image—she or he is likely to be taken over by a primal affect, or by resistance to it, or a logjam of both. At such a moment, the emotional core of the complex is experienced as toxic, even life threatening. At one time, it may well have been that.

Sylvia Perera (1981) writes so beautifully, as she tells the story of our descent to a realm that has been unimaginable and unspeakable:

> Work on this level in therapy involves the deepest affects and is inevitably connected to preverbal, "infantile" processes. The therapist must be willing to participate where needed, often working on the body-mind level where there is as yet no image in the other's awareness and where instinct and affect and sensory perception begin to coalesce first in a body sensation, which can be intensified to bring forth memory or image. Silence, affirmative mirroring attention, touch, holding, sounding and singing, gesture, breathing, nonverbal actions like drawing, sandplay, building with clay or blocks, dancing—all have their time and place. (p. 57)

Because much that goes on in the analytic relationship at this level is preverbal, we will turn to some of our earliest experiences as they appear in dance/movement, and relate them to certain stages of normal development in infancy.

Sources of Movement

An earlier paper (Chodorow 1984) discussed the origins of movement from different aspects of the psyche. Four sources were suggested and illustrated: movement from the personal unconscious, the cultural unconscious, the primordial unconscious, and the ego-Self axis. Although every complex has elements that are personal, cultural, and primordial, themes that emerge through the body are so immediate that it seems possible and helpful to sense from which level or source it is constellated.

Dance/movement is one of the most direct ways to reach back to our earliest experiences. Movers frequently lie on or move close to the ground. By attending to the world of bodily felt sensations, the mover re-creates a situation that is in many ways similiar to that of an infant who swims in a sensory-motor world. The presence of the analyst/witness en-

ables re-enactment and re-integration of the earliest preverbal relation-
ship(s). It is here that images of the transference and the countertransference may be most clearly recognized.

This paper will introduce five symbolic events that appear and reappear in the movement process of many individuals. They seem to represent certain stages of developing consciousness through the preverbal,
presymbolic developmental period of infancy, i.e., from birth to approximately sixteen months. The symbolic actions and interactions are: 1) patterns of uroboric self-holding; 2) seeking the face of the witness and,
when found, a smile of recognition; 3) the laughter of self-recognition; 4)
disappearance and reappearance; and 5) full engagement in the symbolic
process via free imaginative use of mime.

Two sources have been essential to my recognition and understanding of these events. Louis H. Stewart (1981, 1984, 1985, 1986) has been
updating Jung's model of the psyche from the perspective of child development and recent studies of the affects and their expression. Charles T.
Stewart, a child psychiatrist, has been developing a theory of play and
games as universal processes in ego development (1981). Working individually and in collaboration (C. T. Stewart and L. H. Stewart 1981;
L. H. Stewart and C. T. Stewart 1979), they have gathered a wealth of material from Jung, Neumann, Piaget's observations, Tomkins's study of the
affects, and anthropological research into play and games. From these
and other sources, they have brought together certain phases of ego development described by Neumann, with fully embodied observations of
real babies.

Infant and child development is most often studied from the perspective of patriarchal values. For example, Piaget wanted to understand
the development of the intellect, so even though his observations demonstrate a development of both imagination and intellect, his theory
shows a one-sided emphasis on logos functions. Louis H. Stewart and
Charles T. Stewart give us a way to understand the development of the
imagination. Together, both perspectives form a whole, an ongoing dialectic between the twin streams of life instinct. One stream is Eros as
imagination, divine relatedness; the other is Logos as intellect, divine curiosity (L. H. Stewart 1986, pp. 190–94).

In the following pages, we will discuss each theme as it appears in
dance/movement, and explore it from the perspective of infant development. The ego-Self axis is constellated at the threshold of each stage. The
experiential core of each passage in the development of consciousness is
a startling, even numinous moment of synthesis and re-orientation.

Uroboric: Patterns of Self-Holding

Movers tend to expolore a very wide range of uroboric self-holding. We see all kinds of patterns: one hand holding the other; thumb-holding; arm(s) wrapping around the torso to hold rib(s), elbow(s), hip(s), knee(s), foot or feet. All of these seem reminiscent of those earliest body experiences when we at first unintentionally find, then lose, and find again—and gradually discover what it is to hold ourselves. In infancy, the first primal recognition of self may well be that powerful and comforting moment when thumb and mouth find each other:

> We may see that the infant, while sucking its fingers or its toes, incarnates the image of the mythical Uroborus that, according to Neumann, represents the "wholeness" of that undifferentiated state of self-other consciousness that is characteristic of this developmental state. We can also see in this early behavior the earliest evidence of that aspect of the autonomous process of individuation that Neumann, following Jung, has called *centroversion*. In this light we may understand the infant's behavior in the discovery of sucking its thumb as representing the first synthesis of the psyche following upon the rude disruption of life within the womb, which had more impressively represented a paradisiacal absorption in the purely unconscious processes of life itself. (L. H. Stewart 1986, p. 191)

When the mover is immersed in self-holding, his or her eyes are closed, or have an inward focus. There is usually rocking, swaying, or some other kind of rhythmic pulsation. The quality is usually complete self-containment. If the analyst/witness opens himself or herself to a state of participation mystique, he or she may join the mover in a timeless state, and experience a similar kind of rhythmic self-containment. Shared rhythms of holding, touching, lulling, and lullabies are the psychic nourishment of this earliest phase.

If the analyst/witness does not enter into a state of participation mystique with the mover, he or she may feel excluded, irritated, uneasy. Alternatively, or even concurrently, he or she may feel shy, embarrassed to watch an experience of such intimate union with self. As with any other analytic work, witnessing requires opening to the unconscious, and at the same time maintaining a conscious analytic standpoint to reflect on the meaning of the symbolic action and the associated countertransference response.

At times, the experience has a different, perhaps more conscious quality. There is a sense of wonderment as the mover's hands discover and explore the shape of his or her own body. As the mover's hands shape themselves to the bulges and the hollows, the hard bones and the soft flesh, there is a profound sense of self recognition—as if meeting oneself for the first time. Both mover and witness often feel as if they are participants in an ancient ritual form. After many years of witnessing women and men spontaneously discovering the shape of their own bodies with their hands, I learned of a myth that demonstrates so clearly such a return to our uroboric origins. The myth of Changing Woman,[2] who presses and molds her own body as she comes of age, is still re-enacted throughout the American Southwest in the form of an initiation ceremony.

First Smile: Recognition of Other (Approx. Second Month)

The movement process frequently evokes a special smile that is reminiscent of the infant's earliest recognition of the "other." When the movement comes to an end, it is almost always followed by continued inner attentiveness—a period of natural self-containment similar to the uroboric quality. Then, as the mover makes the transition to everyday consciousness, it is as if she or he is gradually waking up. When the mover's eyes open, she or he usually begins to search the room for the analyst. When the analyst's face is found, there is a mutual sense of reconnection and, most often, the smile(s) of recognition. The mover may have just experienced painful emotions; his or her face may still be wet with tears. But as he or she gradually comes back to the dayworld and scans the room for the analyst's face, there is a meeting and a clear-eyed smile. Even when the quality of the therapeutic relationship is primarily that of two adults, any fully spontaneous smile has at its core the infant's smile when she or he first consciously recognizes the now familiar face of the mother or other primary nurturing adult.

Louis H. Stewart (1984) reflects on the infant's first smile:

What are the first signs of love in the infant and child? Our Western image of childbirth has been that the mother must suffer and the child come crying into the world. All this has more recently been questioned and there are those who talk about infants entering the world with smiles on their faces and wide awake mothers ready to smile back immediately upon birth. We are far from knowing then what may be the possible potential of the development of love in the child. However, what is observable today is that the mutual smile of recognition between mother and infant does not occur for several weeks after birth. Before that the child smiles under certain conditions of satiety, half awake, half asleep, but in a dazed, glassy-eyed manner. Then there comes a moment, as early as the end of the first month sometimes, when the infant, awake and clear eyed, smiles in what is unmistakably a pleased recognition of the familiar sounds and face of the mother. Soon, within days or weeks, the infant's first joyful laugh occurs. (p. 1)

First Laugh: Recognition of Self (Approx. 3 Months)

From time to time, usually in the midst of movement, the mover laughs. There are many kinds of laughter. This one expresses joy in the sheer exuberance of bodily motion, and/or a particular image appears and there is the laughter of self-recognition (Stewart and Stewart 1981). Piaget describes such a laugh:

> It will be remembered that Laurent, at 0;2(21), adopted the habit of throwing his head back to look at familiar things from this new position. At 0;2(23 or 24) he seemed to repeat this movement with ever-increasing enjoyment and ever-decreasing interest in the external result: he brought his head back to the upright position and then threw it back again time after time, laughing loudly. (Piaget 1962, p. 91)

Charles T. Stewart draws an analogy between the infant's first laugh and a similar moment in the analysis of an adult, reported by D. W. Winnicott. Winnicott's patient was described as a schizoid-depressive man who could carry on a serious conversation, but lacked any kind of spontaniety. He rarely, if ever, laughed. In the midst of one of his analytic hours, the patient imagined himself doing a backward somersault, similar to the movement made by Laurent when he threw his head back and laughed. Winnicott (1954) writes of his patient:

> On important but rare occasions he becomes withdrawn; during these moments of withdrawal unexpected things happen which he is sometimes able to report. . . . The first of these happenings (the fantasy of which he was only just able to capture and to report) was that in a momentary withdrawn state on the couch, he had *curled up and rolled over the back of the couch.* This was the first direct evidence in the analysis of a spontaneous self. (p. 256)

Joan Blackmer writes of a dream in which two small, agile tumblers, trained acrobats, turn somersaults. Among her amplifications, she describes their trickster quality: "They certainly are transformers. . . . The somersault, in itself a moving circle, is a mandala, a symbol of the Self, which causes change *through human motion.* Psychologically, this represents a change in attitude." (1982, p. 8)

The laughter of self-recognition always turns our world around.

Disappearance and Reappearance: Object Constancy (Approx. Ninth Month)

There are so many ways that the mover/analysand hides from the witness/analyst—and reappears. The dance/movement structure itself is a game of disappearance and reappearance (as the mover's eyes close and open again). But within the movement, even with eyes closed, the mover may turn away and do some small, intricate gestures that the witness cannot see. If the witness follows his or her curiosity and moves to where the gestures can be seen, the mover may turn away again, and the cycle can repeat itself. Often, if the witness stays put, the mover turns around again to where she or he may be seen. Sometimes peek-a-boo and other hiding games and activities emerge as overt, central, conscious themes in dance/movement enactment.

Separation anxiety develops in the third quarter of the baby's first year. At the same time that the infant begins to struggle with the pain of separating from beloved persons, she or he immerses herself or himself in games of peek-a-boo, and intensely investigates problems of disappearance and re-appearance.

> At 0;8 (14): Jacqueline is lying on my bed beside me. I cover my head and cry "coucou"; I emerge and do it again. She bursts into peals of laughter, then pulls the covers away to find me again. Attitude of expectation and lively interest. (Piaget 1952, p. 50)
>
> 0;9(15): Jacqueline wails or cries when she sees the person seated next to her get up or move away a little (giving the impression of leaving). (Piaget 1952, p. 249)
>
> 0;9(20): Jacqueline is lying down and holds her quilt with both hands. She raises it, brings it before her face, looks under it, then ends by raising and lowering it alternately while looking over the top of it: Thus she studies the transformations of the image of the room as a function of the screen formed by the quilt. (Piaget 1954, p. 193)

As the first smile is the beginning of mother-child differentiation, peek-a-boo, and later games of hide-and-go-seek, continue an ongoing process that leads toward the development of object constancy.

Pretend Play: Separation of the World Parents (Approx. 16 Months)

Jung describes this major passage of consciousness as:

> . . . the first morning of the world, the first sunrise after the primal darkness, when that inchoately conscious complex, the ego, the son of the darkness, knowingly sundered subject and object, and thus precipitated the world and itself into definite existence. . . . Genesis 1:1–7 is a projection of this process. (1963, par. 129)

A number of passages in the infant's first year create the base upon which a clear separation of dayworld and dreamworld can occur. Neumann (1954, 1973) refers to this differentiation of conscious and unconscious as "separation of the world parents." In the infant's life, this passage comes not through the word but rather through the discovery of nonverbal, symbolic play—that is, the baby discovers that she or he can pretend. It is this first, independent discovery of *symbolic action* that coincides with the beginning of real curiosity about language.

> Around sixteen to eighteen months of age, the child becomes aware of the semiotic function through the experience of pretense, for example in the miming of an already adaptive behavior pattern like the ritual behavior adopted to ease the transition into sleep (e.g., thumb-sucking and fingering the satiny edge of a blanket). The child laughs with joy at this new recognition of Self; and this is pretend play (Piaget, 1962). But let us reflect for a moment on the sleep ritual. This is not a neutral pattern of behavior. It represents one of the landmarks in the child's development. If the transition to sleep and waking is not easily accomplished, the child may be forever prone to sleep disturbances, to excessive fear of the dark, needing a night light, etc. And why is going to sleep difficult? Because it brings together the child's most feared and distressing fantasies, that of being deprived of the presence and comfort of those most dear, and of being left alone in the dark which is peopled by who knows what ghostly phantoms. Thus we consider it no accident that the child discovers pretense in the recognition of the sleep ritual; pretend play begins with the miming of a behavior pattern which has assisted the child in warding off fear of the unknown and soothing the anguish of separation. Subsequent pretend play will be seen to reenact all the emotionally charged experiences of the child's life. (Stewart and Stewart 1979, p. 47)

Similar to the infant's first discovery of pretend play, the dance/movement process in analysis often begins with the miming of a familiar behavior pattern that has served to ward off emotional pain. Also similar to children's play, imaginative mime can lead the mover toward and eventually through the emotional trauma that lies at the heart of a complex.

The following descriptions are of three women, each in the early stages of analytic work.

A woman begins to move by expressing a happy-go-lucky attitude, "moving on." Then she pauses and her chest seems to collapse. With a feeling of increasing heaviness, she lowers herself to her knees and becomes overwhelmed by a deeply familiar sense of despair.

A professional dancer puts on a show that would dazzle Broadway. She then sinks to the ground, becomes very quiet and begins to move slowly. The slow movement is halting and looks increasingly painful. Her body convulses and she seems to be in a trance.

A busy, active executive enacts her overscheduled life. For a moment, she pauses, looks down to the ground and realizes how tired she is. She struggles briefly with her yearning to lie down, and overcomes it by returning to the portrayal of her active life.

Each woman in her own way struggles with the tension between an overly bright, adaptive persona and its shadow. As in any analytic process, a pair of opposites will be constellated. Out of the experience of that twofold tension, a third reconciling symbol will eventually be born: a new inner attitude that contains yet also goes beyond both perspectives.

Carolyn Grant Fay describes the emergence of such a moving symbol. The mover is a woman who has had many years of analytic work. She does not begin with avoidance of pain, nor does she seek it. She begins by listening deeply:

> I lay for what seemed like a long time, listening inwardly to myself. My throat brought itself to my attention. It hurt and felt constricted and tense, so I let my throat lead me into movement. It led me up to kneeling, then forward, and then slowly across the floor in a sort of crouching position. In my imagination I became aware as I concentrated on the throat that it was red with blood. The heart area was also aching and bloody. Finally my throat brought me up to standing and propelled me farther along. It stopped me suddenly, and I just stood there. At this point, I collapsed onto the floor and lay there motionless. There was no movement . . . not an image . . . nothing.

> After a while I became aware that the color red from the blood was there at my throat and breast. Little by little it became many shades of red from light pink to deep crimson. A rose began to take shape, rising out of the throat and heart through movements of my arms up, out, and around. The rest of my body down from that area seemed, in the fantasy, to be forming the stem and leaves of the flower. All sorts of superlatives come to me now as I try to express how I felt at that moment: warm, happy, fulfilled, in order, at one with myself. (Fay 1977, pp. 26–27)

Closure

More important than whether we use dance as a form of active imagination, is the question of how we can fully engage the imagination. Jung suggests giving free rein to fantasy, according to the individual's taste and talent. Some people have what he called "motor imagination" (1938, p. 474). It is the nature of such an individual to experience life in terms of spontaneous movement activity and to imagine with and about the body. Thus a dialogue is initiated between interest and imagination as twin streams of libido: *interest in the body the way it is,* and *fantasies of what the body might be about* (Stewart 1986, pp. 190–94).

As the process of individuation leads us to become who we are, certain analysts and analysands are inevitably led to use dance/movement as part of their analytic work. For those with a motor imagination, dance/movement is simply the most immediate, natural way to give form to the unconscious. Some find dance/movement essential because they feel alienated from the body, or because they only know how to direct the body and now sense deeply that they must learn to listen to it. Some turn to dance/movement because it is a direct way to work with certain complexes that were constellated in infancy. It seems that complexes of a preverbal, presymbolic nature are less often touched by the verbal aspects of analysis.

Eliade (1963) wrote: "Life cannot be *repaired,* it can only be *recreated*" (p. 30). In analysis, active imagination is that re-creative process; dance movement is one of its forms.

Notes

1. Personality Number One was grounded in the concrete reality of everyday life, the facts of the world the way it is. Personality Number Two lived in eternal time, the world of the ancestors and spirits, a mythic realm. Jung wrote: "The play and counterplay between personalities No. 1 and No. 2, which has run through my whole life, has nothing to do with a 'split' or dissociation in the ordinary medical sense. On the contrary, it is played out in every individual" (1961, p. 45).

2. The initiation ceremony is called the Kinaaldá by the Navaho. The Apache call it the Sunrise Dance (Quintero 1980). It is an elaborate ritual—a time of rejoicing to mark a girl's onset of menstruation. Her passage to womanhood is announced to the whole community in a dramatic four-night ceremony.

Changing Woman had a miraculous birth and grew to maturity in four days. At this time, she had her first menstrual period. The Holy People were living on the earth then, and they came to her ceremony and sang songs for her. She originated her own Kinaaldá. One of the most important parts of the ceremony was molding her body. Some say that at the first Kinaaldá, Changing Woman molded her own body. The pressing or molding was done to honor the Sun and the Moon. Changing Woman was molded into a perfect form.

When the first-born human girl became Kinaaldá, Changing Woman did the same things for her. She pressed and molded the younger woman's body, thus gifting her with beauty, wisdom, honor, and self-respect. The Kinaaldá is part of the Blessing Way Ceremony. It is done today as it was done in the beginning (Frisbie 1967; Henderson 1985b; Sandner 1979, pp. 122–32; Quintero 1980).

References

Adler, J. 1973. Integrity of body and psyche: Some notes on work in process. In *What is dance therapy, really?* eds. B. Govine and J. Chodorow, pp. 42–53. Columbia, Md.: American Dance Therapy Association.

_____. 1985. Who is the witness? A description of authentic movement. Paper presented at movement therapy seminars in Los Angeles and San Francisco, Jan. 1985.

Bernstein, P. L., and Singer, D. L. 1982. *The choreography of object relations.* Keene: Antioch New England Graduate School.

Bernstein, P. L. 1984. *Theoretical approaches in dance-movement therapy,* Vol. II. Dubuque: Kendall/Hunt.

Blackmer, J. D. 1982. *The training and experience of a modern dancer: Exploration into the meaning and value of physical consciousness.* Diploma thesis, C. G. Jung Institute, Zurich.

Chaiklin, S., and Gantt, L. 1979. *Conference on creative arts therapies.* Washington, D.C.: American Psychiatric Association, 1980. pp. 8–10 and 30–32.

Chodorow, J. 1974. Philosophy and methods of individual work. In *Dance therapy: Focus on dance VII,* ed. K. Mason, pp. 24–26. Washington, D. C.: American Association for Health, Physical Education and Recreation.

_____. 1978. Dance therapy and the transcendent function. *American Journal of Dance Therapy* 2/1:16–23.

_____. 1982. Dance/movement and body experience in analysis. *Jungian analysis,* ed. M. Stein, pp. 192–203. La Salle, Ill,. and London: Open Court.

_____. 1984. To move and be moved. *Quadrant* 17/2:39–48.

Eliade, M. 1963. *Myth and Reality.* New York: Harper and Row, 1975.

Fay, C. G. 1977. *Movement and fantasy: A dance therapy model based on the psychology of C. G. Jung.* Master's thesis, Goddard College, Vermont.

Frisbie, C. J. 1967. *Kinaaldá: A study of the Navaho girl's puberty ceremony.* Wesleyan University Press.

Greene, A. 1984. Giving the body its due. *Quadrant* 17/2:9–24.

Hall, J. 1977. *Clinical uses of dreams: Jungian interpretations and enactments.* New York: Grune & Stratton.

Henderson, J. L. 1985a. The origins of a theory of cultural attitudes. In *Proceedings of the 1985 California Spring.Conference,* pp. 5–13. San Francisco: C. G. Jung Institute.

_____. 1985b. Private conversation.

Jung, C. G. 1902. On the psychology and pathology of so-called occult phenomena. *Collected works* 1:1–88. Princeton: Princeton University Press, 1975.

_____. 1907. The psychology of dementia praecox. *Collected works* 3:1–151. Princeton: Princeton University Press, 1972.

_____. 1912. Two kinds of thinking. *Collected works* 5:7–33. Princeton: Princeton University Press, 1967.

_____. 1916. The transcendent function. *Collected works* 8:67–91. Princeton: Princeton University Press, 1969.

_____. 1927. The structure of the psyche. *Collected works* 8:139–58. Princeton: Princeton University Press, 1969.

_____. 1929. Commentary on "The secret of the golden flower." *Collected works* 13:1–56. Princeton: Princeton University Press, 1976.

_____. 1935. The Tavistock lectures: On the theory and practice of analytical psychology. *Collected works* 18:5–182. Princeton: Princeton University Press, 1976.

_____. 1938. *Dream analysis,* ed. W. McGuire. Princeton: Princeton University Press, 1984.

_____. 1940. The psychology of the child archetype. *Collected works,* 9/1: 151–81. Princeton: Princeton University Press, 1977.

_____. 1946. On the nature of the psyche. *Collected works* 8:159–234. Princeton: Princeton University Press, 1969.

_____. 1961. *Memories, dreams, reflections.* New York: Random House, 1965.

_____. 1963. *Mysterium coniunctionis.* Princeton: Princeton University Press, 1974.

Kalff, D. 1980. *Sandplay.* Santa Monica: Sigo Press.

Machtiger, H. G. 1984. Reflections on the transference/countertransference process with borderline patients. *Chiron: A Review of Jungian Analysis* 1984: 119–45.

Mindell, A. 1982. *Dreambody.* Los Angeles: Sigo Press.

————. 1985. *Working with the dreambody.* Boston: Routledge & Kegan Paul.

Neumann, E. 1954. The separation of the world parents: The principle of opposites. In *The origins and history of consciousness,* pp. 102–27. Princeton: Princeton University Press, 1973.

————. 1973. *The child.* New York: G. P. Putnam's Sons.

Piaget, J. 1952. *The origins of intelligence in children.* New York: W. W. Norton & Co., Inc., 1963.

————. 1954. *The construction of reality in the child.* New York: Basic Books, Inc., 1971.

————. 1962. *Play, dreams and imitation in childhood.* New York: W. W. Norton & Co., Inc.

Perera, S. B. 1981. *Descent to the Goddess: A way of initiation for women.* Toronto: Inner City Books.

Quintero, N. 1980. Coming of age. *National Geographic,* 157/2:262–71.

Sachs, C. 1937. *World history of the dance.* New York: Norton & Co.

Sandner, D. 1979. *Navaho symbols of healing.* New York: Harcourt, Brace, Jovanovich, Inc.

Schoop, T. 1974. *Won't you join the dance?* Palo Alto: National Press Books.

Schwartz-Salant, N. 1982. *Narcissism and character transformation.* Toronto: Inner City Books.

Stein, M. 1984. Power, shamanism, and maieutics in the countertransference. *Chiron: A Review of Jungian Analysis* 1984:67–87.

Stewart, C. T. 1981. The developmental psychology of sandplay. *Sandplay Studies,* ed. G. Hill, pp. 39–92. San Francisco: C. G. Jung Institute of San Francisco.

Stewart, C. T., and Stewart, L. H. 1981. Play, games and stages of development: A contribution toward a comprehensive theory of play. Presented at the 7th annual conference of The Association for the Anthropological Study of Play (TAASP). Fort Worth, April 1981.

Stewart, L. H., and Stewart, C. T. 1979. Play, games and affects: A contribution toward a comprehensive theory of play. In *Play as context,* ed. A. T. Cheska, pp. 42–52. Proceedings of The Association for the Anthropological Study of Play (TAASP). Westpoint, N.Y.: Leisure Press, 1981.

Stewart, L. H. 1981. The play-dream continuum and the catagories of the imagination. Presented at the 7th annual conference of The Association for the Anthropological Study of Play (TAASP). Fort Worth, April 1981.

————. 1984. Play-eros. In *Affects and archetypes II.* Paper presented at active imagination seminar in Geneva, Switzerland in August 1984.

————. 1986. Work in Progress: Affect and archetype: A contribution to a comprehensive theory of the structure of the psyche. *Chiron: A Review Of Jungian Analysis* 1986: 183–203.

Tomkins, S. 1962. *Affect imagery consciousness, Volume I.* New York: Springer Publishing Company, Inc.

————. 1963. *Affect imagery consciousness, Volume II.* New York: Springer Publishing Company, Inc.

Ulanov, A. 1982. Transference/countertransference. *Jungian analysis,* ed. M. Stein, pp. 68–85. La Salle, Ill., and London: Open Court.

Whitehouse, M. 1958. The Tao of the body. Paper presented at the Analytical Psychology Club of Los Angeles.

————. 1963. Physical movement and personality. Paper presented at the Analytical Psychology Club. Los Angeles, 1963.

————. 1968. Reflections on a metamorphosis. *A well of living waters—Festschrift for Hilde Kirsch,* ed. R. Head et al., pp. 272–77. Los Angeles: C. G. Jung Institute, 1977.

—————. 1979. C. G. Jung and dance therapy. *Eight theoretical approaches in dance-movement therapy,* ed. P. L. Bernstein, pp. 51–70. Dubuque: Kendall/Hunt.

Whitmont, E. 1972. Body experience and psychological awareness. *Quadrant* 12:5–16.

Winnicott, D. W. 1954. Withdrawal and regression. *D. W. Winnicott: Collected Papers.*

Woodman, M. 1980. *The owl was a baker's daughter: Obesity, anorexia nervosa, and the repressed feminine.* Toronto: Inner City Books.

—————. 1982. *Addiction to perfection: The still unravished bride.* Toronto: Inner City Books.

—————. 1983. Psyche/soma awareness. *Quadrant* 17/2:25–37.

Getting in Touch and Touching in Analysis

Mario Jacoby

One thing, Socrates, I must say which you will find unbelievable, but which is nevertheless true. I never learned anything from you, as you well know. However, I profited when I was with you; even when I was only in the same house, without being in the same room; and when I was in the same room, I would have my eyes fixed upon you while you talked, and I felt that I profited more than when I looked elsewhere. But most of all I profited when I was seated next to you and when I touched you. ("The-ages," apocryphal Platonic dialogue, quoted by J. Hillman, On Psychological Creativity, Eranos Yearbook 1966, p. 384.)

The concern of analysts to help their patients get in touch with body experiences is very understandable. We get patients suffering from somatic complaints such as headaches, bellyaches, constipation, or anorexia. They come with migraines, with skin-rashes, or very often with more nebulous complaints such as "a lump in the throat." Sometimes they are referred by medical doctors who are at a loss to do anything about their symptoms. We also see people without somatic complaints, but whatever comes up in analysis seems only to reach their "heads," so

---

Mario Jacoby, Ph.D., is a training analyst, lecturer, and member of the Curatorium of the C. G. Jung Institute in Zurich. He works as an analyst in private practice and is the author of numerous books and papers in analytical psychology, including *The Analytic Encounter* (1984) and *Longing for Paradise* (1985; German original 1980).

to speak, and does not go to a deeper level touching their "hearts" or "guts." Dream analysis often does not seem to be effective enough for these patients.

Marion Woodman began her body workshops because she rightly saw that "where the split between body and spirit is so deep that the instincts are damaged, the psyche may be producing the healing images, but the instinctual energy cannot connect to the image" (Woodman 1982, p. 86). The primary purpose of these workshops is "simply to make space in which the body can speak to the individual" (ibid.). A. Mindell (1982) also has tried to develop a method to follow and amplify body signals together with dream analysis, to combine the physiological aspects with the symbolic ones. Even as early as 1972, E. C. Whitmont spoke of the necessity of developing techniques of body experience to link with the techniques of analytical psychology, because most people do not know what they feel (1972, pp. 10–12). I am sure there are many more colleagues who have tried various methods of getting in touch with the body (e.g., Gestalt or Bioenergetics).

Apart from the split between body and spirit, there are also many people who cannot develop their symbolizing function, the "as if," due to conditions of early damage, wounds stemming from an unsatisfactory primal relationship with the mother (Plaut 1966; Gordon 1967). They can only grasp what is concrete; dreams have either no reality for them, or only a concretistic one. Intellectualizing or concretizing hinders such people from benefiting from Jungian analysis, with its focus on the symbolic meaning. It seems that when the person is cut off from his or her instincts and is unable to symbolize, the psyche transmits its message by concretizing it into a somatic complaint. The "dialogue with the body" is therefore crucial to any understanding (Woodman 1982, p. 86).

In this context, I remember one of my very first patients who suffered from heavy primary damage, having been an unwanted child and rejected by both (at the time still unmarried) parents. In the beginning of his analysis, he used his time mainly to complain about a great number of unspecific bodily discomforts. Nearly everywhere in his body, inside and outside, he felt pain. Yet he would not take any medication out of fear that it might damage or even poison him. (He was definitely not paranoid in a schizophrenic way.) His dreams circled around two basic themes: one was that he was defecating in wrong places and was heavily reprimanded or ridiculed because of it; the other was that the rector of the place where he had been working as a deacon was undercutting his sense of self or punishing him.

Whenever I tried to bring in a word about a dream, I somehow became the attacking authority figure, and he defended himself by interrupting me with a new complaint. Also, he did not want to discuss such shameful happenings as having to defecate in an unadapted way in the wrong places. Since he was clearly unable to make any use of symbolic understanding, it seemed to him to be real in a concretistic sense, and therefore too embarrassing. All I could do was to listen patiently to his complaints, which centered primarily on bodily discomforts. The ambivalence of his transference feelings was also expressed clearly enough in body language. For quite some time whenever we met, I could see in his eyes fear and mistrust of me, yet at the same time in his handshake there were definite signs of a need to cling. It took some time before his ambivalence could transform to the point that I became trustworthy enough and, at the same time, more and more idealized. The astonishing thing was that by listening to his complaints and taking his physical aches seriously, they gradually just seemed to disappear.

I wondered why this was possible, and offered myself the following hypothetical explanation: I had not followed the rule of thumb regarding not talking about symptoms. By listening to his complaints, taking them seriously, and even asking for more information about them, I was probably, to a certain extent, "in dialogue with his body experiences" and with the implications they had for his psychic state. This man had never had the experience of being listened to and taken seriously, a state clearly reflected in his defecation dreams. Although these dreams may be interpreted in numerous ways, one thing is certain: They give an image of his basic feeling that whatever came out of him ended up in a wrong place and was received badly in the outer world. This experience of being rejected from early on expressed itself also in his various unspecific psychosomatic complaints, showing how "lousy" he felt in his skin. Some of his complaints also had a demonstrative purpose, as a child's cry for consolation from its mother. I had to think of mothers who stroke their children if they are hurt or take them into their arms and perform a little ritual.

At the time, I was astonished by the improvement that occurred without dream interpretation, transference interpretation, or active imagination of "letting the body speak." He was at the time not capable of imagining, and I was not about to impose a task that was beyond him. This was really my first experience of the effect that a therapeutic encounter can have on psychosomatic symptoms. Of course, I do not want to imply that this kind of "miracle" happens frequently and just by listening. In his case, however, he gradually could experience me as being *there* enough to feel more secure, which constellated more security within himself and had an effect on his physical sense of well being.

In general, I must agree with Marion Woodman, Anita Greene, and others that many patients could benefit from some body work in addition to their analysis. In fact, many people today participate in workshops or have private hours with body therapists while seeing their analysts. I have nothing against this if it is done genuinely and is adapted to their basic needs. The experiences can also be productive for the analysis. However, some patients who obviously need body work most refuse it out of feelings of shame, inhibitions about exposing themselves, or fear of arousing the jealousy of a possessive mother- or father-figure analyst and thus losing their love if they see another therapist. Such fears are often deeply rooted and persist in spite of interpretation. Patients with those fears often suffer from a disturbed primary relationship (Neumann 1973), and their resistance to dividing the care of their body and their soul between two persons seems legitimate. The question then arises: What can be done with the ordinary analytical tools to get in touch with the body— meaning the psychic experience of bodily impulses, feelings, sensations.

In the analytic encounter, where the question of tactile contact is much disputed, the only socially and professionally accepted way to get in touch physically is through the ritual handshake. In Switzerland we have the custom of mutual handshakes at the beginning and end of each social encounter, and thus also each analytic session. The handshake can reveal a great deal about the patient's unconscious relationship to his or her surroundings and also to me as analyst, and can vary with the ups and downs of the transference. It can also reveal something about the level of psychic tension in a person, and how this is stored, blocked, or expressed in the tenseness of the muscles. A handshake can be smooth, hard, gripping, cold, clammy, lifeless, too long, or too short. Some people try to draw one closer by their handshakes, others to push one away —all unconsciously. Thus the physical touching of hands tells me a great deal about the way an analysand is or is not emotionally in touch with me and with himself or herself.

I have not had good experiences drawing the patient's attention to his or her handshake and trying to interpret or talk about it. When I have done that, people became self-conscious and inhibited about giving me their hands. Now I merely make my observations, which may help me to refine my empathy for the psychological state of my patient.

In an excellent article, Anita Greene (1984) expresses the opinion that the analytical tools can be expanded and body work may at times be a part of analysis done by analysts themselves, provided they have undergone special training. She cannot see any strong reason against this. According to her experience, touching the patient physically does not necessarily sexualize the therapeutic relationship. (See also Bosanquet

1970.) She feels rather that "the taboo against touching that has prevailed for so many years in psychoanalytic practice came out of a patriarchal age in which body itself was suspect" (Greene 1984, p. 22). Rightly or wrongly, this taboo is a tradition in the analytic profession and is more or less operative among Jungians as well. It stems, as is well known, from Freud's famous abstinence rule and from his recommendation that during psychoanalytic treatment, analysts "should model themselves on the surgeon who puts aside all his feelings" (Freud 1912, p. 115). The only tool an analyst is supposed to use is interpretation of unconscious motifs, of transference, and of resistance.

Today one knows that Freud himself was not a slave to his own rigid rules. A German psychoanalyst even called Freud the first "dissident" of psychoanalytic orthodoxy (Cremerius 1982, p. 496). Concerning his restrictive rules, Freud wrote to Ferenczi:

> I thought it best to demonstrate what one should not do. I wanted to draw the attention to those temptations which are counterproductive to the analysis. As a result of this, the obedient disciples do not realize the flexibility of these guidelines and surrender to them as if they were a decree stemming from a taboo. This will have to be revised one day. (Ibid., p. 503)

The fact remains, however, that Freud strongly discouraged any form of gratification from the analyst, because he considered the infantile drives of the patient to be like a bottomless pit.

Interestingly enough, it was Ferenczi who felt the need for a revision of this strict abstinence rule. He was the first psychoanalyst to allow nearness, interaction, and even body contacts with certain patients in regression. He had taken patients with heavy early damage into analysis, and wanted to find methods of getting in touch with their deep wounds. Classical psychoanalysis did not seem applicable, for they could not be reached from the objective distance of interpretations that were addressed to the patient's capacity for insight. They needed a kind of "maternal care" from the analyst, in order to relive emotional experiences of early infancy (Cremerius 1983, p. 995).

Freud was appalled when he learned that Ferenczi wanted to write publicly about his methods, which allowed physical touch and even the sharing of kisses between analyst and patient. In a letter to Ferenczi, Freud expressed his warning that other colleagues ultimately might go further and "soon we shall have accepted in the technique of analysis the whole repertoire of demiviergerie and petting-parties, resulting in an enormous increase of interest in psycho-analysis among both analysts and patients" (quoted in Jones 1957, vol. III, p. 175). Thus Freud came forward with a patriarchal streak, reproaching Ferenczi for playing "a tender mother role" not only with others, but perhaps also with himself. He therefore has "to hear from the brutal fatherly-side an admonition" (ibid.).

This stress on Freud's fatherly role may support Greene's thesis about the patriarchal background of the analytic and psychiatric establishment and its deficiency "in the differentiated relationship to anima, the feminine, and body that is essential for the discrimination of touch" (Greene 1984, p. 23). Freud obviously could not understand the therapeutic intentions of Ferenczi, who in reality became a pioneer of another more "matriarchal" trend within psychoanalysis, a trend that is linked to the names of M. Balint (a direct disciple), D. W. Winnicott, and H. Kohut in his later years—just to mention the most outstanding and creative practitioners.

Although Ferenczi's experiments with allowing the expression of concrete "mother tenderness" have not been pursued, his work has given rise to a tradition that asks the analyst to be sensitive to the primary needs of his patients. The analyst should be open enough to let himself or herself be experienced as "primary object" (Balint), and be used in a "holding function" (Winnicott), or to reflect the "gleam in the mother's eye" through empathic mirroring (Kohut). In general, however, little is said about body contact; if it is referred to, it is only with great caution. For instance, at the end of his life, Kohut related the following incident. During the worst moment of despair in the analysis of a depressive patient with suicidal tendencies, he gave her two fingers to hold. Though this was, in his opinion, "a dubious manoeuvre he couldn't recommend," he also felt relieved to realize that he had remained an analyst, because at that moment a genetic interpretation had formulated itself in him. It felt like the toothless gums of a very small infant, holding onto an empty nipple. According to Kohut, this incident was not exactly a turning point, but it was an important bridge over a dangerously difficult situation (Kohut 1981).

Balint must also be mentioned here because of his valuable distinction between a *benign* and a *malignant* form of regression. In a malignant regression the patient aims "at a gratification of instinctual cravings," whereas the benign form serves basically to seek "the recognition of the existance . . . of the patient's own unique individuality" (Balint 1979, p. 144). The benign regression leads to a psychic state of *primary love* in which there is "a sort of harmonious interpenetrating mix-up" with the analyst (ibid., p. 136), and the symbolic expression of this "primitive . . . relationship in the analytic situation is often some sort of *physical con-*

tact with the analyst, the most frequent form of which is the holding of the analyst's hand, or one of his fingers, touching his chair . . . etc." (ibid., p. 145). To interpret this as acting out or resistance may undercut the precarious sense of self of the patient. Therefore, such expressions must be allowed and may even be crucial for initiating a *new beginning,* the discovery of a new, better suited way that amounts to a progression (ibid., p. 132).

In this more "matriarchal" trend of psychoanalysis, there is not exactly a taboo against touching; however, any body contact seems condoned only in certain moments of a patient's regression into preverbal areas where words have lost their meaning and sound unempathic to his or her actual experience. Among Jungians, where the restrictions in the analytic relationship are fewer and less well defined, there is all the same—and rightly—a warning against using body contact in an indiscriminate way. The question as to whether an analyst can or should do body work with his or her patients (always under the condition that the analyst is thoroughly trained for it) is one I cannot answer because of lack of experience. I would caution, however, that it depends not only on the transference, but also on the countertransference feelings and fantasies that get constellated by body touch. I would also have difficulties with role confusion, since to my mind the body therapist is in an entirely different role, a more directive and active role than the analyst. But some specially trained and gifted psychotherapists seem to get good results, as they discriminate enough concerning the impact this combination has on patients (Greene 1984; Woodman 1984).

The way for us to get in touch with our analysands is by an attitude that is aptly called empathy. It is worth reflecting for a moment on the function of empathy, which is highly complex and easily disturbed or distorted. In Jung's definition, empathy,

> taken as a whole, is a process of introjection, since it brings the object into intimate relation to the subject. In order to establish this relationship, the subject detaches a content—a feeling, for instance—from himself, lodges it in the object, thereby animating it, and in this way draws the object into the sphere of the subject. (Jung 1921, par. 784)

I think this definition is not satisfactory, because Jung describes the function of empathy as if the object would be animated by my own projected content. In such a case, it would seem doubtful whether by empathizing I get in touch with psychic contents really belonging to the inner life of the other person (the object), or whether I instead just perceive my own projection.

In Kohut's definition, empathy is "the mode by which one gathers psychological data about other people and, when they say what they think and feel, imagines their inner experience, even though it is not open to direct observation" (Kohut 1966, p. 450). If I understand Kohut correctly, he is of the opinion that empathy depends very much on verbal communication. Yet words can never fully render one's inner experiences if one is not a born writer. In most cases the actual experience is much more complex, maybe even different from the words that are or can be used. Empathy means grasping those contents and experiences that can only be hinted at by words. Therefore we need the capacity to put ourselves imaginatively in the place of the other person.

Maybe it is a helpful image to compare empathizing with visiting an analysand in his or her surroundings and trying to feel how the world looks from the analysand's vantage point. As a visitor, while trying to get in touch with the circumstances encountered, I bring myself and my personal equation along. What I experience will depend on my perceptiveness and the sensitivity of my antennae. Being aware of my own reactions, I will quite naturally compare the analysand's house and surroundings to my own and ask myself how I would feel if I had to live in these circumstances. This is what Kohut calls "vicarious introspection." The question also arises of whether the effort of my visit is welcome at that very moment, and to what extent I am allowed to enter the analysand's house. Am I shown only those parts that are respectable enough to be seen by visitors, while the large cellar underneath with its chaotic mess remains locked? Naturally it will take a long time before I am invited to the bathroom—especially when the analysand is sitting in the tub naked, so to speak. I should not force my entry to places I am not supposed to go, and should be sensitive enough not to hurt the analysand's feelings by touching delicate objects that he or she does not want me to handle. In other words, there are fears and resistance to allowing empathy from the analyst, because it has the effect of bringing "the object in intimate relation to the subject," as Jung states.

Yet empathy also means grasping fears and resistances and the distance an analysand may need at different moments and in different states. There will always be failures in our empathic understanding, which in turn may also put us in touch with important complex areas—with the analysand's anger, or inner doubts, or depressive withdrawal as a result of not feeling understood. While recognizing and understanding his or her reactions, these failures are nevertheless crucial for the gradual development of autonomy and self-reliance. They may constellate a gradual withdrawal of the image of the ideal analyst, who by empathy understands just everything. (See also Kohut's concept [1984] of *optimal frustration* in its crucial therapeutic importance.)

Analysts know how strenuous empathizing can be in the course of a long day's practice. If tired or absorbed by some of their own inner contents, analysts may have to fight their resistance to the constant demand to give an empathic response. Experientially, this feels like having to leave one's own house in order to pay a lengthy visit to the analysand in his or her quarters, with its unique surroundings and its specific atmosphere, when in fact one would prefer to stay at home. In any case, because the analyst's subjective equation is always involved to a large extent, empathy as an instrument to gather information is never precise and has to be used with caution. There is always the question of whether one is grasping something in the analysand by empathy, or projecting one's own feelings and fantasies onto him or her. The only way I know to find out whether my empathic response is a perception or a projection is to get the analysand's reaction. Together, then, we may arrive at a genuine enough consensus concerning the atmosphere in his or her inner house.

In the analyst's attempt to grasp and tune in to the otherness of other persons by empathy, perception of body language is potentially very helpful. In most cases, we perceive the body language of other people without conscious focusing, and through this subliminal perception we form an overall impression. The expression of the eyes, lips, and body movement, the way a patient sits in the armchair or moves about on the couch—all make a certain impression on the therapist and often lead to an immediate understanding of the patient's inner state. Observation of body language in a more focused way may thus give us hints about how the patient's inner state is different from our own. Such focusing may be essential to differentiate what is mine and what is the other's in my empathic responses.

On the other hand, the impact of body language can also make it difficult even for an analyst to get into an empathic attitude toward the patient. Let's say we perceive in the body-expression of a patient a pompous and disagreeable inflation, or an exaggerated aggressive reproach of the way the world is treating him or her, or an offensive withdrawal from any communication with us. In such a case it is sometimes difficult not to fall into a natural retaliatory response; empathy with the patient is strained and, in a way, *contra naturam*. The natural reaction would be "to stick a needle into the inflated balloon" by a sharp remark, or to get angry, or to cut off communication. But that would mean acting out or falling into a trap set unconsciously by the patient.

So long as an analysand expresses such inner states mainly through body language, he or she may not even be fully conscious of them. Even if the analyst's acting out or "spontaneous anger reactions" are in most cases counterproductive, it is nevertheless important for him or her to be aware of such feelings and to take them seriously. Through these emotional responses in ourselves, we pick up the manner in which a patient has to provoke his surroundings to certain reactions. Thus we experience what is well known today as a "complementary" countertransference reaction, to quote Racker (Racker 1968; Jacoby 1984, p. 38). Then again, the function of empathy may help us to find the right time and the right words to interpret this to the patient.

There is still the question: What parts of the personality of a patient are we getting in touch with by empathy? What is empathy empathizing with? As I see it, empathy is a conscious focusing on inner experiences of another person. In other words, by empathy I may perceive how psychic contents half-consciously or unconsicously influence the ego-consciousness of an analysand, how they are experienced by his or her ego. This is in contrast to syntonic countertransference reactions (Fordham 1957, pp. 142 ff.) that pop up spontaneously in myself. They are likely to make me aware of contents in an analysand that are not yet linked to his or her ego complex.

In this connection it also is interesting to consider the distinction between *psychic* and *somatic* empathy made by N. Schwartz-Salant. He sees psychic empathy as a "process in which there is an observer (the analyst) acting upon a field of information, the patient's psyche" (Schwartz-Salant 1982, p. 127). On the other hand, our empathy, "when close to the somatic unconscious . . . is very much a function of mutual participation in which both psyches operate simultaneously" (ibid.). I wonder whether Schwartz's observations about somatic empathy do not belong to the common therapeutic field, where the phenomena of transference and countertransference are actively influencing both partners. This may create great nearness, but it is also an opportunity for the analyst to become aware of unconscious contents in the psyche of his analysand.

In my work as an analyst, I try to grasp as much as possible everything coming up in me while I am with a patient, including the phenomena of bodily sensations. So far I have considered this attitude to be an openness toward spontaneous countertransference reactions—in contrast to empathy, which I view as a focused attention on the patient. As I see it, countertransference reactions appear most distinctly in somatic forms, when patients are keeping silent for longer periods. When there is no verbal expression, we still want to grasp whether a patient is in a hostile silence, a painful blockage, or perhaps experiencing a blissful feeling of union on the level of Neumann's *unitary reality* (Neumann 1973).

I want to give an example of a reaction in me that may stem from what is called *somatic empathy* (Schwartz) or *syntonic countertransference* (Fordham). A patient lying on the couch kept silent for quite some time. I felt a great tension mounting in my stomach and began to breathe deeply and to relax the muscles in my shoulders, arms, and legs. At the same time I noticed that I wished my patient would be able to do the same, alternating with a fantasy that I was doing my breathing and relaxing for her as well. I thought: If only she could relax and just be herself with or without talking, in spite of my presence. Interrupting the silence, I said that it must be very uncomfortable and painful for her, having to remain silent. After this intervention she could admit how terrible this felt, and then told memories of having been scolded and locked in her room by her parents for being stubborn when she did not give answers to their questioning. I told her that I had sensed a great tension, and had done breathing exercises while feeling the wish to help her to lower this tension. She replied by telling me about the training she had pursued to learn proper breathing (I had not known about this), and affirmed that she was doing regular breathing exercises at home. Yet when she was in the presence of someone else, the tension was such that it did not work —she was just unable to do it, although the possibility had also crossed her mind. This exchange of what had happened to each of us during her silence helped to ease the tension considerably. There was a moment when we had come in touch with each other on quite a deep emotional level—an important step toward overcoming some of her inner isolation.

Precisely those patients who suffer from a sense of deep inner isolation and who cannot be reached by verbal communication seem to constellate impulses in me to get in touch with them on a more physical level, perhaps by holding their hand or laying my hand on their forehead. Of course, these impulses to touch must stem clearly enough from the syntonic aspects of countertransference (Fordham 1957, pp. 143 ff.) and must feel "right" in order to be put—on certain rare occasions—into practice. As long as the basic core of a patient must be held in isolation and be protected against anybody who tries to get in touch, the analyst has to keep and respect the distance that is unconsciously assigned to him. These are resistances against intrusions that have to do with fears of getting devoured, of losing one's ego, or of falling into the most humiliating dependence if anybody, including the analyst, is allowed to come too near.

I have seen that in women this constellation sometimes can take on the form of a so-called *animus-possession*, whereby the animus, in his function of rationalizing and criticizing, protects against any emotional nearness. This reminds me of those princesses in certain fairytales (e.g., "The Enchanted Princess" in Deutsche Märchen seit Grimm, or the Norwegian tale, "The Comrade") who hold their suitors at a distance by asking them unsolvable riddles invented by a father or "mountain-spirit" to whom they are still tied. If a suitor is unable to solve them, he is to be killed. If, however, a suitor manages miraculously to get behind the princess's secret, it is a humiliating insult in spite of her deep-seated wish for redemption through love. Even after the suitor has solved the riddles, she has to invent more intrigues and set further traps, which should bring death to him as soon he tries to approach her. It always takes a great deal of effort on the part of the suitor before the princess can admit or surrender to her true feelings—to the true self, so to speak.

In this connection I remember a patient, a woman of 28, who had to make herself unapproachable. Whatever I tried to communicate to her was criticized and annihilated. She was full of reproaches that I didn't understand her at all, and that everything only got worse for her if she came to sessions. She continued to come, although she was often late and frequently cancelled her appointments. I felt so castrated or "decapitated"—like the suitors in the fairytale—that I really thought our endeavour senseless and wished that she would find another analyst. But each time I had it in mind to talk to her about this, she came forth just in that session with something that again caught my interest and engagement as an analyst and made me feel that dismissing her would be experienced as a traumatic rejection.

One day I got the distinct feeling that she was sitting in her chair very disarmed and really suffering from her isolation. That touched me, and I had a sudden impulse to reach over to give her my hand to hold onto in her despair. I did not immediately act on that impulse. It came to me as a surprise, as I never had experienced anything like this in relation to her. As we sat there silently, I realized that this impulse in me was growing stronger. I pondered, therefore, whether it stemmed from a need of my own to finally get in closer touch with her at a moment when this spiteful *animus guardian* of hers seemed to be asleep, because her negativity had become intolerable to my own sense of value as an analyst. Or was it really the patient who needed such a gesture from me; was it an impulse from a syntonic countertransference reaction? I knew I should not say anything to her at that moment because of the danger of waking that animus of hers, who would then again distort the meaning of my words and spoil the opportunity. As is often the case, the question of whether my own need or hers was involved was not clearly answered. And as I did not get any strong impulses against it, I risked reaching over and holding her hand. She took it and immediately began to cry. After a while she said through her tears: "And I had hated you so much—I don't have to hate you any more."

This session seemed to be a breakthrough to her true feelings. However, the next day she telephoned, asking for an extra hour the very same day and adding that it wouldn't matter if I didn't have any extra time. I had, with the best will, no free minute the whole day, including the evening, and reminded her that our regular meeting was scheduled the morning of the following day. She came to that session full of reproaches again because I had not been there for her when she needed me, and back she went into her unapproachable habitus.

Had this move towards getting in touch with her been a mistake? As direct verbal communications led again into entanglements of misunderstanding, I could only come up with some tentative interpretations and was not able to check them with her. I tend to consider her telephone call as a new attempt to set up a test that would be impossible to pass. She was testing whether after this moment of closeness I would now be at her disposal, according to her wishes and whenever she needed me. Behind this was also a desperate attempt to get me under her control, something she badly needed as a defense against her fear of falling helplessly at my mercy. Considering her early traumatic experiences with a narcissistic and emotionally unreliable mother, it was more than understandable that the feelings coming up in connection with our "being in touch" had obviously been too hot for her. As a result, either I had to be a figure that was, in a concrete way, *there* only for her and at her demand, or I was to be discarded. With such alternatives, no analyst can win.

As the defenses were put up again, things stayed apparently as they had been before. Yet, gradually, there was some softening and less attacking. "Life" took over. She met a man and could now trust me to a certain extent to help her sort out what this new relationship meant to her. Although our moment of closeness did not initiate a clear move forward, it did not have any damaging effect—probably the contrary.

Some patients, however, experience getting in touch on a physical level in a decisively good therapeutic way. I think here of analysands who tend to get temporarily into a kind of "depressive freeze," a "frozen" state where their own feelings—let alone persons of the outside world—are not reachable. Everything is far away or just lifeless. Images of ice and snow may appear in dreams. Usually there is an intense regressive activation of a severe abandonment complex and a feeling of having fallen out

of the world of human connections. From the point of view of the countertransference, I usually felt not the aggression of an animus guardian, as
in the case I described before, but the despair of a crying child—though
as if encapsulated and very far away. I observed a certain stiffness and
coldness in the body and a voice that resisted reaching out to me. Certain
early memories were connected to this state. One patient remembered
crying endlessly in a big, empty room, hearing only what she now knew
was her echo. Somebody else could recall fears while imprisoned in a
dark chamber. Of course, these memories could not be verbalized and
communicated during the frozen state, only later.

As a response to such a state of being cut off, I felt in certain instances that these patients needed my active help in trying to find them in
their prisons and to reconnect them to humanity. If the abandonment
complex is activated to such an extent, there is usually no way to get in
touch on a verbal level. Whatever the analyst would say would be wrong.
And just sitting silently may be felt as if he or she is not there. It can be an
experience of torture for the analysand. Thus the impulse to reach the
patient by some direct physical touch seems appropriate.

However such a move needs the "right moment," otherwise it may
be felt as ineffective or useless—much to the disappointment of the patient. It also may be felt as an intrusion. The right moment has come
when the patient's wish to get in touch again with life is more or less consciously awakening, yet the feeling of being helplessly cut off still persists.
In such moments, I sometimes have followed my impulse to reach over
to patients, holding their hand, or gently placing my hand on their forehead when the patient is lying on the couch. What usually happens then
is a release of tears and a certain letting go of body cramp. Later they can
sometimes verbalize how important an experience it was to be "found"
in their painful, isolated corners. It seemed to them that this had never
happened before in their lives. Sometimes dreams of blankets being
gently put over them, of warm beds, or of being in a warm country
confirmed the warmth they were able to experience through this physical contact. Maybe I have had good luck so far. But again, one has to take
into consideration that I would risk such a move only with a few carefully
selected patients in moments when it just felt right.

But is "feeling right" a criterion reliable enough for such risky interventions? I think that in the last resort it is the final criterion, provided
that our underlying motivations have been scrupulously differentiated
and honestly looked at. For if it does not feel right, there is no doubt that
one should abstain from any body contact. One simple reason for this is
that we have to stand behind these interventions and have to take full re-

sponsibility for them. A preponderance of doubt in this respect will inhibit us; our physical touching then will signal ambivalence to the patient, who most probably will feel rejected again. The whole procedure will be counterproductive if the touch is not as sensitive as possible to the patient's needs. Such an unambivalent attitude cannot be achieved if it does not feel right to touch a patient.

However, if it seems to feel right, a number of questions arise and further criteria have to be considered. First of all, careful attention must be paid to the analyst's motivation and his or her possible countertransference needs, which can be a potential danger to the analytic process. Especially when dealing with patients in a regressed state who seem to be dependent on him or her for being "found," the analyst may be gripped by an unconscious saviour fantasy and had better be aware of the accompanying power needs. The analyst also may take it as a personal narcissistic gratification when he or she becomes the "most important person" in a patient's life, the one to whom the patient can open up as to nobody ever before. The analyst's own narcissistic needs then may motivate his or her interventions. An honest estimation is also necessary concerning the amount of sexual attraction that can be stimulated by body contacts with a particular patient. Most important is the analyst's capacity to imagine in an empathic way beforehand what physical touching might mean to the patient.

I have found that whenever it felt "right" to me to get in touch with a patient on a physical as well as a psychic level, it also reflected the psychological condition of the analysand. The patient was always consciously and unconsciously (from the Self) cooperative enough with the analytic process. I always genuinely liked the analysand and had trust in his or her basic inner values and richness, even when he or she was passing through phases of apparent emptiness and negativity. The ego-functions—though at times overwhelmed by a complex—were always potentially sound enough to understand and integrate what was happening.

In general, we have to caution against any unconventional body touch in cases where a *delusional transference* is dominant. In such cases, the ego cannot differentiate itself enough from the feelings or ideas that are projected onto the analyst. The analyst is not experienced "as if" he or she were father, mother, lover, persecutor, devilish seducer, or all in one. The analyst just *is* one or more of these figures, and his or her every active move may be interpreted according to such a delusional conviction, so that the danger of all kinds of delusional entanglements arises. Also, if the transference is intensely sexualized and if there are erotic longings, it is usually better not to nourish fantasies that may become vivid through the otherwise harmless touching. Of course, there always is a danger that gratification by the analyst may lead to a kind of addiction. Regression may, among other things, also serve the purpose of obtaining such gratification.

Such pros and cons, where touching is concerned, have great similarity with Balint's distinction between benign and malignant regression. There is, however, some general confusion in depth psychology about what we mean by regression. It is never posssible to become fully an infant again; in regression, early perceptions and responses are contaminated by later experiences and developments. As Winnicott says, "Deeper and deeper does, of course, imply earlier and earlier, but only to a limited extent. In our analytic patients there has been a fusion of early with later elements" (Winnicott 1957, p. 111). To what extent early development is in fact paralleled in states of regression is hard to know and open to speculation. There has been some criticism from modern psychoanalysis of Balint's idea of the new beginning through a benign regression. Because the possibility of a return to a pretraumatic harmony, before the basic harm occurred, implies fixation of a primary creative potential on a retrospective utopia, the creative element in the *here and now* of the analytic situation may be neglected (H. Thomä 1984, p. 530).

This criticism sounds astonishingly Jungian, and one is reminded of Samuels's statement that many of the modern psychoanalysts are in fact "unknowing Jungians" (Samuels 1985, p. 9). From a Jungian point of view, I would say that what happens in most forms of regression is the activation of our *inner child*. This is an archetypal content living in us in the here and now. However this archetypal core has in the course of our lives become a complex, having been formed by specific personal experiences, particularly in the early life history. Most patients experience their inner child unconsciously as a suffering child. It suffers usually from too great a lack of fit between its existential needs and the responses to them, their recognition by the environment. It is true that through the transference, an analysand may get in touch with or sometimes be overwhelmed by the suffering child (which is usually experienced as regression), and he or she may also discover how, and in what way, he or she is under the dominance of the destructive side of the mother- and/or father-archetype. It seems as if such patients have an inner map, where values are engraved in a distorted way so that to have natural longings for tenderness or nearness is felt as humiliating, or to feel the slightest bit of dependence arouses traumatic fears. The patient has eaten the poisoned apple of the witch, so to speak, as told in Grimms' fairy tale "Snow White," and the realm of Eros is poisoned. In other words, the nonfitting surrounding of early childhood has become an inner psychic content (negative parental images) and, finally, also a conscious attitude that is not in tune with the unconscious.

The analytic encounter has—*deo concedente*—the potential to promote new experiences that may transform the destructive and one-sided archetypal pattern to a certain extent. In spite of its traumatic experiences, the inner child may still have a longing for empathic recognition of its existence and its existential needs. If these needs are responded to well enough in the analytic situation, there may be, for the first time, a connection with the positive side of the mother-archetype, promoting security, confidence, and thus growth. The analyst then may function as a mediator to new archetypal experiences.

As is well known, it is easy to write about such an outcome, but in practice it means long and arduous work. One should not be too optimistic that it will be fully achieved. Yet to find the suffering, often isolated *child within* is usually decisive, and if we really want to get in touch with him or her, it may at rare times imply some physical contact.

References

Balint, M. 1979. *The basic fault*, 2nd ed. New York: Brunner/Mazel.

Bosanquet, C. 1970. Getting in touch. *Journal of Analytical Psychology* 15/1:44–58.

Cremerius, J. 1982. Psychoanalyse—jenseits von orthodoxie und dissidenz. *Psyche* 36/6:481–514.

_____. 1983. Sándor Ferenczis bedeutung für theorie und therapie der psychoanalyse. *Psyche* 37/11:988–1015.

Fordham, M. 1957. Notes on the transference. In *Technique in Jungian Analysis: Library of Analytical Psychology*, vol. 2. London: Heinemann.

Freud, S. 1912. Recommendations to physicians practising psychoanalysis. In *Collected works*, vol 12. London: Hogarth Press, 1958.

_____. 1931. Letter to Ferenczi, Dec. 13, 1931. In Jones, E. *Sigmund Freud: Life and Work*, vol. 3, p. 175. New York: Basic Books, 1957.

Gordon, R. 1967. Symbols: Content and process. In *Analytical Psychology: Library of Analytical Psychology*, vol. 1. London: Heinemann, 1973.

Greene, A. 1984. Giving the body its due. *Quadrant* 17/2:9–24.

Jacoby, M. 1984. The analytic encounter. In *Studies in Jungian Psychology by Jungian Analysts*, vol. 15. Toronto: Inner City Books.

Jones, E. 1957. Life and work of Sigmund Freud, vol. 3. New York: Basic Books.

Jung, C. G. 1921. *Psychological types*. In *Collected works*, vol. 6. Princeton: Princeton University Press, 1971.

_____. 1951. The psychology of the child archetype. In *Collected works*, vol. 9/i. Princeton: Princeton University Press, 1959.

Kohut, H. 1966. Forms and transformations of narcissism. In *Search for the Self*, vol. 1, p. 450 ff. New York: International Universities Press, 1978.

_____. 1981. Videotape of his address to the Conference on Progress in Self Psychology, Berkeley, California.

_____. 1984. *How does analysis cure?* Chicago & London: University of Chicago Press.

Mindell, A. 1982. *Dreambody.* Los Angeles: Sigo Press.

Neumann, E. 1973. *The child.* London: Hodder & Stoughton.

Plato. "Theages," apocryphal Platonic dialogue, quoted by J. Hillman in *Eranos Yearbook* 1966.

Plaut, A. 1966. Reflections on not being able to imagine. *Library of Analytical Psychology,* vol. 1. London: Heinemann, 1973.

Racker, H. 1968. *Transference and countertransference.* London: Hogarth Press.

Samuels, A. 1985. *Jung and the Post-Jungians.* London: Routledge & Kegan Paul.

Schwartz-Salant, N. 1982. *Narcissism and character transformation: The psychology of narcisstic character disorders.* Toronto: Inner City Books.

Thomä, H. 1984. Was heisst "Neubeginn" (M. Balint)? *Psyche,* 38/6:516–43.

Whitmont, E. C. 1972. Body experience and psychological awareness. *Quadrant* 12:5–16.

Winnicott, D. W. 1965. On the contribution of direct observation in psychoanalysis. In *The Maturational Processes and the Facilitating Environment.* London: Hogarth Press.

Woodman, M. 1982. *Addiction to perfection: The still unravished bride.* Toronto: Inner City Books.

Body Language and the Self: The Search for Psychic Truth

Judith Hubback

Introduction

Every one of us who presents a professional paper to colleagues is at the same time presenting his or her own personal self as it was felt to be when writing the paper. The hope is that I, as writer, know the state of my personal self as well as possible and am still researching into it, and that I do not write and communicate to others from a ground in which there is still a great deal of personal unconsciousness. Each time a paper is composed it is a voyage of self-exploration, even if it has the appearance of being a search for the best way of understanding and treating patients of such and such a kind, or research into psychological theory. A description and discussion of our work, combined with a continuation of self-analysis behind the scenes, may be of benefit to future therapist-patient encounters and interactions.

The theme of this paper falls into three stages. First, the reality of the

Judith Hubback, M.A. (Cantab.), is a training analyst of the Society of Analytical Psychology. She was editor of the Journal of Analytical Psychology from 1977 to 1986. Before becoming an analyst she studied history, then the problems of university-educated married women (*Wives Who Went to College*, 1957). She worked as psychotherapist in University College, London, for 10 years and is now in private practice. Her papers and poems have appeared in various publications: the Journal of Analytical Psychology, Psychological Perspectives, Harvest, Outposts, and others.

analyst includes body factors of all sorts, as well as psychic ones. The analyst's personality is housed in the material body, which has its characteristics, sex, idiosyncrasies, and vicissitudes. Apart from anything less extreme, he or she might die. I think a great many body factors of the analyst as well as of the patient come into the texture and life of the therapy, into the transference and the countertransference, and not only at the beginning, even though in the long run the psychic ones are probably the most potent for change.

In using the term "body-language," therefore, I am referring to far more than the patient's facial expression, gestures, and other immediate messages, or concealments of meanings. It is usual for the therapist to take note of general demeanor. The perhaps fleeting look in the eyes, of which it often turns out the patient was unconscious, or had not known that it was perceptible, may ask: Is the analyst well? Such a question may indicate self-concern as well as concern for the other. Similarly, the swift or furtive glance all around the room to see if anything has changed or if some danger lurks in the corners; the difficulty in making eye contact; the particular moment at which he or she opens or closes eyes or fists; and no doubt countless other behaviors are ways of speaking without words. Those matters are important, but I wish here to take their occurrence for granted and to explore body language in the broader and perhaps deeper dimension of transference/countertransference. This small study, within which the patient's body language and that of the analyst will be considered, is meant to be linked with contemporary Jungian and psychoanalytic studies of the self. It reflects the difficulty that many an analyst has in relating the archetypal self of the collective unconscious—which is basically a concept and an abstraction—with his or her personal experience of the self, without falling into the grip of the extremes, inflation and denigration.

The second part of the theme is that, along with what might be called the benign aspects of the analyst and the setting, which have evidently a positive nature and effect, body factors must be taken to include those shadow features which manifest in bodily or other material form. The regrettable shadow features I intend to examine are, first, the analyst's occasional illnesses. Are they only physical, or have they also a psychic and synchronistic meaning which may add unbearably (or so the patient feels) to his or her anxieties, which were being analyzed before the intrusion from the analyst's shadow, and which compound together, perhaps at an especially difficult time? Following that, I shall describe a particular violent event that took place when burglars broke into my home during a session with a patient.

The last part of this paper aims to open up the discussion of how those temporarily bad or unfortunate experiences can be integrated with the patient's search for psychic health, for the truth about himself or herself and about the larger self as manifested within, and for improved relationships with others. Those features of the analytic experience are subsumed in the quest for individuation, or an approximation to that potential.

The term "personal self" has been adopted advisedly. A great deal of ink has flowed on the subject of the self. This contribution is an attempt to explore one part of the subject, to describe and comment on some examples of the experienced body basis of the self. While we are still alive we can only know and do anything at all by means of the self, that mysterious factor that holds matter and spirit together, links them and enables them to relate. We are neither disembodied psyches nor mind-less bodies. "The self" has become a marvelously catch-all term that means basically the factor of me, the me-ness of the person I am. It is experienced as the essence of me. Not only has each of us a "me-ness," but also each of us potentially senses that whoever we are talking to has his or her own me-ness. I think it is correct to assume that the personal essence of me is both individual and shared with every other individual in the world. The sharing adds the dimension of relatedness, without which the concept of the self does not make sense for living human beings. Even at the stage when it is an autistic or narcissistic self (at, and soon after, birth) it relates to itself and thereby it has potentially the first, repeatable, expandable, and applicable experience of relating, which becomes relationship with the object, provided that development is fostered by adequate parents and other figures in the environment.

Some people find that the idea of God helps them to be sure they have their own me-ness and to know that every other individual also has that. For example, one of the earliest Christians, St. Paul, wrote: "Know ye not that your body is the temple of the Holy Ghost which is in you, which ye have of God, and ye are not your own?" (I Corinthians 6:19). That is an assertion of the belief that something very remarkable—Holy Ghost, spirit, or self—lives in the body. Other people do not like bringing any god into the matter; they find the boundary of the human dimension suits them better than the difficult combination of boundlessness and comprehensiveness that there is in the deity.

Healthy newborn infants look very self-contained, or even self-sufficient, but in normal development they do not stay isolated either physically or emotionally. Their self-containedness rapidly becomes something much more complicated as they progressively spend more time awake, and they probably only feel integrated again when they are asleep. And as they—we—get going in life, we have the all-in-one integrated experience less and less often; but always it is a possibility. When it comes, it is very powerful indeed, and we can get caught in its power and mistakenly believe we are powerful; or we can fear that it is utterly big and we are utterly small. The language about the self and myself and yourself has to be a translation from the psychic actuality of being it or being in it, first into body language of all kinds, from infancy to the grave, then into spoken language, which involves a further translation. That reminds me of a line in an early poem by T. S. Eliot: "I've gotta use words when I talk to you" (Eliot 1936, p. 131).

The Analyst's Body and the Patient's

After studying at least a small amount of the huge literature on soma and psyche, it seemed to me worthwhile to devote myself first to certain general features of patients' and analysts' bodies. The analyst's physical life affects the patient, the transference, and the countertransference, and attention to this topic leads to larger theoretical issues.

We are creatures of the senses. Our patients can affect us consciously and unconsciously by their looks, their beauty or their ugliness, and we affect them since we also are actual people as well as being receivers of projections. I remember a woman with a face that looked to me like that of a horse; I could not stand more than a few sessions with her as I came to hate her, and I wondered if it was only for that particular body-feature. She was not a kind of female Chiron (with the centaur's body parts reversed) but unfortunately seemed to me to be a concretized horse-woman, and I found no facilitating image to help me out of this fantasy, which dehumanized her in my eyes. At the sixth session she told me her boy friend was odious, so I knew there was too much hate for analytic *agape* to develop (Lambert 1981) and we parted company.

Another woman was very tall but she did not remind me of any animal, and she had a beautifully proportioned body to go with her height. She said she hated her largeness; her father had been large and domineering; and she added that her eldest brother was huge. In a few weeks it emerged that her problem was that she felt possessed, a state similar to that of being in the possession of an evil force. However, early in her therapy this did not appear in the transference/countertransference, nor did I experience her as overwhelming me or as trying unconsciously to deprive me of what I needed in order to be her therapist. I think her boundaries were healthy, so that the possession, or archetypal image of the over-powerful father, could be worked with.

Patients for their part are affected by the sense impression they get of their therapists. One of my patients was, early in her analysis, convinced that my hair was just the same color as her mother's had been. She suffered from an unconscious and dangerous identification with a deeply depressed mother, and that was one of her main impediments to change. The extent to which I reminded her of her actual mother got in the way of thoroughly working through some of the fusion periods in the analysis, in which she was omnipotently using me as an idealized good mother whom she wanted desperately to be a total contrast to her bad internal mother.

My impression is that more male analysts have spoken and written about the attractiveness, or the opposite, of female patients than have female analysts about male patients (Stein and Alexander 1959). And I do not know whether the subject of the objective good looks or ugliness of the analyst, as compared with the transference projections, has been given any attention. Presumably the use of the couch, which maximizes the transference as compared with the impact of sense perceptions, results in the actual face and body of the analyst being relatively unimportant, particularly once the analytic relationship is thoroughly engaged. The French phrase *joli-laid* (pretty-and-ugly) which is, perhaps surprisingly, applied to men more often than to women, could be applicable to some analysts. But the presence of that composite characteristic is fairly rapidly superseded by transference fantasies, so its actuality is only a relative factor in analysis.

I am writing about body factors evident in the first place to the senses, but carrying a large component of psychic meaning. It is a combination of the analyst's body as it actually is and of "the living body" that affects the transference. In *Spirit and life*, Jung wrote of the need both to separate conceptually the material body proper from "the living being," and to integrate in our thinking the fact that the body is "a material system ready for life and making life possible with the proviso that for all its readiness it could not live without the addition of this 'living body'" (Jung 1926, par. 605).

The sense impressions that the analyst and the patient have of each other are immediately changed into images, which either of them (but more likely the patient) may express at the time that that happens; or they may keep them inside, the analyst probably consciously suppressing the expression of them, and the patient either doing the same, or repressing them. They may then later reappear in imagery or even with a symbolic quality to them, when they will be available for transformation. If they have attracted to themselves archetypal images that are waiting for a form, then changes can occur within the transference/countertransference, which can be brought to light. The material and the concrete become symbolic.

At her first meeting with me, a certain woman patient "thought" —i.e., fantasized—that I looked like a lioness. Without revealing the reason, she said she did not want to come again, and fled back to the colleague who had referred her to me. Fortunately she was encouraged to return and talk about it. I thought, but did not say, that in the psychic circumstances her flight was understandable. She gradually managed to allow me to become, for her, human, and her fantasy became analyzable.

Jung considered that

> . . . the psyche consists essentially of images. It is a series of images in the truest sense, not an accidental juxtaposition or sequence, but a structure that is throughout full of meaning and purpose; it is a "picturing of vital activities." And just as the material of the body that is ready for life has need of the psyche in order to be capable of life, so the psyche presupposes the living body in order that its images may live. (Jung 1926, par. 618)

I think a close analogy to, or an illustration of, the foregoing remarks of Jung is to be found in many aspects of therapeutic work with patients. The patient often brings physical pains to the session and needs the psychic response of the analyst, who will most likely be able to find both the meaning and the purpose, by way of what is happening in the transference and the countertransference, and to relate it to earlier life events or old familial constellations. For example, a patient arrived looking pale and clutched his abdomen as he sat down and huddled into the chair. He said it was indigestion caused by eating too much popcorn the evening before. He did not mention it again and I made no comment. As the session developed it became possible to see that the "indigestion" was an internal experience "caused" by an excess of something otherwise good, and the bad from outside met some inner malfunctioning which, in the analysis, carried the significance of a negative archetypal image. It would not have been possible to interpret the opening remark without all that happened in the session, by which time the similarity had emerged between the genesis of the physical pain and of his very difficult current life-pains, which he considered were being caused by other people but which he also knew went back to childhood interactions and attitudes he had developed during those stressful years.

I can again refer back to Jung:

> There is, in a certain sense, nothing that is directly experienced except the mind itself. Everything is mediated through the mind, translated, filtered, allegorized, twisted, even falsified by it. We are so enveloped in a cloud of changing and endlessly shifting images that we might well exclaim with a

well-known sceptic: "Nothing is absolutely true—and even that is not quite true." (Jung 1926, para. 623)

The reader will remember that one of my intentions in this paper, expressed in the title, is to search for psychic truth.

Psyche-soma

Up to now I have been offering some examples of the sense aspect of the body-psyche theme, stressing the interconnections and interactions of the two in analysis and therapy. Another aspect is contained in the large field of illness classified as psychosomatic. Here again the literature is voluminous and growing every year. In it the medical doctor speaks with authority of a different kind from that which someone can offer who came to analytical psychology from the arts side of learning. It is increasingly noticeable, at any rate where I work, that many general practitioners—basically physicians—are more willing than they were some years ago to discuss the origin and the meaning of the illnesses suffered by people who are both their patients and mine. The old mana-based medical superiority is on the decrease, but the present "psycho-somatic fashion," in C. A. Meier's words (Meier 1962), is not simply a re-action against medical materialism but a modern version of a view of illness held by many ancient Greek physicians. Even then the conundrum of whether the truth is that bodily ills are independent of psychic states, or that affects bring about those ills, was carefully considered. It is the view of analytical psychologists that unconscious complexes produce symptomatic actions and accident-proneness, and somatic symptoms that can result in genuine organic damage. A simplistic psychosomatic approach or interpretation may lead to the apparent remission of the symptoms, but if serious organic disturbance has become independent of the psycho-dynamics, the view of the matter as psychogenic will no longer be effective enough and physical treatment will be necessary. The Freudian concept of conversion, according to which the psyche produces the physical symptom, is perhaps better known than Alfred Adler's theory of the link between neuroticism and unacceptable organ inferiority, whether that is actual or fantasied. The somatic factor was usefully acknowledged in Adler's view, without being considered to be necessarily causal on its own; it often brought it within range of treatment which could result in the patient's undertaking further and deeper therapy, exploring more areas of the unconscious.

As well as referring cursorily to psychosomatic illnesses, it is worth mentioning Leopold Stein's paper, of major importance in the study of psyche-soma, "Introducing not-self" (Stein 1967). He "postulates a psy-chosomatic unity superordinated to the body and the mind" (p. 110). He points out that etymologically, the very early pre-Latin word *fendēre* means to beat, to protect, and to beat back, which leads him to write that "the hostile attitude bound up with destructiveness, and thus for beating back and slaying, presupposes the ability of the self to recognise not-self," although "defence is often tacitly regarded as a mechanism characteristic of the reasonable ego" (p. 103). Also, he writes that from what little is known of "the etymology of most of the words standing for the concept of the self as we or as ordinary folk understand it . . . we can glean two motifs . . . : one, that of omnipotence; another that of belonging to a clan" (p. 101).

Stein's "psychosomatic unity" is of particular interest when manifes-tations of transference/countertransference are being examined, particu-larly in the context of synchronicity. The patient's defense system and the analyst's are each at work, both in their own areas and in interaction. The analyst's perhaps defensive shadow—uncaringness—his or her not-understanding which the patient may be at one and the same time imag-ining and instigating, because it suits the patient to make out that the ana-lyst is a cold fish—those shadow factors may well be connected with phases in the analysis when the analyst is not liking the patient, since the patient is literally being unlikable as a result of his or her persecutory at-tacks. Yet the problem is a shadow one. The shadow of the "good" analyst is the uncaring one, who cannot but look forward to the end of the difficult session, or even to the resolution of the long phase in the analy-sis when he or she does not know what is happening, after which the ana-lyst "feels himself or herself" again—no longer ill, or ill at ease. The working-through of these events or stages may be quite painful.

The Analyst's Illnesses

These views on interactions between patients and analysts are of-fered as a background to the attempt to find out how useful the concept of synchronicity can be in throwing light on the situation when there is a psychosomatic relationship between two people: patients' reactions to the analyst's physical illness. It would be more correct to call that simply "the analyst's illness" and not to beg the question in advance of whether it is a physical or a psychic illness.

It is easy enough, if facile and unprovable, for an analyst beset with a harsh super-ego, or with judgmental parent-imagoes, to believe that suc-cumbing to a flu virus, for example, means that he or she does not want to see such and such a patient for a few days—perhaps a patient who has not yet worked through some psychopathology from which the analyst also suffers. An actual flu infection can occur to an analyst whose range of patients at any one time includes more than one whose transference projections are particularly apposite. The flu then temporarily rescues the analyst who, assuming he or she takes some days off work, can probably gather enough strength to withstand what is being experienced as persecution, by means of analyzing a not-yet-healed wound, or as an obstinate personality defect. It could be that flu hits the analyst just as he or she needs, yet once more, to pay serious attention to a recurrent tendency to a narcissistic but unconscious omnipotence. If the illness is interpreted as flu getting power over the analyst, he or she is thereby offered the opportunity to deepen the ongoing personal analysis.

I think such a mild physical illness can operate valuably if the analyst can perceive whence comes the internal mental attack. It is not coming from the patient, who is probably needing an uninterrupted series of sessions to attack *within the transference*. This does not disturb the physically well analyst unduly if he or she is skilled at seeing when attacks are happening; the analyst probably finds it more difficult if he or she is succumbing to a virus attack. It is the analyst's job to discern the subtle and the devious aggressions; then the true psychic target can be interpreted.

I am of course not alone in thinking that the psychogenic factor in the analyst's illness can and must be worked on. However, as in all matters of a psychosomatic nature, the difficulty lies in finding out convincingly what led to the choice of illness, particularly if the analyst has not suffered from it before, as that is not always obvious. The questions that any illness raises for the analyst are: what is the analogy offered, what is the meaning, and what is the symbol?

Illness and the Self

There are many medically more serious illnesses than flu that an analyst may get, and many that result in far longer interruptions of analytical therapy. I am writing here of intensive therapies where the patient comes three, four, or five times a week, anxiety is not shunned or otherwise bypassed, and deep structures are affected. For such patients with not yet firm enough boundaries, even a short gap caused by the analyst's illness may bring on extremist fantasies of abandonment—the patient is being abandoned—or of death—the analyst is going to die. The impact of a rather longer gap can be almost impossible to tolerate.

Two psychoanalysts, Dewald (1982) and Abend (1982), have recently published papers closely connected with this theme, in which each of them describes transference and countertransference considerations that arose as results of serious illness in the analyst. My contribution to this subject is to relate how, some time ago, after a series of minor interruptions that built up a mood of emotional irritation and fear in a certain patient who was struggling to tolerate and work through anxiety about a lump in one of her breasts (her mother had had a mastectomy), I had unfortunately to stop work for two weeks owing to having developed shingles, *herpes zoster.*

I had been unaware that a rash on my right arm was shingles. When acute pain attacked my shoulder I thought it was a renewal of an earlier arthritic condition and I had consulted my doctor about it. I only casually told him about the skin condition, which he then diagnosed. The shingles was, medically, very minor, but the pain was fiendish.

What resulted psychologically was an experience of almost total loss of interest in almost everything and everybody, of a nature and quality quite different from run-of-the-mill tiredness or depression. Some people would call it loss of soul. The patient who was so anxious about her breast lump had to go into hospital just then, and my complete inability to do more than listen to her on the telephone and to remind her that if she felt even worse she could go to her doctor, had a long-lasting bad effect on her. Her lump was not malignant, and my recovery duly took place. But her reproaches about how deeply I had hurt her recurred at intervals over several months. The pain in her psyche seemed to dig right into her feeling of herself. She felt I had hit her, as well as abandoned her to her fate. Her reaction seemed to me to indicate that she had regressed to a very early state—in developmental terms it had a pre-paranoid quality—and the very young infant girl in her desperately needed me to care for her and to nurse her back to health.

During the days when I had almost completely lost interest in everything and when I could not apply any thinking capacity to how things were, what was happening had nothing to do with "being interested" in the usual or thinking sense of the words. All I did was to be, for nearly two weeks. And I was greatly helped by a friend and colleague who quickly and simply said, "You are having a self experience." I had not been consciously afraid of losing my self, or my soul, and I had not reached the stage where I might have feared losing my life. The I-feeling was still there and by simply waiting, the greater self and the smaller me were both restored and became viable again.

Retrospectively, it could be thought that, where I was concerned, I had an absolute need for the loss of soul experience, and the fact that it cut across my patient's need for me to be fully available to her had to be lived with and lived through. That view of the matter cannot be satisfactorily validated if the rational angle is predominant; it smacks of justifying the occurrence of the events by saying they "had" to happen. Yet that view can also lead on to seeing that she had another need which the synchronicity helped: the need to discover my limits, to find out that over-protracted intensive care can become unhelpful *participation mystique*. And that is not relationship. There was a need not to have *coniunctio* at that turning point, and for her idealization to decrease. That way lay development for her and emergence from the power of early infancy fantasies, archetypal ones.

When I resumed analysis with the patient who feared cancer, I did not interpret much, nor did I communicate to her directly anything of my own experience. As the weeks went by her belief in herself as an alive person who was valued and who was going to continue living was restored. It seems to me virtually impossible to decipher the truth about the synchronous quality for her and for me of the weeks lived through in that summer. As her analyst—previously trusted, but less and less idealized as her attacks of envy were worked through—I felt sure that she was getting the benefit of somehow absorbing through her psychological pores the discovery that the fear of loss of life can be faced. The body events came into relation with their psychic counterparts, and the psychic experiences seemed to need body form for their impact to reach deep enough. It has appeared to me to be a series of events in her life and in mine in which the immensity of the self dimension was presented first in a very malign form; then, thanks to the synchronicity, it was possible for the action of the self gradually to become benign and available as libido for going on in life.

It is somewhat invidious to select one quotation from among so many possible ones about cancer (or the fear of cancer) and the psyche, but this one is especially valuable. I think it illustrates some of what occurred in the foregoing case, in the transference/countertransference:

> The phenomenology of cancer is full of images of guilt and retribution ("What have I done to deserve this?") and promises to one's self and others that, should there be a recovery, sacrifices will be made, and there will be a *change of ways*, life will be lived properly. (Lockhart 1983, p. 63; italics added)

I did not feel pathologically guilty about what I had done to this patient, and the whole episode certainly led to an increase in consciousness ("a change of ways") for me as well as for her. Then in another passage Lockhart wrote:

> Cancer as an image in dreams or as a reality in the body signifies something wrong in one's relation to life, and so cancer is both a warning and an opportunity to seek out the paths of unlived life—in whatever period of time one has remaining. (Ibid., p. 63)

It seemed to me that while I had merely had shingles and she had had a breast lump, both of us had some more "unlived life" to live, though my period of remaining was most likely going to be shorter than hers.

A Violent Incident

The second clinical event that illustrates the interactions of body and psyche in analytical therapy is one that occurred some years ago. At intervals colleagues have suggested I should try to write about it. I would like now to offer the bare outlines of the violent episode of the burglars in order to link the material incident with the forward-reaching concepts of analytical psychology. What it has in common psychologically with the first case is that there was considerable danger (though of a different kind) and fear. An additional factor of uncertainty was introduced the next day when a psychoanalyst who lives in the same road as I, gloomily predicted that I "would lose the patient," i.e., it would be the death of the therapy. I took that to be his (unsolicited!) interpretation that I had killed it. I certainly hoped he would be proved wrong, although I could see it was a possible forecast to make.

The body side of the incident is that two men broke into my house through the front door, upstairs from where I was seeing a patient (whom I will call B) in my consulting room, which is at garden level. Instead of using my ego and calling the police when I heard two sets of footsteps in the room above, which I was certain could only belong to intruders, I put not only myself but also my patient at risk by acting on the basis of instinct. I went upstairs to investigate.

The intruders were surprised, and the nearest of the two hit out when he saw that they were going to be frustrated in their intention of burgling undetected. They had believed they had the house to themselves. There followed a fight in which both B and I—he was a tough male psychiatrist—were injured. We were lucky that the burglars were not armed. My first reaction had been anger, hence the fight. When the battle began to turn against B and me, and the intruders demanded that he should hand over whatever cash he had on him and that we should both lie down on the floor, fear replaced anger. I think I had never before in my life punched and kicked anyone with such anger, nor have I ever been quite so physically afraid as I was in the second stage of the affair. Both were simply instinctual and body reactions. However, B did not hand over any money, nor was either of us willing to lie down on the floor, and (or was it "so"?) the intruders departed.

Discussion

This very physical event was in every sense a violent intrusion into B's analysis, and it was unique in its nature and range. As a psychiatrist working partly in the community, B had often had to handle aggressive people physically, so to some extent he knew that there is no hard and fast distinction between body and psyche in psychiatry. But I have had no experience of body-work with patients, and could be described as seeing and keeping analysis totally different in that respect from almost any other aspect of life today.

The first psychological reaction of both I and B was that we had had a shared experience, a bad one, and one that had perhaps dangerously broken through the usual boundaries. The actuality of "being in the same boat" could never again be denied. It was henceforth a bond in which action had featured. The question arises as to whether some previously inexpressible factor had been acted out, inadvertently, and certainly against our wills (Hubback 1984). It was not sexual acting out, at least not in any obvious way, but I wondered whether there was some obscure sexual quality, using the term sexual in the broadest possible sense. Throughout the analysis there were the two parental transference projections, so the acting out would have been both of male homosexuality and of mother-son incest.

B and I each took a week to recover. When sessions resumed, his main communication was of great self-reproach. The intruders had managed to do what he never had, to break in and really go at me. He felt he had never attacked in such a way as really to hurt me, and that was irrespective of a deeper need not to knock me so hard that I was eliminated. The parent/analyst is required to survive all onslaughts.

His deep anxiety about passivity surfaced in a way that an analysis of five-and-a-half years' duration had not made possible until then. I felt awe about how he and I were talking about the material version of the sort of thing that some—and perhaps many—analysts say quite glibly: "You wanted to kill your mother," or your father, as it might be.

Flesh and blood homicide might have happened in my house, though not by B, and there was B saying that in hitting me, the intruders had shown that they had something he had not. That "something" was phallic bravery, expressed with arm and fist. He had not yet been the hero who literally fights the dragon-mother.

The boundary between talk about physical events and psychological-symbolic ones was temporarily lost. It was restored in the course of the following months, yet I think it took a long time for B to get over what amounted to a deep envy, experienced at an instinctual level, of the two men who had done with their physical fists what he had never done by psychic punching. So the intruders had acted out for him. What was ultimately important was that they had physically hit him as well as me, and that his negative hero had at last the possibility of turning into a positive one. B had not, in the youthful years, been able to free himself from certain depressing features in family life. His experiences with each of his parents had been unsatisfactory at that stage. In relating to them in middle and late adolescence, the positive hero had not been in evidence. He had found himself unable to go forward constructively, but had become increasingly depressed, in a way that many young people do when the passage through that archetypal stage is not well negotiated. It can be more like the death of the three hundred Spartans at Thermopylae than the achievement of the young runner from Marathon to Athens.

Where I was concerned, I felt far from heroic. I had punched the nearest intruder almost as much as (if less effectively than) I had been punched, and I had kicked, hoping to kick where it would hurt a man. But that was foolish, as it made him angrier. I had never in consciousness wanted to attack B in a big way, but I realized retrospectively that there had been times, early in his analysis, when I had felt like shaking him. It is possible that I had not released in the transference enough of the pent-up attack from which he was suffering, and that my desire to shake him (that is a fairly mild form of attack, compared with breaking someone's nose, which is what the intruders did to him) was an indication of far more aggression than I had been prepared to acknowledge in myself.

My main anxiety about my part in the events was that by acting from primitive instinct when my cave was entered by wild animals, I had caused B, for whom I was responsible, to be at physical risk. I was well aware of his having a wife and several children. So, where I was concerned, the intruders had acted out my shadow: the fear or the risk of increasing a patient's illness. The bad analyst, being the representative of the bad parent, can do a great deal of harm—can spoil the patient's chance to return to health, or, where narcissistic disturbances are concerned, can forever prevent the discovery that healing, growth, and change do exist. I was partly haunted by the remark of my psychoanalyst friend, and partly found it a challenge. B had been harmed. Was his analyst, who had inadvertently played such a part in the harm, going to be able to work through with him the emotions that had been aroused?

The factor of having acted on instinct was one that at the time exercised me strongly, perhaps excessively. It was not much use to me that everybody said it was natural not to have considered using my telephone to call for help. I was worried about that particular point; analysis is a non-natural experience (unless I split hairs with a minute investigation of "nature" and "natural," which will be reserved for another time), and the open enacting of either aggressive or erotic instincts does not take place in what should be the symbolic *hieros gamos* of the therapeutic relationship. *Agape* is what we strive for. Just as we do no more than read *Mysterium Coniunctionis* and pore with fascination over the illustrations in the *Rosarium Philosophorum*, so should neither the erotic nor the aggressive instincts be acted out in analysis. Damage is damage, whichever unbridled instinct it comes from.

The next challenge, however, was to emerge from what had gone before. One of the most valuable features of analytical psychology is, I think, the dual concept of the personal and the archetypal shadow. For B, his passivity and inability to move forward into the hero phase of developmental life was a shadow problem. The equivalent, or parallel, personal shadow for me at that moment was impulsiveness. I had not then, developmentally, nor indeed have not now, reached the stage of life when the archetype of the wise old woman can perhaps be constellated. It remains to be seen whether B will ever be as free from passivity, or I as free from impulsiveness, as each of us would like. In his outer life he is active and effective; in mine there is these days a welcome indication of slowing down. I know that even moderately wise old women do not dash about like youngsters; they have to be wary of broomsticks that would seduce them from reflectiveness. The psychological point here is that because of the intruder incident, a deeper understanding became possible of day-to-day shadow and body-and-psyche shadow. The instinctual and the psychic poles of the archetype had both been in evidence. And developmental energy was released by being, inadvertently, channeled through the electrical currents of the shared experience and the transference/countertransference.

Most of the interactions and intrapsychic events in analysis are not known to anyone but the two people concerned. Many drop into oblivion, and it is best if the *vas bene clausum* is indeed kept well closed, even if that is a counsel of perfection. Where long-term deepening of understanding is concerned, combined with the possibility of continuing change of perception of, and attitude toward, psychic events, one outcome of the intruder incident was that while it could not be concealed, it was available for detailed examination.

Over time the main focus of interest, where I am concerned, goes toward drawing attention to the fact that even the most sustained attempts to analyze omnipotence are never quite effective enough; the fantasy of omnipotence is such an early feature of the human psyche. Throughout my time of being an analytical psychologist I have been interested in finding out how to be effective in analyzing that fantasy. I am concerned with the problem of how the analyst can maintain his or her knowledge of established, and of new, theory and technique, combined with constant vigilance over the danger of omnipotence. The search for psychic truth is, I suggest, at the core of the work, the effort toward consciousness of as many factors as possible from which to build a profile of what actually happens in the body or in the soul. While there cannot be certainty of truth or absoluteness, it always has to be sought.

Conclusion

It was ambitious to direct attention to the search for psychic truth; it even has a grandiose ring to it. All the same, it seems to me that to bear in mind the very broad issues of our work as psychotherapists and analysts, as well as the details, helps us to keep a sense of proportion. "The search for psychic truth" refers to both the research and the therapy aspects of analysis. The need to relate them to each other can only be met effectively if more and more factors are brought in; the main ones in most of our current research are theories of the self and transference/ countertransference.

We can also usefully place those words and terms in the reverse positions, since one of the main courses to pursue is the analyst's subjectivity interacting with that of the patient and generating archetypal forces. In other disciplines (for example, physics, anthropology, and history), as well as in our own, the standpoint, the attitude, and the person of the observer are now being taken into account most valuably. Much if not most of analytical therapy hinges on trying to find out the real psychic happenings and to set them in a framework and model of the psyche that improves the likelihood of taking a few more steps toward a true understanding of interactions or the lack of them. By taking the body fully into account we are, I think, demonstrating an intention of keeping analytical psychology as sane as possible.

References

Abend, S. A. 1982. Serious illness in the analyst: Countertransference considerations. *Journal of the American Psychoanalytical Association* 30.

Dewald, P. A. 1982. Serious illness in the analyst: Transference, countertransference, and reality responses. *Journal of the American Psychoanalytical Association* 30.

Eliot, T. S. 1936. *Collected poems.* London: Faber & Faber.

Hubback, J. 1984. Acting out. *Journal of Analytical Psychology* 29/3.

Jung, C. G. 1960. Spirit and life. In *Collected works,* vol. 8.

Lambert, K. 1981. Individuation and the personality of the analyst. In *Analysis, repair and individuation,* London: Academic Press.

Lockhart, R. L. 1983. Cancer in myth and dream. In *Words as eggs: Psyche in language and clinic,* Dallas: Spring Publications.

Meier, C. A. 1963. Psychosomatic medicine from the Jungian point of view. *Journal of Analytical Psychology* 8/2.

Stein, L. 1967. Introducing not-self. *Journal of Analytical Psychology* 12/2.

———, and Alexander, M. 1959. *Loathsome women.* London: Weidenfeld & Nicholson.

The Body in Child Psychotherapy

John A. B. Allan

The body has long been an area of neglect in psychotherapy. I remember that throughout my own training in child psychology in the
early 1960s, we were told that on no account must we touch the child.
Obviously there were some deep-rooted fears about the unconscious
confusion of sexuality, affection, aggression, and control. Indeed, these
shadow components have represented and continue to represent huge
problems for western civilizations.

In this paper I want to describe two ways of incorporating the body
into child psychotherapy. One approach has to do with the use of physical holding and the other with the bodily enactment of fantasy images,
where the child "acts out" inner dramas in the play therapy room and the
therapist is actively involved in the play as a participant. Examples from
case studies will be mentioned to illustrate various stages of the individuation process that occur during fantasy enactment.

Background

In my first job as a psychotherapist, I worked in a residential treatment center for disturbed children in California. As it happened, there

John A. B. Allan, Ph.D., is a member of the Department of Counselling Psychology,
Faculty of Education, University of British Columbia.

were a considerable number of autistic and psychotic children in care. While many of the children responded to play therapy, progress with some was slow. Instead of using the play media for exploration and growth, the autistic child tended to get stuck in repetitive and persevera-tive movements that went on session after session. After a year of working this way, I slowly came to the realization that my approach was not ap-propriate for some of these children. What they needed was a different method of treatment.

While searching and pondering what to do, I met Professor Robert Zaslow, of San Jose State University, who was in the process of develop-ing a new holding technique called "Z-process attachment therapy" (Zas-low & Breger 1969; Zaslow 1981). I was trained by Zaslow and worked with him for a year before I went to the University of London to do my doctorate on the use of holding as therapy (Allan 1972).

Zaslow's main areas of specialty included developmental child psy-chology and child psychopathology. While observing austistic and psy-chotic children, he noticed many signs of fixation on early sensory-motor levels of development, including the neonatal period. These children of-ten exhibit a high level of motoric arousal, the presence of dorsal arch-ing, tonic-neck and startle reflexes, the use of peripheral vision, twirling, and the "pill-rolling" of fingers with thumb. Also, like normal babies, these children tend to watch their fingers move, especially when the hand is held up to lights.

Another central characteristic of autistic and psychotic children that Zaslow observed was their conditioned avoidance behavior toward peo-ple and non-compliance with verbal requests. These children did not like to be held or cuddled, seldom smiled with appropriate affection, and ac-tively avoided both face and eye contact. Zaslow stated that the condi-tioned avoidance response occurred very early in development and fixated these children at the sensory-motor level of development, i.e., at a preverbal stage. Thus, successful therapeutic intervention would neces-sarily involve the sensory-motor system of the child. With this in mind, Zaslow started picking up and holding children. Immediately he noticed their tendency to struggle to disengage. However, he simply said, "I'm going to hold you until you relax and sit quietly on my lap." This typically resulted in an intense struggle for forty-five minutes before the child could relax. Zaslow noticed that after the struggle there was a reduction in aggressive and destructive behavior, greatly improved face and eye contact, and the development of some exploratory play.

Theory

The underpinnings of Zaslow's work rest mainly on Bowlby's attachment theory (1958). It is through parent-child attachment that regulation of the central nervous system occurs as well as the internalization of feelings of trust and security, approach and initiative behavior, acquisition of speech and play, and a movement away from parents into play with other children and skill mastery.

Breaks of attachment, on the other hand, lead to feelings of anger and sadness, and the learning of negative motivational sets. Infants and children who have had many breaks of attachments, or whose attachment bonds have been weak, often fail to internalize deep feelings of love, acceptance, and trust. Instead of moving away from parents into healthy play with peers, these children become stuck in disturbed behavior patterns that signal a need for attention and help. Zaslow (1981) argues that the feelings of anger and sadness become trapped in the child's body or sensory-motor system and result in a negative motivational core. The strong negative feelings are acted out in a repetitive, compulsive fashion, often without growth or new learning.

What causes these breaks in attachment depends on a number of factors. Essentially, one is looking at the interaction between the characteristics of the parents and the child (Zaslow & Berger 1969). This includes genetic-constitutional factors of the infant and the psychological make-up of the parents as well as breaks of attachment caused by such physical separations as hospitalization, death, divorce, and other trauma. Zaslow argues that these situational crises activate intense feelings of hurt, anger, and sadness that maintain alienation. The parents are unable to reduce or transform the distress and the maladaptive tension in their infant or child. Zaslow hypothesizes that in the case of the austistic or psychotic youngster, the parents become associated with tension production and, from the infant's or child's perspective, are to be avoided. This avoidance is manifested by the child's arching and pulling away and by the withdrawal of energy from the surface of the body.

Holding becomes one way to change this pattern of avoidance and disengagement. That is, the child is held on the adult's lap through the struggle to disengage, until relaxation is achieved. The experience of intense feelings of anger and sadness that are expressed in this struggle break up the pattern of resistances and defensive behavior. Hyperactive children show a great deal of natural protest behavior when held, and the holding achieves rapid results. With hypoactive children, rocking and tickling allow the holder to overcome passive resistances and to increase the child's expressive energy through gentle tactile stimulation. The goal of holding is to break up the negative and locked system of the child in order to activate positive human interaction so that attachment and learning can occur.

From a Jungian perspective, this early conditioned avoidance response to the primary caretakers has a profoundly negative effect on the development of the Self. Some infants develop a very thick "stimulus barrier" (Bergman & Escalona 1949) around the Self which protects the child from many forms of environmental stimulation but also prevents the Self from developing emotionally and symbolically.

Michael Fordham, who has worked extensively with psychotic and autistic children, sees these conditions as reflecting:

> A persistence of the primary Self, an integrate which in healthy growth de-integrates to produce a symbiotic relation between the infant and mother. Since the integrate persists, no distinction can develop in the child between environment, ego and internal world because these three entities are not distinguished but remain one whole Self. (Fordham 1966, p. 299)

My view is that some forms of autism arise when parents fail to interfere with and disturb an infant who persists in a state of primary Self, a state of non-emergence and non-relating. One purpose of the holding, then, is to intrude into the primary Self and to break up the integrate so that attachment and relating occur.

Touching and Holding Methods

The three holding techniques described next do not involve merely holding a child. They are highly purposeful techniques that have as their goals the release and transformation of difficult or painful emotions and the stimulation of a sense of relaxation, attachment, and pleasure. The holding sessions usually last about one-and-a-half hours and consist of three phases: catharsis, understanding, and behavioral practice. The therapist uses different skills during each stage, but in an overall context of sensitivity and empathy. One common goal is to help the child put his or her feelings (and wants and wishes) into words. There is always an attempt to bring about a developmental shift from the acting out of feelings to the verbalization of them in a face-to-face context.

The holder's lap is the main "container" where the "work" is done. Within one holding session, a child's emotional rhythms may fluctuate many times from intense struggle and rage, to fear, to deep grieving, and into relaxation. The holders must adapt their responses (i.e., tactile and verbal) to match the child's reactions. Holding is a fluid, open system of interaction that should lead to an end state of positive attachment. The holders must never hurt the child, allow the child to hurt himself or herself, or let the child hurt the adult holder.

Holding is always done in the presence of one or both parents. First the approach is described to them in some detail. Photographs and videotapes are shown before holding is initiated, so the parents have a clear understanding of the method and what is involved. Parents are given the choice of whether they want to take the lead and hold the child on their laps or whether they want the therapist to do the holding.

Although the child may be the main focus of treatment, holding is also a form of family therapy, as the holder is treating the parents, and the interaction and communication between the child and the parents.

Methods

Three methods of holding are described: *vertical holding, horizontal holding*, and *holding for pleasure*. These methods were devised specifically for the use of holding with autistic and psychotic children. Recently refinements have been developed that focus on the use of holding with less severely impaired children, where an emphasis is also placed on the appropriate verbalization of feelings (Allan 1976, 1984).

Vertical Holding

The therapist meets with the child and the parents and works toward establishing rapport. Once mutual trust is achieved, the therapist says to the child: "David, I can see that you are very upset, and I am going to hold you in my arms to comfort and calm you. I'll put you down when you're quiet."

> Pick the child up in your arms [in this example, a boy], sit down, and place him on your lap, sideways to you, so that his feet dangle down over your thighs and then take his socks and shoes off. Place your left arm over his shoulder, tuck his right arm in between your bodies and then place your left thumb in the palm of his left hand, curling his fingers around your thumb at the same time. Put your right hand around his left ankle so that your forearm is touching his right ankle as well.
>
> In this position you resist the child's attempts to disengage from you by holding him until he relaxes. For example, if he tries to release his hand from yours, you increase your finger pressure to a point that is sufficient to maintain his hand in yours. If he kicks with his legs your right arm provides a barrier for him to push against. If he stiffens his legs and holds them straight out, you apply pressure with your hand, inward, on his ankle until his knees

bend. If his whole body becomes stiff and rigid, you place the palm of your hand on his waist and apply pressure downward with your hand until you feel him release his tension and relax his muscles. [See photograph, p. 166.]

During the first thirty to forty minutes, you will find that you are constantly shifting your attention and hands from one part of the child's body to another to confront and reduce the rigid tensional states and to prevent the child from climbing off your lap.

The method of holding is not that of a straight jacket, but it is sensitive, fluid, and yet firm when indicated. Although you are in control, you take your cues from the child; that is, the area that the child tenses or struggles with is the one you move to and interact with. When the child relaxes, you relax your pressure, but you do not remove your hands.

This type of holding raises the child's level of arousal; that is, the child tends to become more tense and screams and struggles to a much greater degree than before. This is desired, as one of the purposes of the holding is to increase the activity level of the child in order to bring about an end state of relaxation. I have observed that the greater the struggle, the longer the subsequent period of relaxation.

When a child starts sobbing, you will find that the child is now accessible to comforting. At this point, you cradle the child comfortably in your arms, tilt the head forward slightly so that the chin rests on the chest, and say sensitively and softly: "That's okay, David; it's good to cry." Likewise, when he rages, you do not stifle his rage by holding him in a straight-jacket fashion, but instead you try to use your arms and body as a "movable barrier" for him to rage against. This time you could say: "That's the boy; it's good to get angry and fight."

These responses may seem unusual, but the purpose is to try to encourage both weeping and raging while the child is in your arms. These are "letting-go" reactions that tend to reduce the overall body tension and are followed by the state of relaxation-in-human-contact. This is likely to strengthen the child's attachment to you, because the end state is one of comfort and pleasure, and because you are the person who brought about the transformation.

By the end of the session, when the child relaxes, you relax too and allow him or her to rest comfortably against your chest. A quiet period usually follows, which allows the exchange of warmth between your bodies. The child tends to become receptive to you and may start to visually explore your face and the rest of the room. I have found it best to let the child take the initiative during this period. Also, I have noticed that after the weeping and rage, face and eye contact improve significantly.

Horizontal Holding

This holding method is more advanced and should only be used when you feel competent with the *vertical* position. It demands more of the holder and tends to increase both sobbing and rage. It is an additional method to use once the child is able to relax in the *vertical* position but when you feel there is still some excess tension in the child's body.

> First determine whether you or a parent will hold the head of the child [in this example, a boy]. Then from the sitting position on the holder's lap, you lift the child up and gently place him on his back across your legs so that his head, neck, and back are comfortably supported. Hold his arms so that the parent or therapist can turn the child's face toward their faces so that eye contact can be established. Keep the child in this position until he relaxes, at which point you return him to the upright sitting position on your lap.
>
> This horizontal position enables you to handle and reduce more directly the variety of avoidance and tensional postures that the child may show during the holding. For example, if he turns his head away from your face, you turn it back. If he throws his head back, you lift it up. If the child stares at a distant object, you move your head in line with his eyes' gaze. If the child tries to watch his fingers move in a manneristic fashion, you hold his hand out of view and if he tries to "pill roll" (i.e., rub the fingers together repeatedly), you hold his fingers firmly so that it cannot be done. If his mouth is "frozen" open, you close it by applying an upward pressure with your thumb from underneath the chin. When the child ceases to resist, you release your thumb pressure. [See photograph, p. 166.]

In other words, whenever the child shows a tensional posture, whether it be in the form of continuous movement or static tension, you use your hands to provide a superior pressure to dominate or reduce those bodily tensional states. The purpose of this pressure is to prevent the child from continually discharging tension by repetitive movements or from maintaining a state of high arousal by the use of startle or "freezing" postures. The repetitive movements and static postures of the child do not in themselves bring about a state of relaxation. However, the use of holding essentially shifts the energy output of the child up to a much higher peak, which is then followed by a decrease in movement and a swing down toward relaxation. The session ends with relaxation and the use of pleasurable holding.

Holding for Pleasure

Unlike the normal child who smiles and laughs when tickled, many children with severe social and emotional problems tend to turn or pull away from pleasurable stimulation (Allan 1972). Smiling and laughing are important responses, because they reflect happiness and also tend to reduce bodily tension. The feelings of tension reduction tend to become associated with the parents and tend to increase a child's approach behavior to them.

The purpose of *holding for pleasure* is to get the child to respond to holding with smiles and laughter. Once this has been achieved, the aim is to extend the number of holding methods that bring pleasure and to increase the duration of pleasure. One of the goals is to develop in the child feelings of physical trust, as this may reduce the need to be in control. Several methods are described in greater detail elsewhere (Allan 1977), but mostly they involve tickling, swinging, and cuddling, rocking backwards, and jumping and bouncing together.

> The child may at first actively resist or show no positive response to your movements. Do not be put off by this, but continue to try to elicit smiles and laughter. If the child keeps resisting, continue the tickling, but now also imitate and echo the cries and screams in a playful, friendly, and teasing way. When you do this, you are letting the child know that the cries and actions do not frighten or upset you, and that you can continue to play despite the child's opposition or refusal to do so. Once the first smile or laugh appears, other pleasurable responses tend to come quite quickly. The element of "surprise" (or startle) that is experienced in tickling, falling backwards, and bouncing, I believe, helps the child to feel safe and to respond spontaneously to you and the environment in other situations.

It is from these playful situations that the child finds out that spontaneity is not harmful. In others words, the relaxation and pleasure experienced in the holding can be seen as starting points or foundation stones out of which other, more normal, responses may emerge.

Results of the Use of Body Methods

Over the past fifteen years I have used holding in many different ways. Three examples follow.

Example One: A Group of Autistic Children

My first major project involved treating a group of seven autistic children in residential care, ranging in age from three to nine years. All the children were profoundly autistic. They avoided eye contact, had ritualistic and stereotyped forms of play, used no language, and demonstrated severe and sustained impairments in emotional relationships prior to treatment.

Each child was seen once a week for two hours over a nine-month period. All three holding positions were used, with the therapist serving as the holder. Because the children were in residential care, the parents were not involved in this treatment series.

Over the nine months, certain patterns emerged that were common across the sample. As the sessions progressed, the children changed in their responses to being held. First they tried to escape or detach from the holder's lap; then they wept; then the weeping turned into rage. Relaxation and attachment followed both weeping and raging. This complete sequence of detachment, weeping, rage, and relaxation only became apparent after the child had been held in this way for twenty to thirty sessions. Generally speaking, for the first two to three months the tension was paramount and there was little indication that the child relaxed afterwards. However, after about three months of treatment, a new pattern emerged. The child would struggle and tense up throughout the early part of a session, the struggling would reach a peak of intensity, and then the child would weep briefly and relax for a moment before beginning to tense up again. Weeping became more of a feature as time went on, and each time the subsequent degree of relaxation was more profound. Weeping, in fact, became so pronounced that three of the children wept on several occasions, with little interruption, for as long as one hour. However, during this period they were accessible to being comforted and sought contact with me. It was at this period that relaxation became part of the child's response to being held and, as will be seen later, this was accompanied by other quite dramatic changes.

Enragement first occurred toward the end of the sessions in which crying had taken place and followed a similar pattern to crying, being very brief initially and in later sessions lasting up to one hour in some children. Eye contact improved noticeably after both weeping and rage.

In the last three months, the use of horizontal holding declined, and in most cases relaxation occurred quickly, often following token gestures of weeping or raging (but not the prolonged bouts noted earlier on).

Parallel changes occurred in the second part of the session during *holding for pleasure*. At the start of treatment, all children resisted the attempts at pleasurable interaction by trying to climb out of the cradling arms, pulling away when tickled, and making continuously forced crying sounds. When the brief periods of relaxation were experienced, and after twenty to thirty minutes of gentle but constant stimulation during these periods, all of the children began to smile and laugh, but for only ten to twenty seconds before they became manneristic again. Over the several sessions, and with increased relaxation, the children became more responsive and spent as long as fifteen to thirty minutes smiling and laughing in response to the stimulation. Eventually, some of the children began to explore the therapy room and to play with some of the toys. At first they played alone with the therapist, but only after some initial body contact. Later, play extended to the start of the session before either of the holding conditions was used and then generalized to the residential care environments. However, though some normal patterns developed, the children were by no means cured.

The observations of the child care workers suggested that the younger children (three to five years) showed a slow but continual improvement, while the older ones at first tended to improve and deteriorate at the same time, that is, they showed an increase in awareness (improved eye contact, visual interest in people and the environment) and an increase in mannerisms. In some cases, eating and sleeping significantly improved, as did the ability to show and express a variety of feelings—sadness, assertion, jealousy, anger, and affection. Recognition of people and places was observed, along with improvements in vocalization—the emergence of some words and the use of sound for initiating purposeful social interaction. When the children were fully able to relax under my holding, their caretakers reported that the children became very physically attached to them, becoming menneristic only when separated from them. At this point, the children began to respond slightly more to physical and verbal controls and to pleasurable stimulation, smiling and laughing when tickled. Gradually, mannerisms in most children decreased slightly, while exploratory behavior and constructive play increased. In sum, the changes indicated increases in social responsiveness and awareness of the environment rather than in the acquisition of specific task skills.

Example Two: A Seven-Year-Old Autistic Boy, Tim, and His Mother

The more I have used holding, the more I have come to focus on treating the mother and child together, and sometimes the father as well. In this case, I want to describe a critical incident between a mother and child which seemed to greatly facilitate improvement for both. The mother posited the onset of autism as having occurred immediately following the boy's hospitalization at fifteen months for major eye surgery.

At the start of treatment, Tim was very autistic as evidenced by poor eye contact, twirling and manneristic behaviors, severe temper tantrums, no speech, and no symbolic or emotional play. However, once or twice a year, when extremely frustrated, he would say three or four coherent words.

Treatment consisted of holding him in the horizontal position with the mother present, orienting his face to my face and working on simple words: "Say 'No'"; "say 'Go'"; "say 'Mom'"; "say 'Dad'"; "say 'Yes'." During this time the mother sat next to me, holding his legs and hands.

Tim's response to this position and the verbal requests was to arch his back, flail out with his arms, turn his face from side to side, and screech. I reflected his feelings and repeated the request: "Tim, you don't like me holding you like this, do you? Say 'No' and I'll lift you up." His reaction was more intense struggling, and after forty-five minutes he said "No-on," whereupon I lifted him up and put him on his mother's lap.

Over the next ten sessions, it became quite easy to shape "No-on" to "No" and to get him to say all of the other requested words. His behavior at home greatly improved: Temper tantrums decreased and spontaneous language increased.

Once Tim had mastered single words, both when on my lap and when he was sitting alone, I moved to get him to say such paired words as: "I go," "Me up," "Stop it," "I love Mom," "I love Dad," etc. During the eleventh session, when asked to say "Me up," he struggled, fought, and suddenly said very clearly: "Umbrella . . . umbrella . . . umbrella." I looked around in amazement, thinking someone had left an umbrella in the room, but I could not see one. I checked with the mother and she said:

> Isn't that strange? I don't like to see him struggling with his pain, so I cut out and let my mind wander. I saw this photograph of a colorful umbrella on your bulletin board [Tim could not see it because it was behind his back] and I was thinking how depressing the picture was except for this one bright, colorful umbrella. Then Tim said "umbrella."

When she said this I understood, on one level, what was happening. The mother experienced difficulty in handling some intense emotions. She would repress such feelings, and the boy would experience them from the transference situation (Jung 1946). There was apparently a very strong unconscious bond between them. Tim could literally "read" his mother and respond to some of her images, thoughts, and feelings in an almost reflexive, subliminal way. Based on this experience ("umbrella") and my understanding of it, I immediately changed my line of interaction with Tim. While still maintaining him in the horizontal position, I said to him:

> Tim, your Mom really wants you to speak. It means so much to her. It's her biggest wish in life that you will start to talk. [Tim began

to intensify his struggle to get off my lap.] Tim, you know this wish of your Mom's, but you've decided not to speak. You're mad at your Mom and you want to hurt her. [At this point he broke down and sobbed deeply for the first time.]

Also, I had an understanding of the changes I wanted the mother to make:

Mother, during this week, when it seems appropriate, I want you to say to Tim, "Tim, I know you're mad at me [for leaving you at the hosptital]. It's all right to be mad. Let me help you with your anger.

I told the mother not to push speech for a while, but to share her feelings with Tim. If she felt sad and hurt, then she should allow herself to cry in front of him.

When Tim and his mother came back two weeks later, there was a positive change in both of them. Tim was emitting a great deal more spontaneous speech, playing ball with his sister, and sleeping well at night. His mother had cried twice in front of him. Each time, he had gone over and touched her face and said very clearly: "Tears for Tim." When I had the next holding session with him and his Mom, I elicited all of these words very clearly and quite quickly: "No," "Yes," "Dad," "Mom," "Yes, Mom," "No, Mom," and "I go home." The words also generalized, for a while, off the lap and while sitting on the couch by himself.

It seemed that because Tim's mother really wanted him to speak, he was determined not to. Once this surfaced, I was able to help the mother let go of the immediacy of her wish for him to talk. Another interesting aspect was the mother's trapped feelings of her grief over Tim's disability (i.e., his autism) and her guilt. I felt that by holding in her feelings, she had bound Tim to hold in his feelings as well. When I encouraged her to cry openly in front of Tim, it took the pressure off Tim's control of his emotions and released approach behavior, i.e., he went up to her, touched her tears, and said: "Tears for Tim."

*Example Three: Use of the Body in Fantasy Enactment with
a Young Girl*

This example describes a different use of the body in child psycho-therapy. Although I used physical holding in the treatment of this child, Luci, I wish to emphasize here the use of the body in dramatic play and fantasy enactment. By itself, holding is an insufficient form of therapy; it is a useful starting point. After holding, one is still faced with helping the child to deal with deeper manifestations of the Self. These emerge quite readily in some children through play. A more detailed background on Luci will be found elsewhere (Allan & Macdonald 1975).

Background

Luci was five-and-a-half years old when she was referred to a Child Guidance Clinic for treatment of bizarre and destructive behavior. She thought she was a "seagull," a boy named "Danny," or a "barking dog." She had considerable speech, but much interactive speech was echolalic. To "Hi, how are you, Luci?" she would reply "Hi, how are you, Luci?" Also, she carried around with her a seagull feather that she held close to her eyes and twirled constantly back and forth. If you held her hand, she would say: "How do you like my fluffy white wing?" At other times she said, "What's the deer doing jumping through the refrigerator with its lights on?"

The kindergarten teacher found that the behavior that was the most difficult to handle was when Luci ran around the floor on all fours, "barking like a dog," biting other children on their ankles, and attacking mothers when they came to drop their children off or pick them up. She would pull babies out of their mothers' arms saying: "No hold babies. Babies don't like."

Like many psychotic children, Luci expressed a rich and bizarre symbolic life. Though there were many autistic mannerisms and perseverations, it seems that there was some fragmented ego development, but the ego was essentially still immersed and imbedded in the Self. This resulted in ego identification with aspects of the archetype of the Self (Perry 1965) and the corresponding inflation, i.e., "I'm a seagull," "I'm a boy," "I'm Supergirl" (Edinger 1973).

Treatment Approaches

Four main treatment approaches were used in this case: (1) holding therapy with Luci and her mother and father; (2) individual therapy with the mother; (3) fantasy enactment with Luci, myself, and a female therapist; and (4) art therapy. I will allude briefly to the holding therapy, but focus mainly on the fantasy enactment sessions, as it was there that her psychological and symbolic life unfolded. Following each fantasy enactment session, Luci did some art therapy with a female therapist.

Holding Therapy

Both parents stated that Luci had been non-cuddly as an infant and refused to let them hold or cuddle her when she grew older. I initiated the holding in order to help Luci overcome her resistances to being held and to help her to put her feelings into words and talk about them.

Initially, in response to being held, Luci would start to cry, shake her head from side to side, try to fight her way off the lap, and say, "You're not holding me. I'm a bird. I'm outside flying around. I'm a boy named Danny." In response I would say: "It's fearful to be held, isn't it? Let yourself say: 'I am Luci and I feel afraid.'" This would result in an increase in struggle, rage, and attempts to kick, bite, and scratch. This pattern lasted for about forty-five minutes, by which time there was considerable calming and she was finally able to say: "I'm Luci and I'm afraid. I'm Luci and I feel safe."

At first the effects of this were very short lived and she would revert back to being Danny or a seagull. However, over four to six sessions there was a definite change. She could cry a little more easily, relax longer, and her speech became less echolalic and less rigidly metaphorical. Her speech became more interactive on a fantasy level, and she wanted to include us in the fantasy play rather than exclude us. Also, her drawings changed considerably and seemed much more grounded. At this point I initiated fantasy enactment on a weekly basis, as well as continuing the bimonthly holding sessions when indicated.

Fantasy Enactment

The purpose of this form of treatment was to give Luci the chance to dramatize or enact her fantasies in the play therapy room. I enlisted the help of Rita, a woman therapist. We removed all the toys from the playroom, brought Luci in, and said: "We are here to play with you. What do you want to do?" Immediately she said, "I'm Danny, you're Joanna [pointing to me], and you're Lawrence [pointing to Rita], and I want to tie you up."

As Luci exhibited a great deal of acting-out behavior, we decided to use this method of play as a basis of treatment. We let her enact her dreams in the playroom, and let ourselves follow them and be actively involved in them. In this way her mind, body, and actions led or directed the dramas, while our bodies responded to and followed her leads. Our minds could then process the experiences we felt as we played out the roles she assigned to us. Our goal was to go along with her dramas for forty minutes and then spend the last ten minutes reviewing and reflecting on the session. Following this, Rita would spend ten to fifteen minutes with Luci in art therapy.

Treatment lasted for a year. In retrospect, it seemed to be characterized by five major themes: rage, depression, fear, dependency, and individuation.

Rage

In the first few sessions, Luci pretended to tie us up and to attack us. Although she did not actually hurt us, there was a tremendous intensity to her actions. She lined us up, pushed us down to the floor, sat on a little bench above us, and shot arrows into us. We had to scream with pain, plead for mercy, and die many times.

The feelings were so strong that Luci could not stop her wish to hurt us. After forty minutes, against her wishes we crawled to the other end of the room where we erected an "invisible shield." Behind this shield, we stepped out of the role-playing and commented on the session: "Danny really wanted to hurt Joanna and Lawrence today. He wanted to see them cut up and he didn't want to stop. . . . I guess Danny feels hurt by the big people and wants to hurt back."

The rage continued over the next few sessions and became more bloodthirsty. She cut our arms and legs off with swords, and fired pins into our eyes, mouths, and sexual organs. We were lying in blood. Then "poo" emerged as a main theme: our bodies were rotting, worms appeared, and we were floating in a sea of poo and blood. Later, while we were still emitting cries of agony, Luci sat above us eating deluxe hamburgers while we had to eat poo-burgers. Again, at the end of the sessions when we stood behind the shield, we reflected Danny's power and our pain, and wondered whether "once Danny had felt hurt, powerless, and poisoned by bad food and bad feelings." In her drawings, Luci now depicted herself as grounded, but she was very small in comparison to Rita and me.

Depression

Following this aggressive phase, Luci arrived one day for therapy in a very lethargic and depressed state. She spoke only in a whisper and related a dream:

I'm visiting the "dead land." There are no people, no fires in the fireplaces, no food in the refrigerator, no beds in the bedrooms, and no furniture in the living room. Outside there are no flowers, no grass, only rocks.

She stayed in the depression for about three weeks, lying most of the time on her bed, unable to go to her special school, but still coming in for therapy. In the playroom she turned out all the lights, closed the blinds, and totally darkened the room to create the "dead land." We wandered around the room with her, complaining about the deadness of everything. Later, when behind the shield, we reflected the feeling tone: "Danny's very sad. There's nothing to eat. It's cold and empty here. He's all alone and there seems to be no hope."

Slowly, over the sessions, Luci's mood changed and she divided the room into "good" and the "dead" place. Her mood changed as she traveled between the two.

> My mother is with us now and we're flying by jet to the good land. There's flowers, trees, grass, and dirt and lots of food in the kitchen. . . . Oh dear, it's time to go back to the dead land. Let's pack up and go. . . . It's so dark and cold here in the dead land. I'm shaking with cold.

Eventually a small, windowless washroom off the playroom came to be used as the dead place because it could be made completely dark. By this time the depression had lifted, but it was replaced by fear.

Fear

This phase, too, was heralded by a dream. She dreamed:

> I am sleeping in my bed in my room. Above my bed are two posters, a happy face and a monster person with hands, who wants to touch me. Suddenly I wake up and there are monster "pumps" on top of me, above me, below me, all around me, squeezing my stomach and suffocating me. My Mom and Dad hear me yell and come running in.

The mother reported that this was the first time that she had ever seen Luci tremble or be afraid. The fear lasted for about two months. During this time Luci drew several muscular "Supergirls" who were never afraid and could always fly away. [See illustration, p. 166.] The washroom became the "pump room," and Luci would sit on our laps, relaxing for two to three minutes before attacking us with flying pumps. When this happened, we all had to become afraid, tremble, and cry out with fear.

By having her sit on our laps, we could experience the genuine sensations of fear in her body. In this position, Luci reenacted the dream over and over again, directing the pumps to attack all of us in different parts of our bodies. Later, she pretended to be the pump and to suffocate us, and to clutch our legs and necks and land on our stomachs. Over time it became apparent that feelings of fear had changed to feelings of power and the wish to hurt us. Her drawings showed the movement from pumps to pumpkins, and then to pumpkin people chasing her.

It slowly dawned on Rita and me that the angry pumps had become a defense against experiencing relaxation, human contact, and intimacy. She seemed afraid of the experience of affection. At this time, too, we wondered whether she had been sexually abused or molested, because the pump energy, activity, and symbolism was very sadistic and phallic in nature ("The pump goes in your pee hole and pees on you"). We wondered also whether this pump activity could be the reexperiencing of intrauterine sensations of the sexual act. The sexual abuse hypothesis seemed very real, but it did not fit our experience or intuitions about the family.

As we worked with this material, certain thoughts became clarified. Emotional closeness and intimacy were experienced as a thrusting, forceful pump that was frightening and to be avoided or directed elsewhere. We were faced with the problem of how to handle the therapeutic situation where the pumps were actively preventing relaxation and contact. All our attempts at reflection of feeling and interpretation did not stop the pumps in their attacks.

Eventually we found ourselves becoming annoyed and angry. Our verbalization of our feelings did not help. ("Danny, we're getting angry at the pumps and wish they would stop attacking us.") Finally, I felt we had to set limits: "Danny, if the pumps attack us once more, we'll all have to leave the pump room for today." The pumps were quiet for a few minutes and then attacked us again. We immediately terminated the session.

A week later, back in the same room, we heard a new sound, a gentle swishing, which Luci informed us was a friendly baby pump who wanted to cuddle. This was the start of a new phase, characterized by dependency.

Dependency

Luci brought a blanket into the pump room, sat on our laps, and pretended she was a baby puppy in a dog family where they all had breakfast, lunch, and dinner in bed. This theme was played out time and time again. Her drawings now changed completely. There were scenes of incubation and hatching, pregnancy, birth [see illustration, p. 166], a new baby, and nursing mothers. Supergirl totally disappeared.

At this point we felt there was no longer any need for the fantasy en-actment, as Luci was now playing with objects and toys in age-appropriate fashion.

Individuation: The Last Phase of Treatment

Rita saw Luci in play therapy for two more months. She worked on farmyard themes—separating the wild animals from the domestic ones —and cowboys and Indians. At this time, she came to see herself as an Indian Princess who was loved and treasured by the tribe. She was re-turned to the public school system, and after an adjustment period ther-apy was terminated. Follow-up some twelve years later indicated a happy, well-adjusted teenager.

Discussion

Holding entails many risks for both the therapist and the child. Transference and countertransference issues are strongly activated be-cause of the intensity of involvement. I remember especially my cycles of inflation-deflation and utter hopelessness in the early phase of using the holding method (i.e., for the first three years). Fortunately, I was in analy-sis during this period and received considerable help in understanding my own rage, loss, deep despair, and many of my own "autistic" qualities. There was a feeling of power, a conviction that we were on the verge of a new discovery, that I could significantly help these children, which alter-nated with feelings of powerlessness, failure, and the feeling of "not be-ing good enough." The children's pathology had developed so early and was so profound that whatever impact I could make would surely be too little and too late. We saw changes, but would they ever be sufficient to change the condition, to release normal development?

Also, I was having some conflict with the man who was developing the technique. On one hand, I admired him. I felt I learned a tremendous amount from him, and that I would never have anything original or dif-ferent to offer because he had said it or done it all before me. On the other hand, I was worried about his inflation and lack of judgment. He felt he had "the missing link" in psychotherapy and wanted to use hold-ing to treat all types of disorders. I thought he should slow down and de-tail the results of a few cases for publication.

Many times I wondered how the children perceived the holding. This was something they did not want or choose. I had to be very careful not to hurt them, and at times I had to control and watch my anger. And yet, in a certain way, I *was* hurting them; that is, by blocking their mannerisms, reducing their stiffness, and not letting them crawl off the lap, I was forcing them to feel pain. They cried deeply and got very angry. Was I making them cry *my* pain and express *my* anger? And then there was fear. They were very afraid of the world. Once their defenses were reduced, this fear became very apparent and many would then cling to their caretakers and actively seek mothering. Although I believe what I was doing was helpful, there were many times when I questioned myself, my motives, and the value of my work.

Slowly my own method and style of working evolved and was significantly different from Zaslow's. I choose not to stimulate actively for rage as he did, but to wait more for the child's reaction to holding and to use play therapy in conjunction with holding therapy. I tried to get a real feel for the child's experience while being held, and to reflect and interpret those experiences in an effort to reduce anxiety and to help the child understand what was occurring.

Another area of concern centered around the issue of the etiology of the disorder. Basically, I believe that autism and childhood psychosis can be caused by both physiological and psychological factors. Some cases I have worked with seemed to have clear-cut organic causes, others a mixture of physiological and psychological factors, while still others appeared to have purely psychological causes. I have written elsewhere about the concept of "difficult babies" (Allan 1976) and their early negative effects on attachment bonding. In some families I have worked with, after two or three months of treatment the parents have revealed critical negative incidents that would have had a profound effect on the infant and child. Some of the comments included such statements as: "I didn't want her and I repeatedly hit her"; "I sexually abused her"; "He looked like his father and I hated him"; "I told him I wished he would die"; "I refused to hold him because my mother never held me." I am sure that profound negative emotions, including the experience of physical and psychological abandonment, produce biochemical changes of a very toxic quality sufficient to produce autism. The converse is also true: the experiences of deep love, effective holding, and connectedness result in positive biochemical changes sufficient to result in normal growth and patterns of behavior.

I have also seen many cases where the autistic or psychotic child was dearly wanted and where the parents had other normal, healthy children. In such cases there was often an incident of severe trauma and shock (hospitalization, the death of a parent, the birth of another sibling), and autism followed. My view is that if the condition is identified early enough (within the first two to three years of life), then, with professional help involving treatment not only of the child but also of the couple and the family, the condition can be significantly ameliorated. Many parents do need help transforming the intense protest and despair reactions of the child and in eliciting laughter and pleasure in human contact and in establishing appropriate social control and responsiveness in the child. When "secrets" and painful emotions have been shared in couple work (or in the psychotherapy of one parent), something very beneficial happens to the child. It is as if the child lets go of a certain negative control, and affective approach behavior is released (see the case of Tim above). The "confession of a secret" seems to have a profound healing effect and is often the turning point of treatment. Another key component is helping to alleviate the parents' sense of shame and guilt. Even though in some cases parents did not and could not "cause" the autism, there is the painful analytical work of helping them to face and express deep-seated feelings of guilt and shame.

The treatment of Luci clearly shows how the child turned away from the outer world and attempted to achieve some stability, gratification, and pleasure from the inner world. There was a tremendous psychological split in Luci between instinct (the "dog") and spirit (the "seagull") and an attempt by the fragmented ego to deal with powerful feelings of chaos and anger, fear and violation, alienation and shame, and sadness and anguish. The therapeutic alliance, holding, limit-setting, and interpretation helped Luci face those feelings and slowly integrate them. Throughout this case, I always had a strong feeling that Luci would come through.

In summary, the case of Luci clearly shows the healing power of the archetype of the Self and how this becomes activated by the process of transference. The holding therapy seemed to release the Self from its hold by the negative body ego (i.e., by the early sensory-motor conditioned avoidance reactions). Once the Self was freed, Luci actively sought contact with us through words and dramatic play. By following her fantasies and dreams, the Self led her through a journey of rage, depression, and fear to growth and health.

References

Allan, J. 1972. Characteristics of autistic behavior. Unpublished doctoral dissertation. University of London.
_____. 1976. The identification and treatment of difficult babies: Early signs of disruption in parent-infant attachment bonds. *Canadian Nurse* 72/12:11–16.
_____. 1977. Use of holding with autistic children. *Special Education in Canada* 51/3:11–15.
_____. 1984. *Handicaps and holding.* (Published in Japanese.) Nagoya, Japan: Fubaisha Press.

_____, and MacDonald, R. 1975. Fantasy enactment in the treatment of an autistic child. *Journal of Analytical Psychology* 20:57–68.

Anthony, J. 1958. An experimental approach to the psychotherapy of childhood autism. *British Journal of Medical Psychology* 31:211–55.

Bergman, P., and Escalona, S.K. 1949. Unusual sensitivities in very young children. In *Psychoanalytic study of the child* 4:333–452.

Bowlby, J. 1958. The nature of the child's ties to his mother. *International Journal of Psychoanalysis* 39:350–73.

Edinger, E. 1973. *Ego and archetype: Individuation and the religious function of the psyche.* Baltimore: Penguin Books.

Jung, C. G. 1946. The psychology of the transference. In *Collected works* 16:163–323. Princeton: Princeton University Press, 1966.

Perry, J. 1953. *The Self in the psychotic process: Its symbolization in schizophrenia.* Berkeley: University of California Press.

Zaslow, R. 1981. Z-process attachment therapy. In R. Corsini, ed., *Handbook of innovative psychotherapies*, pp. 900–16. New York: John Wiley & Sons.

_____, and Breger, L. 1969. A theory and treatment of autism. In L. Breger, ed., *Clinical-cognitive psychology: Models and integration*, pp. 246–91. New York: John Wiley & Sons.

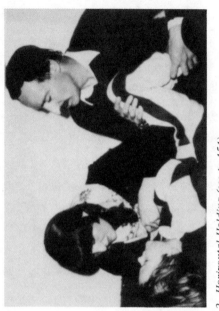

2. *Horizontal Holding (see p. 151).*

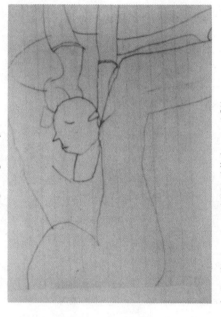

4. *Luci's drawing of "Birth" (see p. 161).*

1. *Vertical Holding (see p. 150).*

3. *Luci's drawing of "Supergirl" (see p. 160).*

Bare Bones: The Aesthetics of Arthritis

Ronald Schenk

Fleshing Out the Body

A conference on "the body in analysis" is a strange thing. For years I have been thinking to myself and talking with people about the need for *body* among Jungians. Now I find myself saying, "My, what a strange corner we have painted ourselves into!" A conference on the body is strange because ninety percent of the time we don't *have* bodies, in analysis or anywhere else. We simply *are* bodies. We live our bodily being. We are beings living through our bodies. The body is the bearer of our material being. We are lived bodies. Consciousness is embodied to begin with. Why worry about the body?

As we know, this peculiar situation has come about through a long conceptual tradition that teaches us to separate body and psyche. This split inevitably forces the body into analysis (don't forget it was the hysterical body that brought our profession into being), while at the same time it drives both analyst and analysand to body work. This tradition, grounded in a language system that keeps body and soul separate, is not

---

Ronald Schenk, M.S.W., is a Jungian analyst in private practice in Dallas, where he works with both adults and children. His initial clinical training was in psychoanalytic therapy in New Haven; he is now a Ph.D. candidate in psychology at the University of Dallas. His article, "Navaho Healing: Aesthetics as Healer" is in press.

merely as old as Descartes, but is as old as Western consciousness itself. Homer uses the word *psyche* to refer to that part of the individual that is active only when the body is dead or inactive. Plato's thought goes through several transformations—soul and body as interaction (Charmides), body as "tomb" of the soul (Gorgias), and body as "vehicle" of the soul (Timeaus). For Aristotle, body is the appearance of soul in matter for the sake of the soul's achievement. The Christian tradition is ambivalent toward the body. On the one hand, it is the "temple" of the Holy Spirit (I Cor. 6:19), the image of God himself. On the other hand, there is a long tradition linking the body to Satan. In all of these conceptions, body and soul are separate, with the body at best serving the ends of the soul.

I would now like to take a lateral arabesque out of the Western tradition that splits body and soul, to bring into the arena of depth psychology the work of Maurice Merleau-Ponty, a post-modern philosopher who has attempted the integration of body and soul in concept and language. In his early work (1962, 1963), Merleau-Ponty thought of body and soul as co-significations, co-relative factors. Body is the mode through which we are present to soul, and at the same time the means through which soul is present to the world. Body, soul, and world are each indispensable moments of the lived interactional structure that embraces them. Our intentions toward the world find their form in body, while at the same time we perceive in conformity with that very body. As consciousness presents itself through a body, the body becomes the perspectival aspect of being. Body is the mode of actuality of the individual, his or her concrete way of being and manner of inhabiting space and time.[1]

Body is neither pure thing nor pure idea, but the "bearer of a dialectic" between the two (Merleau-Ponty 1963, p. 204). Body and soul are not entities, but perspectives, contingent upon each other, flowing into and out of each other. But body is also distinct. It becomes distinct when it is "known"—through dysfunction, for example. When body is dysfunctional, "the world is doubled," becoming inner and outer (ibid., p. 190). World, body, and perception become distinct entities, and then gradually merge back into a unity. El Greco's paintings are not elongated because El Greco was astigmatic, but El Greco's disorder was integrated by him into a distinct way of being.

The body has autonomous being for Merleau-Ponty.

> [It] is and is not ourselves. The body does everything and it does nothing. Neither end nor means, always involved in matters which go beyond it, always jealous of its autonomy, the body is powerful enough to oppose itself to any merely deliberate end, yet has none to propose to us if we finally turn toward and consult it. (1973, p. 112)

The body is itself a "complex." The body as a "prepersonal cleaving to the general form of the world, as an anonymous and general existence, plays, beneath my personal life, the part of an inborn complex" (Merleau-Ponty 1962, p. 84).

As complex, body is a unique structure of experience, the experience of material being. As complex, body carries history. The pastness of experience is carried into the present through the body, or, through the body the present remains in the past. The ambiguity of being in the world in both the past and present simultaneously is taken up by the body.

> It can now be said that, a fortiori, the specific past, which our body is, can be recaptured and taken up by an individual life only because that life has never transcended it, but secretly nourishes it, devoting thereto part of its strength, because its present is still that past. (Merleau-Ponty 1962, p. 85)

The body is the "third term" in the figure-background structure between consciousness and world (Merleau-Ponty 1962, p. 101). It is the ground for experience, the darkness upon which experience is inscribed, the flesh of the world that inscribes upon the world. Body is what makes space, what makes world. It is our opening onto the world, our "rising toward the world" (ibid., p. 92), the "collecting together of itself in pursuit of its aims" (ibid., p. 101).

Existence realizes itself in the body. It is not that my red face or clenched fist signify anger. The face and the fist *are* the anger. The meaning is not behind the gesture, but is "intermingled with the structure of the world outlined by the gesture" (Merleau-Ponty 1962, p. 186). Neither the body nor consciousness can be considered originative nor causative, since they presuppose each other to begin with. Body is existence solidified, and existence is a perpetual incarnation. Body is the "woven fabric" of existence (ibid., p. 166), the "mirror of being" (ibid., p. 171). It is the unique manner in which I relate to the world and through which my experience is shaped and styled, while at the same time the world is encrusted in the body.

> The experience of our own body . . . reveals to us an ambiguous mode of existing. . . . I have no means of knowing the human body other than that of living it, which means taking up on my own account the drama which is being played out of it, and losing myself in it. I am my body, at least wholly to the extent that I possess experience, and yet at the same time my body is as it were a "natural" subject, a provisional sketch of my total being. (Ibid., p. 198)

In summarizing Merleau-Ponty's thought thus far, body as paradoxically lived and known, autonomous, complex, drama—all mirror Jung's notions of *psyche*, giving us a clue to the psychological being of body, body as the unconscious itself, or body as the depth in the surface.

In Merleau-Ponty's later work (1968), body is no longer an interactional element with soul or the medium of the dialectic between experience and world; it is at once the "intertwining" or the "chiasm" between the two. It is neither matter nor signifier of psyche, but the visible and the invisible at once.

> We mean that carnal being, as a being of depths, of several leaves or several faces, a being in latency, and a presentation of a certain absence, is a prototype of Being, of which our body, the sensible sentient, is a very remarkable variant, but whose constitutive paradox already lies in every visible. (Ibid., p. 136)

Body as a "prototype of Being" would parallel body as a prototype of the Self in Jungian terms. For Merleau-Ponty, body has now become "flesh," not corpuscles nor psychic material brought into being, but the reciprocity between the seer and the seen, so that one no longer knows which is which.

> To designate it, we should need the old term, "element," in the sense it was used to speak of water, air, earth, and fire, that is, in the sense of a general thing, midway between the spatio-temporal individual and the idea, a sort of incarnate principle that brings a style of being wherever there is a fragment of being. (Ibid., p. 139)

Flesh is the prototype of Being that circles between visibility and invisibility. It is the "bond between the visible and the interior armature which it manifests and which it conceals" (ibid., p. 149), the lining and the depth of the invisible.

The thickness of body is the opening into the world. It is not so much that which perceives, but that which is "built around the perception that dawns through it" (Merleau-Ponty 1968, p. 9), the "cohesion of depth of the world" (ibid., p. 112). As entrance into the world, it is not so much adherent to the here and now, but the "inauguration of where and when, the possibility and exigency of fact" (ibid., p. 139). Flesh is the invisible "encrusted" (ibid., p. 134), the "furrow" (ibid., p. 151), or the "occasion" (ibid., p. 150) of ideas. "It is the invisible of the world, that which inhabits this world, sustains it, and renders it visible, its own and interior possibility, the Being of this being" (ibid., p. 151).

In summary, through Merleau-Ponty we have moved from a notion of body as an integral part of body-soul dialectic to body as a third realm, a chiasm, a mode of vision, a style of being. Merleau-Ponty has helped us to fashion a way of seeing body, namely, body as a way of seeing, through which we may now envision one particular mode of being, that of the arthritic.

The Arthritic Aesthetic

I am
    tracked,
Unbending in view,
    resolute,
        duty-bound, wrapped in responsibility,
Ever upholding of obligation,
    commitment,
        like a titan
            supporting
even the heavens.
    When source is within,
        where can Psyche show,
    how display?
She must come slowly, come secretly,
    come relentlessly
        from the bony core
wearing away at the links
    until they have disappeared
        like the tread of a tire travelled
too far.
    Through the bones showing forth
        Psyche presents
            in sculpture forged in fire and ice
                grotesque as the underworld.
    Through the skeletal core
    Psyche says, "no more, no more."

Etymologically, *arthritis* comes from the Greek word meaning inflammation of the arthron, or joint. The word first appears in medieval times to designate pain caused by a faulty flow of the humors. *Rheumatic* means to suffer from a flux, a flow, a rheum or fluid. The Greek word *rheumatismos* designates an evil humor or mucous that was thought to flow from the brain to the joint. Galen used the term to designate pain caused by one of the four humors being in faulty connection with the others, or flowing from the brain into the blood and being discharged into the cavities of the body.

Arthritis is a disease of autoimmunity, the body becoming allergic to itself. It begins insidiously and progresses slowly, bringing about a relentless metamorphosis of the body into a skewed and rigid form. Lymphocytes from the blood stream begin to attack not only antigens or foreign substances, but also the structural tissue around the joint. Another group of blood cells, macrophages, are called to the scene in increasing numbers. These cells secrete enzymes that eat away at cartilage. The joint has become a scene of war, the body attacking itself. Symptomatically, there is much stiffness, pain or tenderness in the joint, swelling, nodules under the skin, cloudy fluid in the joint lining, and cold, clammy skin. Inflammation and liquidation, fire and water appear as one. The patient has a mild fever and a vague feeling of malaise. As the cartilage or intermediary tissue is eaten away, bone ends come to grind against each other, eventually fusing. Muscles atrophy, the joint becomes useless, and bizarre deformities of bone appear.

The etiology of arthritis is unknown. It is not communicable, no particular blood factor can be found, nor has it been linked to genetic origins. Recently, medical psychologists have hypothesized neurological dysfunction in regard to two traits of arthritic patients: the inability to express feelings and the inability to fantasize (Achterberg and Lawlis, 1980, pp. 266–73). To be unable to express feelings is referred to medically as *alexithymia*, meaning "without words for feelings." The medical or causal view would see this condition as due to a structural defect rather than to self-imposed restraint or unconscious repression of feeling. This structural defect, it is suggested, is a lesion in the prefrontal lobe or frontolimbic pathways. The neural pathways of the soma would then be seen as responding exclusively, without evoking a response in the cortical areas that interpret sensory events. In other words, what is hypothesized is a short circuit from the lower to the higher pathways, feelings transcribed directly into physical symptoms rather than words.

Arthritis is also linked to an inability to fantasize, known as *pensé operatoire*. This condition is exemplified in the relatively meager drawings that arthritic patients make of their disease. Again, the causal view of this condition would look for a structural defect or learning disability as a source.

Perhaps as much as any disease of the soma, arthritis has been linked causally with factors of the psyche. Two of the early explorers in psychosomatic medicine worked in the field of arthritis. Stanley Jeliffe, an Austrian psychoanalyst in the 1920s, analyzed an arthritic patient. He took "before-and-after" X-rays of the bone structure of his patient's leg to prove the efficacy of psychoanalysis. Richard Halliday was a British medical insurance investigator in the 1930s and '40s who was among the first to come up with a cohesive personality profile of the arthritic patient. Among his findings was the fact that in Scotland, people of the Calvinist faith were much more likely to develop arthritis than the population at large.

Medical literature over the past few decades abounds in various descriptions of the "arthritic personality" profile, but there is much controversy over methodology. Central to the arthritic mode, however, seems to be an inherent conflict between flexibility and rigidity. The individual is tirelessly active, seeming to work day and night, on the job and at home, in self-sacrificing service to others. At the same time, the personality of the arthritic has been described as emotionally restricted, calm, quiet, and excessively patient. He or she has difficulty verbalizing feelings of anger, and often seems emotionally restricted or indifferent to his or her situation.

The background of the arthritic patient typically includes an early life characterized by an excessive amount of physical activity and athletics. The patient has an affinity for orderliness, punctuality, and tidiness. His or her past characteristically includes a strict and uncompromising mother and a weak or absent father. There is evidence of an inadequate sense of individual identity, and severe emotional deprivation in early life. The patient is said to have strong dependency needs that are kept hidden behind a rigid facade of character armor that proclaims autonomy and independence.

An aesthetic view of arthritis would see through a causal notion of the disease, whether the source be somatic or psychic, to its mythical and classical background. The figures and motifs found in myth and history give body to the disease, and validate it as, in itself, a "form" or way of life. The fiery attack of the lymphocytes on the joint lining speaks of heroic activism gone beserk, Hercules madly slaying even his own. The rigid upholding of obligation bespeaks Atlas, whose name is derived from the word meaning "to bear." (The word for the cells that eat away at the cartilage is "macrophage," literally meaning "giant eater.") The interplay between the dynamic and the rigid in the arthritic state, then, can be seen as an interplay between the Herculean mode on the one hand, and that of Atlas on the other.

As the chronic disease par excellence, the disease of middle and old age, proceeding on a slow, relentless, linear course toward making the body concrete, arthritis would be seen primarily as a revealing of the old king, Chronus. His is an image of exile and fixedness. His temperament is cold, reflected in a cold, distant affect, as well as in the cold, clammy skin of the arthritic. Coldness is cold reality—no fantasy here, just things as they are. Chronus's concern is for structure, upholding tradition and order. The rigidity of Chronus is not just the stiff upper lip and stiff-joint-edness of the arthritic, but also the ego-certainty of "I know" reflected in the arthritic's invulnerability to change through such means as psychotherapy. The perpetual suffering of Chronus is reflected in the chronic pain of the arthritic, a certain style of suffering that is impervious to change.

Immediately adjacent to the configuration of Chronus, and in my opinion even more revealing of the arthritic consciousness as a way of life, is the philosophical doctrine of Stoicism. (Here I am following and expanding upon the insights of Alfred Ziegler [1983].) Stoicism existed as an active school of philosophy from the beginning of the Hellenistic Age, 300 B.C., to the decline of the Roman Empire in 300 A.D. As the arch-philosophy of the spirit, it was the chief rival of Epicureanism, the arch-philosophy of the material. The main precept of the Stoic view was "life according to nature," or life in accordance with cold reality, we might say. Like the Epicurean, the Stoic strove to attain autocracy or self-sufficiency in the face of the ever-expanding ancient world. The Stoic rejected the divine by identifying himself or herself with it. The body was considered to be an encumbrance to divine reason, and the Stoic strove to treat it with indifference. Stoic apathy is an imperviousness to perturbations from both the concrete, outer world and the inner world of emotion and fantasy. A person must pay attention only to what is within his or her power, namely will.

In the lives and writings of Zeno, Epictetus, and Marcus Aurelius, we can see the Stoic aesthetic as a background for the psychology of arthritis. Zeno was known for his great powers of abstinence and endurance. His habits were simple; he lived on uncooked food and wore a thin cloak no matter what the weather. A poem about him reads:

> The cold of winter and the ceaseless rain,
> Come powerless against him; weak is the dart
> Of the fierce summer sun, or fell disease,
> To bend that iron frame. He stands apart,
> In nought resembling the vast common crowd,
> But, patient and unwearied, night and day,
> Clings to his studies and philosophy.   (Hadas, ed., 1961, p. 11)

This description attests to the consciousness of the Stoic and the arthritic, namely, that interior virtue is sufficient regardless of the external circumstances. The rigidity and hardness of this personality reflect the rigid structuralization of the arthritic body.

Epictetus was a slave who spread his message by evangelizing to crowds. His manual was transcribed from his oratory by one of his disciples. Among his sayings are the following:

> Disease is an impediment to the body, but not to the will unless the will itself chooses. Lameness is an impediment to the leg, but not to the will. (Hadas, ed., 1961, p. 87)

> Remember that in life you ought to behave as at a banquet. Suppose that something is carried round and is opposite to you. Stretch out your hand and take a portion with decency. Suppose that it passes by you. Do not detain it. Suppose that it is not yet come to you. Do not send your desire forward to it, but wait until it is opposite you. (Ibid., p. 88)

For Epictetus, a person has no say in the course of his or her life. Ever self-effacing, one plays the role chosen for him or her by another. Emotion, body, and world are all "enemies" from which to be distanced: ". . . [the philosopher] watches himself as if he were an enemy" (ibid., p. 99). It is as if those heroic warrior lymphocytes were under the direct command of Epictetus as they attack the joint lining.

We speak of alexithymia, the inability to express feelings in words, as a symptom, but Epictetus says, "And let silence be the general rule, or let only what is necessary be said, and in few words. Rarely and when the occasion calls say something" (ibid., p. 95).

In contrast to Epictetus, the slave who spoke to throngs, Marcus Aurelius was an emperor who wrote only for himself. In his diary he advocated abstinence from pleasure and desire, and he emphasized the transitory quality of life and the bounds of nature. His image of the ideal person is like the rigidly protruding arthritic bone: "Be like the promontory against which the waves continually break, but it stands firm and tames the fury of the water around it" (ibid., p. 131).

Aurelius writes in more detail:

> Are you angry with him whose armpits stink? Are you angry with him whose mouth smells foul? What good will this anger do you? He has such a mouth, he has such armpits: it is necessary that such an emanation must come from such things. (Ibid., p. 139)

We speak of the arthritic's inability to fantasize as a symptom, but in regard to imagination, Aurelius says, "Wipe out the imagination. Stop the pulling of the strings. Confine yourself to the present" (ibid., p. 155).

In summary, in the same way that the notion of an "arthritic personality" takes us away from an organic causal view of symptomatology, the aesthetic view that sees the mythic and Stoic perspective in the background of arthritis moves us away from the notion of arthritis as merely pathology or the psyche's compensatory measures. Instead, arthritis becomes the presentation of the body itself, soul bodying forth and reflecting a way of being, the "being of Being," in Merleau-Ponty's words.

To see the aesthetics of arthritis requires what Beaudelaire calls the "intimate eye." The intimate eye is the eye of the sculptor Henry Moore, who speaks of the importance of the emotion inherent in the form of an art object rather than its representational value. It is the eye of the impressionist painter Pierre Bonnard, who says that the subject of a painting is its surface with colors and laws over and above those of the object. The intimate eye would see the arthritic body much as T. S. Eliot describes body generally in "Burnt Norton": ". . . the enchainment of past and future/woven in the weakness of the changing body." With the intimate eye, ornamentation would not be seen as the adornment of joints with bracelets, wristbands, and neckware, symbolically representative of the relationship between articulation and rigidity. Rather, the bones themselves would be seen as adornment, not signifying Psyche's meaning, but being Psyche's ornamentation, Psyche's display of herself in one particular mode for the beholding eye.

If sculpture is the artistic medium that most purely combines dynamics and structure, then the arthritic form becomes the blending of the dynamics of heroism with the titanic upholding of structure. The arthritic body becomes both the sculpture and the artist. *Pensé operatoire* would be seen not with psychology's bias toward the rich, vivid, burgeoning imagination that one finds in cancer patients. Rather, it would be seen with an appreciation for the bare-boned imagination, the imagination of no imagination. Rather than seeing alexithymia through a view biased by a tradition of talking as cure, the aesthetic eye would perceive silence itself as a mode of being. The silence of the arthritic would bespeak a level of experience for which words fail. Through the tight jaw and the stiff upper lip, the arthritic would be telling us of that which is unutterable in our day-to-day existence, unutterably private, unutterably unique, unutterably horrific. Here, the showing forth of bones becomes that which is art itself, the necessarily inarticulate cry. Here aesthetics becomes something not separate from nor tangential to understanding, but that which is the meaning itself.

To appreciate the arthritic aesthetic, we would need to start from a place other than that which sees the feeling function as the only or even the primary mode of eros or empathy or healing.[2] We would need to see the pain of the arthritic as a style of suffering inherent in a particular mode of being, and honor the potential in that pain, just as we honor the

potential in the form of modern sculpture. It is an approach that is neither cruel nor kind, one that seeks connection not in feeling but in seeing. Our starting point, like that of the Greeks, is not the separation of the
good from the beautiful, or the beautiful from the useful, but in the vision of them as one and the same. We would need to leave aside notions
of beauty as harmony, balance, or symmetry, and adjust our gaze to see
the perfection inherent in the individual form. Like Rilke in the First
Duino Elegy, we would see that "Beauty is nothing/but beginning of Terror which we are still just able to bear." We would come to an appreciation of the aesthetic particular to the grotesque—the gnarled, knotted
forms of the grotto, cave, or underworld. These forms can be appreciated
for themselves, not by an eye that penetrates, seeking meaning in an ultimate source, an eye anchored in a system of transcendent wholeness, but
by the eye adrift, sensuous in its touch, the eye of the eroticized mind.

The Voluptuous Gaze

The following passage appears in Yukio Mishima's autobiographical
novel, *Sun and Steel*:

> Yet why must it be that men always seek out the depths, the abyss? Why must
> thought, like a plumb line, concern itself exclusively with vertical descent?
> Why was it not feasible for thought to change direction and climb vertically
> up, ever up, towards the surface? Why should the area of the skin, which
> guarantees a human being's existence in space, be most despised and left to
> the tender mercies of the senses? I could not understand the laws governing
> the motion of thought—the way it was liable to get stuck in unseen chasms
> whenever it set out to go deep; or whenever it aimed at the heights, to soar
> away into boundless and equally invisible heavens, leaving the corporeal
> form undeservedly neglected.
> If the law of thought is that it should search out profundity, whether it
> extends upwards or downwards, then it seemed excessively illogical to me
> that men should not discover depths of a kind on the "surface," that vital bor-
> derline that endorses our separateness and our form, dividing our exterior
> from our interior. Why should they not be attracted by the profundity of the
> surface itself? (Mishima, pp. 22–23)

Something there is in the Western mind that distrusts surface. Platonic vision places essence beyond appearance and moves from appearance itself to universals beyond. Gnosticism calls for the release of soul
from within the prison of the body to the heavens above. Christianity de-
clares the Kingdom of Heaven to be within. Technological investigation
looks for causes in inner workings. Modern medicine probes into the
body, as does depth psychology into the psyche. (Both Freud and Jung
likened the analyst to the surgeon.) Our language system, that through

which our very being is formed, is based upon the metaphysical movement from word to meaning. The quest for the source—above, below, behind, and beyond—works to prevent recognition of what is most obvious, *appearance*. The vision of quest serves to hinder the revelation that occurs in the immediate presentation of things as they are.

In talking further about an aesthetic mode of perceiving, and relating it to the body, I would now like to go to the field of biology and the work of the Swiss biologist Adolf Portmann (1964, 1967). Portmann's observations of plants and animals have led him to postulate an innate urge toward self-expression in nature. He sees in the multitude of the varied outer appearances of animals and plants, not primarily a species-preserving function, but a display of "self." The "self" is the living form of the animal, which not only maintains its life and propagates its kind, but also presents its special manner of existence, its world.

The philosopher Alphonso Lingis delineates "world":

> A world, a cosmos, is the order, the ordinance extending according to axes of close and far, intimate and alien, upwards and downwards, lofty and base, right and left, auspicious and inauspicious, within which things can have their places, show their aspects and stake out paths. (1983, p. 3)

For Portmann, the most modest plant expresses its independent being, its world, in the shape and coloration of its leaf, flower, and fruit. Tiny aquatic organisms express their essences in a host of splendid forms and colors. The simplest of mollusks manifests itself in the most splendid and ornate of shells. Portmann asserts that this urge toward display in nature operates independently of anything related to functionality. The survival of species cannot explain the ornate coils and elaborate racks of antlers. The splendid feather patterns of the peacock do not play an important part in mating, but seem to be exhibitionism for its own sake.

In sum, Portmann takes seriously the fact that prior to all utilitarian conceptions of the preservation of species, what we encounter first and foremost is the straightforward appearance of the living being in its full form, what Lingis calls the "logic of ostentation" (1983, p. 8). Nature serves the beholding eye of the other. Lingis writes:

> Glory is for its witness, the spectacle is for the spectator, the screen of phenomenal effects produced in reality are for a sphere of lucidity, an eye, a mind! With this inference one makes even the gloss of appearance intelligible, and one posits oneself as an essential and necessary factor in the sphere which one enters. One appropriates even this film of semblance and this vanity of appearances. *Omnia ad maiorem gloriam deo*—God himself

was said to have been obliged to create man to receive the splendor of his glory. (Ibid., p. 9)

Freud saw libido's original manifestation as being a matter of *surface* excitement, the pleasure of the polymorphously perverse infant in couplings for the sake of surface effects, a horizontal movement from one contact point to another. From the first, eros seeks form in appearance.

The aesthetic view would not look to the surface as a "forest of symbols," as Baudelaire characterizes Western consciousness, deflecting one's view off into the depths, on toward the horizon, out toward the universal where their signified referents, sources, and meanings are posited to be. Instead it is a gaze that caresses and is caressed in reciprocity with the world. It is the gaze of the sensualized mind, in foreplay with the surface.

In order to give us a glimpse of what the eroticized universe is like, Lingis takes us to the ancient Hindu temples of Khajuraho in India. Here one finds wall upon wall of friezes depicting a universe of possibilities of coniunctio: "dual and multiple cunnilinctio, penilinctio, copulation, homosexual and bestial intercourse circulate about the temple walls without primacy of place or of artistry given to any one figure" (1983, p. 59).

Here the 8,400,000 forms of animal positions that are the foundation for the 8,400,000 asanas of Patanjali's classical hatha yoga are all taken as possibilities of human intercourse with nature. Here the human body not only makes contact with every other organic form, but each separate and unique form of the individual body has relationship with each unique form of every other body. "The human form here is not treated as a single design whose spatial configuration expresses statically a dynamical axis or nexus of force" (ibid., p. 63). Rather, each peculiar form is portrayed in its own perfection. Here the dissymmetry of sexes is not a practice of power or ascendance, as men bearing vulvas and women bearing penile erections alternate and reciprocate in initiation and reception. Here one makes love with animals, not descending, and with the gods, not ascending. The gaze does not ascend nor descend, penetrate nor detach: it circulates aimlessly, drifting, holding the reverberations between forms.

What is revealed at Khajuraho through the depiction of human bodies in supple, erotic connection with the universe is a bodily way of seeing, being as seeing, seeing as embodied, seeing/being/body—all one. Seeing erotically eliminates the question "What do we do as therapists?", because this vision sees all doing as inherently seeing. We do as we see. Seeing here is not passive observation and acceptance, any more than the vision of the artist is passive. The therapist creates a container and sees. If he or she sees erotically, he or she will see what presents itself—in interaction between therapist and patient, in the imaginative realm of the subtle body, in the psychological life of the patient, or in the reverberations of the therapist's own psyche—and respond as his or her instincts, experience, and training dictate.

Like the artist, then, we would not be able to say what we do, so much as what we have done, given our vision of the circumstance. We cannot say how to do therapy, only how not to do it. The work is not an application of technique, but a deconstruction of what gets in the way of seeing.

The interpretive mode and "body work" go hand in hand, manifesting and perpetuating the central split of our cultural heritage, body and soul, surface and source. But the medium is the massage. The rub is in the gaze. This is not to discount analysis and body work, which I believe in as healing practices precisely because they do emanate from our prevailing consciousness, like curing like. I believe, though, that the problem lies in this very consciousness itself, which we carry with us every day and which renders the analytic mode arthritic. It is the consciousness of oppositions and divisions: body-soul, inner-outer, lower-higher, objective-subjective, surface-depth, profane-sacred. It is the consciousness that separates aesthetics from epistemology, art from understanding, what I do from how I see, clinical technique from way of seeing. To speak of links between the unconscious and the body, between imaginative consciousness and bodily perception or of "imaginative body" or "body ensouled," only maintains the split, only serves the vision of Satan, in William Blake's opinion. The "body in analysis" is no different from the body anywhere else. All perception, all imagination is bodily perception, bodily imagination, while at the same time the body *is* the imagination, *is* the view.

"The body?"

"No need to worry. It's there—in the gap . . . in the chiasm . . . in the intertwining. Now visible, now invisible. Here."

"Where?"

"Here. It's in the vision, floating in 'happy copulation,'[3] seeing a world in a single bare bone."

"Body? Where?"

"There."

"Gone."
"Don't worry, it's here. Just play ball."

Notes

1. Jung's view of the body, although at times dualistic, also echoes the phenomenological view. In the *Visions Seminars*, vol. II (Zurich: Spring Publications, 1976), p. 475, he writes, "the body is the visible expression of the here and now." James Jarrett, in *Spring 1981* (Dallas: Spring, 1981) pp. 199–200, quotes Jung: "The body is merely the visibility of the soul, the psyche, and the soul is the psychological experience of the body; so it is really one and the same thing." (Jarrett, however, misplaces the reference as being *Collected works*, vol. 3 pars. 41–42.)

2. Jung, in the *Visions Seminars*, vol. II, p. 326, attributes the influence of feeling on the Western consciousness to Christianity.

3. William Blake, "Visions of the Daughters of Albion."

References

Achterberg, J., and Lawlis, F. 1980. *Bridges of the bodymind*. Champaign, Ill.: Institute for Personality and Ability Testing.

Hadas, M., ed. 1961. *Essential works of Stoicism*. New York: Bantam Books.

Lingis, A. 1983. *Excesses: Eros and culture*. Albany: State University of New York Press.

Merleau-Ponty, M., 1962. *The phenomenology of perception*. C. Smith, trans. New Jersey: The Humanities Press.

——————. 1963. *The structure of behavior*. A. Fisher, trans. Boston: Beacon Press.

——————. 1968. *The visible and the invisible*. A. Lingis, trans. Evanston: Northwestern University Press.

——————. 1973. *The prose of the world*. J. O'Neill, trans. Evanston: Northwestern University Press.

Mishima, Y. 1970. *Sun and steel*. J. Besser, trans. New York: Grove Press, as quoted by A. Lingis in *Excesses: Eros and Culture* (Albany: State University Press, 1983).

Portmann, A. 1964. *New paths in biology*. New York: Harper and Row.

——————. 1967. *Animal forms and patterns*. New York: Shocken Books.

Ziegler, A. 1983. *Archetypal medicine*. G. Hartman, trans. Dallas: Spring Publications.

Work in Progress

Affect and Archetype: A Contribution to a Comprehensive Theory of the Structure of the Psyche

Louis H. Stewart

At the age of 19, I wished to become a painter, or so I thought, and I soon imagined myself apprenticed to Paul Cézanne and a spiritual disciple of Vincent van Gogh. But after a year and a half of study, the Germans invaded France and I returned home to the United States to prepare myself for what was to come. After the interlude of military ser-·vice, I found myself totally adrift. My aspiration to be an artist had been well founded in my interests and talents, but unfortunately, not by the motivation of a Cézanne or a van Gogh, nor those among my classmates whose dedication to art I had envied. What was I to do? A devoted friend who, I now realize, must have sensed that art was not my true vocation, convinced me to join her in teaching nursery and kindergarten children in a private school. This experience was the turning point in my life. It revealed to me my true profession as a psychologist and directed me to Jung and analysis and to training as an analyst.

At the deepest, most unconscious level, I myself went back to kin-

Louis H. Stewart, Ph.D., is a founding member, former president, and training analyst of the C. G. Jung Institute of San Francisco. He practices in Berkeley and in San Francisco. He received his Ph.D. in clinical psychology at the University of California, Berkeley, and is professor of psychology at San Francisco State University, and clinical professor of medical psychology at the University of California, San Francisco. He is the author of "Sandplay and Jungian Analysis" in *Jungian Analysis* (M. Stein, ed., 1982).

dergarten, the kind of kindergarten any child would wish to attend—the kind I had never experienced. At a more conscious level, I learned through my experiences with the children and through the guidance of my friend, the true teacher, what it meant to be educated through the arts. She created for the children an atmosphere that I now understand to be the educational equivalent of the analytic temenos, within which the archetypal images of the collective unconscious could be constellated and realized in symbolic transformation. Even then I could see that the children were passing through stages of an autonomous process of creative development that found expression in their painting, dancing, singing, dramatics, and play. The process followed orderly, regulated stages of exploration and assimilation, which led to imaginative play and creative work, and to a centering process that found expression in typical mandala paintings. I saw similar forms in their play and other creative activities.

This was a revelation. I suddenly saw that the development of the whole individual was the same process as the process we call creativity, which we envy and honor so much in the creative artist, poet, religious innovator, philosopher, and social reformer. When years later I had become immersed in Jung's analytical psychology, and experienced his ideas embodied in my own analysis and in my analytic work with others, it was always self-evident to me that what he described as the individuation process, which rests upon active imagination, was precisely what I had observed years before in the kindergarten children. In that context we called it "development."

Over the years it has become clear to me that my experiences in the kindergarten revealed not only the autonomous creative process of the life instinct, but also its relationship to, and dependence upon, the mirror of culture as it is first experienced in the family and then in educational and other settings. What gave a final impetus to my understanding of this function of culture was Joseph Henderson's concept of the cultural unconscious. Then I was able to see that the kindergarten children were finding just those images and experiences in the rich cultural atmosphere of the kindergarten that they were in need of, in order to give form and articulation to the images of the collective unconscious that were directing their development.

The dominant ideas by which I was seized in those "kindergarten" days were the realization that play and the creative imagination were of ultimate significance to the development of the individual, as well as to an understanding of the process of psychotherapy, and furthermore, that these two processes were mirror images of each other. I rushed out into the field of psychology with a missionary fervor to spread the good word. Fortunately, I soon discovered Jung and realized that I didn't have to reinvent the wheel. Between Jung's works and my analysis with Joseph Henderson, I was set on the right course.

Just after I became a Jungian analyst, three major contributions to my understanding of analytical psychology came along. Two of them sprang from that seminal International Conference of Analytical Psychologists held in Zurich in 1962. They were Henderson's conception of the cultural unconscious and the cultural attitudes (1962), and Dora Kalff's *Sandplay* (1962). The third was the publication of Jung's *Memories, Dreams, Reflections* (1961). What hit me most directly in that remarkable book was Jung's recounting of his confrontation with the unconscious in midlife. Here I found confirmation of my own tentative thoughts about the relationship of play and creativity to the functioning of the individuation process, as well as their role in fostering a return to the early childhood nucleus of affective/archetypal experiences that have not been integrated into the personality.

It took some time for me to assimilate these revelations: Jung's self-analysis as the paradigm of individuation, and its relationship to the developmental process; Henderson's conceptualization of the function of a cultural level of the unconscious that provides the necessary mediation between the personal and collective levels; and finally, Kalff's sandplay, which provided a technique of active imagination that directly reflected Jung's original *rite d'entrée* to the unconscious. The fruits of my immersion in this learning process were the papers I have published over the past few years on sandplay as active imagination (1977, 1981a, 1981b, 1982).

Jung's Theory of Emotion

What is an affect? What is an archetype? For more than half of his long life, Jung was preoccupied with these questions. His study of affects came first, as part of his study of emotional or feeling-toned complexes in his experiments with the association test. In *The Psychology of Dementia Praecox* he affirms the fundamental importance of the affects: "The essential basis of our personality is affectivity. Thought and action are, as it were, only symptoms of affectivity" (1907, p. 38).

This remained Jung's basic standpoint until he began his studies of myth and symbolism around 1909 (1961, pp. 158–62). The concept of the archetype was probably incubating during his own self-analysis and "confrontation with the unconscious," but found expression only tangentially up until 1919. When the concept of the archetype did begin to appear in Jung's writings, it carried from the beginning a strong emphasis on the universal image/ideas. To be sure, in his formal definitions Jung notes that the archetype and archetypal image may both be characterized by a numinous charge that derives from the affects, but the distinction between archetype *per se* and archetypal image/idea becomes increasingly explicit, and the archetypal image/ideas as identified in myth and fairytale did not of necessity carry an emotional charge. We shall return to these issues a little later, since it is just in this distinction between archetypal experience and archetypal image/idea that there is room for confusion and misunderstanding.

We may well ask at this point just what is meant by an affect. One of the interesting aspects of the state of psychology when Jung was writing on affects and archetypes is the assumption that an affect is somehow a well known phenomenon. After all, emotions and affects have been referred to by the philosophers of all epochs. Affects are those disturbing aspects of human nature that can run away with us, to use Plato's metaphor of the horses and chariot. On the other hand, the emotions are the source of human feeling and of our highest values. But what, in fact, is an emotion, an affect? In his formal definition, Jung says:

> By the term affect I mean a state of feeling characterized by marked physical innervation on the one hand and a peculiar disturbance of the ideational process on the other. I use *emotion* as synonymous with affect. I distinguish—in contrast to Bleuler—*feeling* from affect, in spite of the fact that the dividing line is fluid, since every feeling, after attaining a certain strength, releases physical innervations, thus becoming an affect. For practical reasons, however, it is advisable to distinguish affect from feeling since feeling can be a voluntary disposable function, whereas, affect is usually not. Similarly, affect is clearly distinguished from feeling by quite perceptible physical innervations, while feeling for the most part lacks them, or else their intensity is so slight that they can be demonstrated only by the most delicate instruments, as in the case of psychogalvanic phenomena. . . . I regard affect on the one hand as a psychic feeling-state and on the other as a physiological innervation-state, each of which has a cumulative effect on the other. (1921, pp. 411–12)

Significant in this definition are the following elements: a strong *feeling state*, marked *bodily innervation*, and a transformation of ego-consciousness through the *abaissement du niveau mental* caused by the affect. One other factor is implied in any affective experience, and that is an *image* that constellates the affect. In Hillman's review of the theories of affect, these elements become symbol (*image*), energy (*bodily innervation*), psyche (*feeling state*), and transformation (*abaissement du niveau mental*) (Hillman, 1961, p. 286).

Play and the Affects

In my studies in sandplay, I have for a long time been interested in the complex relationship between the emotions, and play and imagination. The first fruits of this interest was a paper entitled "Play, Games and the Affects," written in collaboration with my brother, the child psychiatrist Charles Stewart (1979). (I should record that my own thinking owes much to his in ways that I can no longer firmly tease out.) The first task of the paper was to identify the ways in which play and the affects are enmeshed:

- First, play is a voluntary activity engaged in purely for the fun of it, for the joyful pleasure that play is. It may even be argued that play is the prototypical response to the emotion of joy.
- But play is entwined with the emotions in another way, familiar to anyone who has observed children: play is cathartic, liquidating, and compensatory. It is often a recapitulation of an experience that in another context was emotionally upsetting or exciting. (This kind of play occurs after a visit to the dentist's office; in the played-out version, the roles are reversed and someone else becomes the patient.)
- Play itself generates internal tensions of disequilibrium polarized around dimensions of success and failure, acceptance and rejection, etc. This is a feature of structured games, which inevitably evoke strong emotional reactions in the players. The play of childhood is often interrupted by emotional outbursts that cannot be contained in the play itself and that lead to "hurt feelings." As children mature, these tensions may be contained for longer and longer periods of time and are even transformed into aspects of the play itself, as in the taunting and gibing that allow for playful expression of otherwise disruptive emotions.
- Any commonly played game has rules that involve the deliberate evocation of one or more specific emotions that are transformed in the playing of the game. (Perhaps a game survives because it performs this function.) Take, for example, even so tranquil a game as solitaire, played by oneself alone. It engenders a mild tension compounded of equal parts of enjoyment and anxiety, which fluctuates with varying degrees of intensity as one starts to supplicate Lady Luck. There is a parallel tension of potential guilt and shame in the temptation to cheat, knowing that no one is watching but the shadow.

- Play can incubate an emotional seizure in which an image suddenly becomes numinously charged and results either in what Erik Erikson has called a "play disruption," or what Frobenius has suggested may be a potentiation of the imagination leading to a creative cultural innovation. Joseph Campbell drew upon this notion to account for the remarkable explosion of cultural development that took place in the early period of the Sumerian and Egyptian civilizations (1959).

There can be no question that play is inseparably entwined with the emotions. Play and the emotions are related in two major ways: one has to do with the *motivation* of play itself; the other has to do with the function of play and games in the *transformation* of the affects and in the potentiation of creative imagination.

Taking the question of motivation first, we have suggested above that play is motivated by the affect of joy. I would suggest further that the prototypical form of play is to be found in the behavior pattern, so easily identified when observing a happy infant, that is directly evoked in the affect of joy itself, namely laughter accompanied by that unique total bodily response of exuberance. As we know, the developmental sequence in human infants is for the first laugh to follow close on the heels of the first smiles of recognition of the mother. Although it may be the case that the laugh is first evoked in playful modes of stimulation initiated by the mother, nevertheless the laugh also appears when the infant is alone. This last point is important, since we believe that the smile is a joyful recognition of the Other, whereas the laugh is a joyful recognition of Self, and occurs first in active appreciation of self-motion. This total reaction of laughter and unrestrained bodily exuberance is, we believe, the spontaneous expression of the pure joy of being alive and is, as we have said, the prototype of play. To be sure, this joyful play develops further in the temenos of the mother's loving presence, and evolves with her leadership into a joyful dialogue of mutually induced playfulness, which is subsequently enacted alone and with playmates.

As for the function of play and games in terms of affective transformation, it is the more negatively valued emotions that are involved. As we have seen, the child plays out all of the emotionally charged experiences of its life. Moreover, an analysis of games shows that they also evoke emotions that are negatively valued, but that are transformed in the fun of the game. Simple early childhood games such as musical chairs, for example, are obviously structured around the experience, for most of the children, of being left out, and a resulting sense of rejection and shame, or envy of the "lucky" one.

Affect Theory: Sylvan S. Tomkins

The complexity of the relationships between play and the affects suggested the need for a careful assessment of the meaning and function of the affects. In a review of theories of the affects, the most promising and comprehensive theory was found in Sylvan Tomkins's *Affect Imagery Consciousness* (1962, 1963). This seminal work has been the stimulus to the recent work of Izard (1977), Ekman (1972), and other former students of Tomkins, who have been restoring the study of emotion to some respectability in the field of psychology through their research into the universality of emotional expression. Tomkins proposed a thorough-going revision of psychoanalytic affect theory based on an exhaustive study of the nature of the affects. Although this aspect of his theory is interesting and thoroughly documented, it is apparent that Tomkins has but restated the theory proposed by Jung as early as 1907, namely that the affects are the primary motivating system of the psyche, and that they are the source of imagery and consciousness. What Tomkins has to offer that is new is a carefully worked out hypothesis of the evolution of the affects that specifies a particular set of affects and their particular functions. It was this aspect of Tomkins's theory that proved of value in this study.

Before proceeding further I would like to respond to a question that may arise concerning the limited number of affects that will be discussed here, since our personal experience suggests that the affects appear in myriad forms. It is my belief, however, that these "myriad forms" of the affects are transformations of the primal, innate affects, that take place in the crucible of the family (Stewart 1976).

Briefly stated, Tomkins's hypothesis is that: 1) the affects are the primary motivational system, and the drives are secondary, depending on the affects for amplification; 2) the affects are the energic factor that brings imagery and initiates new consciousness; and 3) in the evolutionary process three kinds of affects have evolved: positive life-enhancement affects, negative survival affects, and a resetting affect. The affects of life enhancement are Enjoyment/Joy and Interest/Excitement; the negative survival affects are Distress/Anguish, Fear/Terror, Shame/Humiliation, Contempt/Disgust, and Anger/Rage. The resetting affect is Surprise/Startle. (Each affect represents a continuum of increasing intensity that is indicated above as Fear/Terror, etc.)

My brother and I found it necessary to make some slight modifications in Tomkins's theory in terms of archetypal theory. First, it appears that the life-enhancement affects are better understood as aspects of libido, archetypal affects of the life instinct. Second, the survival affects can hardly be considered negative, which led us to designate them first as crisis affects, and then as the archetypal affects of the primal Self. Third, with regard to the affects Shame/Humiliation and Contempt/Disgust, our view, in accord with Lynd (1958), is that they represent the two faces of a single bipolar affect evoked by rejection directed at the self or the other. Finally, we think Tomkins's resetting affect, Surprise/Startle, is better understood as a reorienting affect, an archetypal affect of the centering process.

As stated above, in Tomkins's hypothesis there is a distinction between the affects of life enhancement and the crisis affects. In our modification, these become the archetypal affects of libido (the life instinct) and the archetypal affects of the Self. This relates them to the affects that *motivate* play, on the one hand, and the affects that are *transformed* through play, on the other hand. At this point we also wish to draw attention to curiosity which, in our view, is motivated by the affect Interest/Excitement. In what follows, we shall discuss the hypothesis that Joy-play and Interest-curiosity are the twin aspects of libido, and that developmentally they represent the earliest forms of expression of the principles of Eros and Logos.

We further postulate that the archetypal affects of the Self—Sadness/Anguish, Fear/Terror, Anger/Rage, and Contempt/Humiliation—represent the fourfold archetypal/affective structure of the primal Self, and that they underlie the evolution of the functions of the ego and the symbolic cultural attitudes. Finally, we see the archetypal affect Surprise/Startle as the centering and reorienting affect of the Self, as the underlying affect related to the evolution of the ego complex, the center of consciousness, and the function of attention and orientation. The question that naturally arose at this point was what the relationship of this hypothesis might be to Jung's views.

Libido: Joy-play and Interest-curiosity

In this discussion it should be borne in mind that, in our view, play and curiosity are the prototypical behavior patterns of the affects Joy/Ecstasy and Interest/Excitement. In addition, play and curiosity are related to each other in an ongoing dialectical process that reveals their functions as the early developmental forms of Jung's two kinds of thinking, fantasy thinking and directed thinking, and the principles of Eros and Logos. It should be noted that it is not our purpose to limit this hypothesis to the developmental period of childhood, since the dialectical process we are discussing is a never-ending aspect of the psyche.

Let us first examine the concept of libido. My focus will be on Jung's views as abstracted from his writings, but I shall include corollary information that is in accord with those views. In his "heretical" chapter on libido, in *Symbols of Transformation*, Jung traced the libido back to its ontogenetic origins in the rhythmic activity associated with the affects (1956, pp. 142–70). The child's earliest interest in the world is most strongly associated with nursing and the activities of sucking, swallowing, etc. It is in this oral mode that everything within the infant's grasp is explored. But in addition there is interest in the wider world experienced through vision, smell, etc. As Piaget documents (1962), the first task of development for the infant is to bring these various modes of exploration into a coordinated system.

Nevertheless, in addition to the early adaptive interest in the oral exploration of the world and the integration of other sensory modes, the infant also is interested in rhythmic activity in and for itself. Most obvious is the sucking behavior that occurs in the intervals between feedings. In this "sucking in the void," to use Piaget's evocative phrase, we can recognize the nascent origins of imagination, for in this purely functional pleasure of sucking on its own self the infant discovers the reality of the inner world of Being. To be sure, the developmental stage that we are describing begins within a few days of birth, and the infant has as yet no separated consciousness of itself or of the world. Yet whatever this experience may be like for the infant, it nevertheless brings together with this primal sucking the inner and outer worlds, and therein lies the germ of all future experiences of the two realms of Being and Becoming.

Moreover, we may see that the infant, while sucking its fingers or its toes, incarnates the image of the mythical Uroborus that, according to Neumann (1973), represents the "wholeness" of that undifferentiated state of self-other consciousness that is characteristic of this developmental state. We can also see in this early behavior the earliest evidence of that aspect of the autonomous process of individuation that Neumann, following Jung, has called *centroversion*. In this light we may understand the infant's behavior in the discovery of sucking its thumb as representing the first synthesis of the psyche following upon the rude disruption of life within the womb, which had more impressively represented a paradisiacal absorption in the purely unconscious processes of life itself.

But these life processes are not without distinctive qualities of form, of which rhythm is a fundamental, if not primary element. The pulsing of the heart and the rhythmic ebb and flow of the blood, the mother's rhythmic breathing, and so on, are dominant features of prenatal life for the fetus. And although it seems improbable that the infant has any conscious experience of all this, nevertheless the rhythmic nature of its experience of the outer and inner environments in the womb do leave unconscious imprints. This we know from the results of recent research that demonstrates the soothing and health-promoting aspects of the sound of the heartbeat and of rhythmic rocking, particularly in the case of infants born prematurely. Of course, mothers have not waited for modern research to alert them to these facts. From time immemorial infants have been carried in close contact with the mother's body, which provides a bridging experience, both auditory and tactile, from womb to world. In addition, rocking and singing are among the most ubiquitous of mothering activities, especially at crucial moments of potential distress, such as the uneasy transition from day to night, from waking to sleeping.

Having established to his satisfaction the origin of libido in these rhythmic pulsations of the life instinct, which finds expression in the affects, Jung proceeded to elaborate in a rich and scholarly amplification the various ideas and symbols that have arisen in human consciousness in its efforts to confront and understand libido. The end result of this *tour de force* is his concept of psychic energy:

> . . . We know far too little about the nature of human instincts and their psychic dynamism to risk giving priority to any one instinct. We would be better advised, therefore, when speaking of libido, to understand it as an energy-value which is able to communicate to any field of activity whatsoever, be it power, hunger, hatred, sexuality, or religion, without ever being itself a specific instinct. (Jung 1956, p. 137)

In yet another context, in *Memories, Dreams, Reflections* Jung presents his view of the nature of the psyche, which emphasizes its innate basis in the life instinct:

> Throughout life the ego is sustained by this base. When the base does not function, stasis ensues and then death. Its life and its reality are of vital importance. Compared to it, even the external world is secondary, for what does the world matter if the endogenous impulse to grasp it and manipulate it is lacking? In the long run no conscious will can ever replace the life instinct. (1961, pp. 348–49)

In this statement about the life instinct, Jung captures precisely the viewpoint we have been proposing: ". . . What does the world matter if the endogenous impulse to grasp it and manipulate it is lacking?" (1961, pp. 348–349). It is for just this purpose that the archetypal affects of Joy and Interest have evolved: to guarantee that the world will be grasped and manipulated in fantasy/play and curiosity/exploration. In this dialectical process that takes place throughout the course of infancy and childhood and on into adulthood, the structures of imagination and of memory are developed. As functions of the psyche, imagination and memory appear in the two kinds of thinking, fantasy thinking and directed thinking. As we shall see later on, fantasy thinking is perhaps best throught of as Eros consciousness, the source of myth, while directed thinking is best thought of as Logos consciousness, the source of language.

I would now like to make comparisons between play and curiosity, on the one hand, and Jung's two kinds of thinking, on the other. For this purpose I have extracted some of the most salient themes of Jung's discussion of the two kinds of thinking from *Symbols of Transformation* (1956). With regard to directed thinking, he says that it is thinking in words; it develops with language and ". . . is an instrument of culture. . . . The clearest expression of modern directed thinking is science and the techniques fostered by it. . . . Its focus is on adaptation, innovation, copying the 'real' world, and changing it." There could be no better description of the function of curiosity/exploration.

Now on to fantasy thinking. According to Jung, it may be understood as mythical thought. He draws a parallel between "the thinking of ancient man and the similar thinking found in children, primitives, and in dreams." But this is not to demean myth: ". . . myth is certainly not an infantile phantasm, but one of the most important requisites of primitive life." Moreover, this kind of thinking "also occupies a large place in modern man and appears as soon as directed thinking ceases." With regard to the content of mythical thought, he notes that the fantasies that arise in this fashion are compensatory to the individual's felt inadequacy, yet the themes, although subjective, derive from mythological themes that are rooted in the "instinctive, archaic basis of the mind." It does not seem difficult to identify in these statements the essence of fantasy/play (1956, pp. 7–33).

With Eros and Logos, and anima and animus, we are dealing with concepts of a different order. Eros and Logos are cosmogonic principles that Jung relates to his concepts of anima and animus, while at the same time expressing the view that they are not to be considered as identical concepts. He offers many examples in a wide-ranging amplification of Eros and Logos, which he prefaces with the following comment: "Numerous mythological and philosophical attempts have been made to formulate and visualize the creative force [libido] which man knows only by subjective experience" (Jung 1956, pp. 137–38). Jung himself equates anima with Eros and animus with Logos:

> The autonomy of the collective unconscious expresses itself in the figures of the anima and animus. They personify those of its contents which, when withdrawn from projection, can be integrated into consciousness. To this ex-

tent, both figures represent *functions* which filter the contents of the collective unconscious through to the conscious mind. . . . Together they form a divine pair, one of whom in accordance with his Logos nature, is characterized by *pneuma* and *nous* rather like Hermes with his ever-shifting hues, while the other, in accordance with her Eros nature, wears the features of Aphrodite, Helen (Selene), Persephone, and Hecate. Both of them are unconscious powers, "gods" in fact, as the ancient world quite rightly conceived them to be. (1959b, pp. 20–21)

Referring to this equation of Logos with the masculine consciousness and Eros with the feminine, Jung defines what he means by Logos and Eros:

By Logos I meant discrimination, judgement, insight, and by Eros I meant the capacity to relate. I regarded both concepts as intuitive ideas which cannot be defined accurately or exhaustively. . . . [They are] intellectually formulated intuitive equivalents of the archetypal images of Sol and Luna. (1963, pp. 179–80)

There is much of interest in these comments on the anima/animus syzygy, which we must leave for another time. For the purposes of the present discussion we find the general formulation by Jung entirely consistent with the hypothesis of the functions of play and curiosity, which through the developmental period of childhood are instrumental in the structuring of the symbolic cultural attitudes (Henderson 1984) as categories of the cultural unconscious. It is also possible to think of the anima and animus as personifications of the cultural unconscious, just as the shadow is the personification of the personal unconscious.

The Fourfold Structure of the Self

If there is any Jungian dogma, it is certainly the fourfold nature of the Self. The mandala as a symbol of the Self appears early in Jung's thought and gradually acquires a central position. In the chapter on the Self in *Aion*, Jung gives a brief summation of his views at a late period in his life. He stresses that the "empirical" nature of his concept of "wholeness" is assured by the fact that

. . . [i]t is anticipated by the psyche in the form of spontaneous or autonomous symbols. These are the quaternity or mandala symbols, which occur not only in the dreams of modern people who have never heard of them, but are widely disseminated in the historical records of many peoples and many epochs. Their significance as *symbols of unity and totality* is amply confirmed by history as well as by empirical psychology. (1959b, p. 31)

The question raised for us is: Whence comes the anticipation? Is it that the symbols arise from a ground plan that maps out the future development? Or is it that the nature of the innate psyche is itself a "wholeness?" Surely if the Self is a dynamic function that directs development, it must have somewhere in its nature the qualities it anticipates. For example, DNA functions as a ground plan for the development of the organism, and contains in itself the "map" and the dynamics for producing that development through a transmission of "information." We may note here that DNA itself has a fourfold structure, with its four amino acid compounds, adenine, guanine, cytosine, and thymine, which, in the words of Elizabeth Osterman,

> constitute an *alphabet* by means of which *matter communicates* with *matter*. In combination with sugar, ribose [which holds the compounds in the double helix form], they make a long, threadlike compound, deoxyribonucleic acid (DNA), which is present in the central portion, the nucleus, of every living cell—of amoeba, flower or man. (1965, p. 18)

What, then, is the nature and structure of the innate primal self? Of course, we can never expect to know the "true" or noumenal nature of the Self. That will always remain a mystery. To limit the scope of our question: What can we know about the structure and function of the phenomenal nature of the innate primal Self?

In many of the references Jung makes to the myriad forms in which the fourfold structure of the self appears, we can ascertain a certain consistent emphasis. When speaking of the ego functions or any other clearly delineated fourfold structure, e.g., the cardinal directions, the four elements (earth, air, fire, and water), etc., Jung consistently makes reference to ego-consciousness, as if to deny any evidence of a fourfold structure in the primary self. Nevertheless, there are other references that bring this into question. For example:

> Experience shows that individual mandalas are symbols of *order*, and that they occur in patients principally during times of psychic disorientation or re-orientation. . . . The mandala at first comes into the conscious mind as an unimpressive point or dot, and a great deal of hard and painstaking work as well as the integration of many projections are generally required before the full range of the symbol can be anything like completely understood. (1959b, pp. 31–32)

Elsewhere he appears to affirm an innate fourfold structure that can appear in the dreams of young children:

> On the one hand, in the products of the unconscious the self appears as it were *a priori*, that is, in well-known circle and quaternity symbols which may already have occurred in the earliest dreams of childhood, long before there was any possibility of consciousness or understanding. On the other hand, only patient and painstaking work on the contents of the unconscious,

and the resultant synthesis of conscious and unconscious data, can lead to a 'totality,' which once more uses circle and quaternity symbols for purposes of self-description. (1959b p. 190)

A similar statement occurs in reference to the dream series reported in *Psychology and Alchemy*:

> As to the question of the origin of the mandala motif, from a superficial point of view it looks as if it had gradually come into being in the course of the dream-series. The fact is, however, that it only *appeared* more and more distinctly and in increasingly differentiated form; in reality it was always present and even occurred in the first dream. . . . It is therefore more probable that we are dealing with an *a priori* 'type,' an archetype which is inherent in the collective unconscious and thus beyond individual birth and death. The archetype is, so to speak, an 'eternal' presence, and the only question is whether it is perceived by the conscious mind or not. I think we are forming a more probable hypothesis, and one that better explains the observed facts, if we assume that the increase in the clarity and frequency of the mandala motif is due to more accurate perception of an already existing 'type,' rather than that it is generated in the course of the dream-series. (1968, pp. 221–22)

On the basis of my review of Jung's writings on this subject, I can only conclude that his seeming ambivalence about the structure of the innate primal Self is due to his reluctance to hypostatize the concept, and, in addition, his insistence on the "irrepresentable" nature of the archetypes. My own assessment of the alchemical and gnostic symbolism he has gathered together, as well as the models of the phenomenology of the self he has constructed, leads me to anticipate that further research, particularly with respect to the archetypal affects of the Self, will confirm an innate fourfold structure of the Self. At the present time I consider this to be a viable working hypothesis, and shall proceed on that basis. With this we are brought back to the question of the nature of the affects and archetypes.

Affects and Archetypes: Jung's Views

If there is any distinction with regard to affects and archetypes that remains constant in Jung's writings, it is the distinction between the archetypal image and the numinous quality it acquires from the affects. In his late article "Synchronicity: An Acausal Connecting Principle," he states:

> The archetypes are formal factors responsible for the organization of unconscious psychic processes: they are 'patterns of behaviour.' At the same time they have a 'specific charge' and develop numinous effects which express

themselves as *affects*. The affect produces a partial *abaissement du niveau mental*, for although it raises a particular content to a supernormal degree of luminosity, it does so by withdrawing so much energy from other possible contents of consciousness that they become darkened and eventually unconscious. Owing to the restriction of consciousness produced by the affect so long as it lasts, there is a corresponding lowering of orientation which in its turn gives the unconscious a favourable opportunity to slip into the space vacated. Thus we regularly find that unexpected or otherwise inhibited unconscious contents break through and find expression in the affect. Such contents are very often of an inferior or primitive nature and thus betray their archetypal origin. . . . (1952, pp. 436–37)

It is important to keep in mind the oft-repeated statement that the "charge" and the "numinous quality" of the "archetype" find expression in the "affects." I purposely enclose the word "affects" in quotation marks here in order to keep in mind that it occupies an indispensable position as a factor of the equation: *archetype + affect = charge + numinous quality = archetypal experience*. From this perspective it seems that the term "archetype" must refer to unconscious archetypal image/ideas that have been prepared by the previous accumulation of unconscious contents. By definition, these archetypal image/ideas are capable of becoming the "conscious meaning" of the archetype, only needing the energic charge of an appropriate affect to achieve consciousness.

In the light of these observations, which are confirmed throughout Jung's works, we must recognize that the affects, if not themselves what is meant by archetypes, are nevertheless an indispensable aspect of an archetypal experience. Jung, of course, has never suggested that affect and archetype could be identical. On the other hand, in his early writings, before he had begun to conceptualize the archetype, we have seen that his view of the affects is hardly distinguishable from later views of the archetypes, with one exception. The exception has to do with the regulative or organizing factors attributed to the archetypes: "The archetypes are formal factors responsible for the organization of unconscious psychic processes: they are 'patterns of behaviour'" (1952, p. 436). In the context of describing Janet's concept of *abaissement du niveau mental*, which is produced by every emotional state, he notes that: "The conscious then comes under the influence of unconscious instinctual impulses and contents. These are as a rule complexes whose ultimate basis is the archetype, the 'instinctual pattern'" (1952, p. 446). Such statements are found in all of Jung's formal definitions of the term archetype.

What are we to make of this? In our review of Jung's writings, we have over and over again found that in any particular example of an archetypal experience—for instance, the vision of Brother Klaus (1959a, pp. 8–12)—the emphasis is on the numinous affective qualities that focus consciousness on a particular image or transformation of behavior. It is in the prior unconscious preparation for the experience, and in the post-conscious elaboration of the experience, that we see the workings of the unconscious complex with its archetypal base in the collective unconscious. When the focus is on this aspect of the experience, we are brought in touch with the ongoing unconscious processes that continually produce fantasies, which may contain the motifs of myth and fairy tale. This is essentially the dream process, which draws its materials from the images of life experience and from the endopsychic images of psychic functions, primarily the archetypes and affects. This unconscious "dreaming/fantasy" function of the psyche is also the source of the images that are available to consciousness through the functions of play and active/creative imagination. It is this elaboration of unconscious images of an archetypal nature that accounts for the creation of all of the cultural forms of art, religion, theoretical thought, and society.

As we can see from the foregoing, there is no question that throughout Jung's writings, the affects and the archetypes are inseparably enmeshed. Even in his very earliest works, when he is writing about affects, before he has conceptualized the archetypes, the descriptions are almost identical to his later descriptions of archetypal experiences (1907, pp. 41–42). In Jung's first use of the term *archetype* in "Instinct and the Unconscious" (1919, pp. 133–138), basic issues are prefigured that preoccupied Jung throughout the latter half of his life, namely, the relationship of archetypal image to the "archetype," the relationship of archetype to "instinct," and a precise definition of archetype. In his last formulation, late in his life, we find the same issues considered in terms of a spectrum, the colors of which symbolize the relative positions of instinct and archetype:

> The dynamism of instinct is lodged as it were in the infra-red part of the spectrum, whereas the instinctual image lies in the ultra-violet part. . . . Violet is the "mystic" colour, and it certainly reflects the indubitably "mystic" or paradoxical quality of the archetype in a most satisfactory way. . . . Now, it is, as it happens, rather more than just an edifying thought if we feel bound to emphasize that the archetype is more accurately characterized by violet, for, as well as being an image in its own right, it is at the same time a *dynamism* which makes itself felt in the numinosity and fascinating power of the archetypal image. . . . The archetypal representations (images and ideas) mediated to us by the unconscious should not be confused with the archetype as such. The archetype as such is a psychoid factor that belongs, as it were, to the invisible, ultra-violet end of the psychic spectrum. It does not appear, in itself, to be capable of reaching consciousness. . . . (1947, pp. 211, 213)

With this we reach the limits of Jung's views. Again we ask how are these views related to the hypothesis we are proposing. First, it should be recalled that with regard to the relationship of image and dynamism, the affects appear to function in the same manner as the archetype, as described by Jung. In fact, the examples he gives of archetypal experiences, particularly his lengthy discussion of the vision of Brother Klaus (1959a, pp. 8–12; 1933), involve discussion of the affective-numinous experience without any reference to other factors. It is only in the reference to regulative aspects of the archetypes, which appears in his formal definitions, that one can discern any clear distinction between affect and archetype. One might conclude, and perhaps correctly, in view of contemporary studies, that the affects are the instincts to which Jung refers.

Summary

On the basis of the foregoing evaluation, I believe that Jung's writings strongly support the correlation of play and curiosity with the two kinds of thinking, fantasy and directed thought. And although Jung never brings together his thoughts on the concept of libido and the two ways of thinking, it seems to me that they are related as energy to expression. Thus the affects Joy and Interest, as twin aspects of libido, the life instinct, anticipate and foster the cosmogonic principles of Eros and Logos, through the dialectical syzygy of their expressive dynamisms, play and curiosity. Although Jung's writings are unclear as to his view of the innate nature of the primal Self, he supports the view that much is still to be learned about the empirical nature of the Self. The fourfold phenomenology of the Self, which Jung describes in such detail, and the spontaneous images of the mandala, strike me as support for the hypothesis that is being presented here of four primal archetypal affects: Terror, Anguish, Rage, and Disgust/Humiliation. In addition, I suggest that Jung's paradoxical formulation of the Self as center and totality finds support in the nature of the archetypal affect Startle, with its function of centering and reorientation, and in its relationship to the other archetypal affects.

In closing, I will speak briefly about the constellation of the archetypal affects. Everything suggests that the primal stimuli of the affects are the following.

- For the affects of the Self, they are the *life experiences* of: the unknown (Terror); loss (Anguish); frustration of autonomy (Rage); and rejection (Humiliation/Disgust); for the archetypal affect of centering and reorientation: the unexpected (Startle).
- For the affects of the libido, they are the *life experiences* of: the familiar and cherished (Ecstasy), and the novel (Excitement).

(In the foregoing, and in the discussion to follow, I have indicated in parentheses the affect associated with the stimuli or the image; each affect is listed in the extreme form of intensity that is appropriate to the primal state.)

But these conscious stimuli of "life experiences" must be "met," so to speak, by unconscious, innate image/imprints, or the potential for such image/imprints. In a search for what these images might be in myth and symbol, as well as the experiences of analysis, we arrived at the following "universally" recognized images as most expressive of these primal unconscious potentials for affective experience. With respect to the archetypal affects of the Self, these are:

- The affect Terror: the abyss (the unknown),
- The affect Anguish: the void (loss),
- The affect Rage: chaos (restriction of autonomy),
- The affect Disgust/Humiliation: alienation (rejection).

With respect to the archetypal affect of centering and re-orientation:

- The affect Startle: disorientation (the unexpected).

And with respect to the archetypal affects of the libido, these are:

- The affect of Ecstasy: diffuse illumination, bliss (the cherished),
- The affect of Excitement: focussed illumination, insight (the novel).

From this perspective, one can see that the "symbol" that constellates the archetypal affect is partially represented in consciousness by the "life experience" and is partially unconscious in the form of the innate "expectation or image/imprint."

This brings us to consideration of the psyche's propensity for the experience of opposites, and to the question of what compensatory opposites may be implied in these image/imprints: the void (loss/Anguish), the abyss (the unknown/Terror), chaos (restriction/Rage), and alienation (rejection/Disgust-Humiliation). (The fourfold archetypal affects of the Self will be the only ones discussed here, since the compensatory images of the other affects are, as yet, less well understood.) Consideration of these images puts us in touch with the dimension of value, which we know to be a function of the emotions. In the transformation of ego consciousness that occurs when an affect is constellated, a "new" state of consciousness results that is representative of one of the innate primal images. It follows, then, that the opposites must be images that represent compensatory states of consciousness.

We have seen that the innate images of the archetypal affects of the Self represent the most dreaded of human experiences—the void of Anguish, the abyss of Terror, the chaos of Rage, and the alienation of Disgust/Humiliation. Thus we expect the compensatory opposites to be images representing highly valued experiences. Looked at as a totality, then, the innate primal images and their compensatory opposites would consist of pairs of images that represent the heights and the depths of human emotional experience. If this be so, it would appear that the compensatory opposite image of the void must be nature in all its glorious beauty. Surely this is the counterpoise to the barren wasteland of Anguish that is experienced in loss. In like fashion, the abyss of Terror conjures up its opposite in the form of the holy mountain, the heights of heaven, the empyrean, residence of the Gods. The chaos of Rage is surely set in opposition to the "true" order of a cosmos, while the opposite of the alienation of Humiliation is without doubt utopian *communitas*. In the end, this little exercise in imagination has led us to thoughts about the cultural attitudes, in that these compensatory images are obviously the age-old categories of the highest human values: the beautiful, the holy, the true, and the good, which are mirrored in the cultural forms of art, religion, philosophy, and society. Moreover, these cultural attitudes must be assumed to be the "normal" set, which is displaced to the unconscious by the *abaissement du niveau mental* created by the affect.

My latest thoughts have to do with the relationship of the primal affects to the differentiated, more conscious functions of the psyche. Here we are approaching a frontier of knowledge, and it is obvious that much further research is necessary. Nevertheless, I can indicate the direction my thought is taking. At this point it seems probable that in the narrowed and concentrated focus of attention caused by an affect, one may identify a potential for the development of the ego functions as follows: the unknown possibilities in Terror (Intuition); the only too well known object of loss in Anguish (Sensation); strategies to remove the frustration in Rage (Thinking); and the evaluation of self and others in terms of sympathies and antipathies in Disgust/Humiliation (Feeling).

It may be suggested, further, that Henderson's cultural attitudes develop out of the expressive aspects of the primal affects of the Self. A good example of research in this area is Rudolph Otto's ground-breaking study in the affective phenomenology of the religious attitude, *The Idea of the Holy* (1923), the book from which Jung took his idea of the numinous. In this classic tour de force, which stands as a paradigm for research in this area, Otto has demonstrated just how much can be learned through an analysis of historical developments when the analysis is illuminated by a psychological attitude. The original task Otto set for himself was to identify the quintessential element of religion—of all religions, without exception. This he found in the experience of the numinous. Following out the development of the numinous in religious feeling, Otto discovered that its primal form is demonic dread, which arises in the experience of primitive terror. The power of his study lies in just this realization that a primal affective experience of terror is transformed, through the aeons of reflection by awestruck humanity, into the highest forms of religious experience.

It is to be expected that a similar derivation of the philosophic, the aesthetic, and the social attitude can be demonstrated from the other primal affects, which in our view belong to the psyche's fourfold structure.

Notes

This is an edited version (with appreciation to John Beebe for his help) of the paper presented in March 1985 to the California Spring Conference and appearing in the Conference Proceedings published by the C. G. Jung Institute of San Francisco.

References

Campbell, J. 1959. *The masks of God: Primitive mythology.* New York: The Viking Press, Penguin Books, 1977.

Darwin, C. 1892. *The expression of the emotions in man and animals.* Chicago and London: University of Chicago Press, 1965, fifth impression, 1974.

Ekman, P. 1972. Universals and cultural differences in facial expression in emotion. *Nebraska symposium on motivation, 1971,* J. K. Cole, ed. Lincoln: University of Nebraska Press.

Henderson, J. L. 1962. The archetype of culture. *The archetype, proceedings of the second international congress of analytical psychology, Zurich.* Basel/New York: S. Karger, 1964.

_____. 1984. *Cultural attitudes in psychological perspective.* Toronto: Inner City Books.

Hillman, J. 1961. *Emotion: A comprehensive phenomenology of theories and their meanings for therapy.* Evanston: Northwestern University Press.

Izard, C. E. 1977. *Human emotions.* New York: Plenum Press.

Jung, C. G. 1907. The psychology of dementia praecox. In *Collected works,* vol. 3, pp. 1–151. Princeton: Princeton University Press, 1972.

_____. 1919. Instinct and the unconscious. In *Collected works,* vol. 8, pp. 129–38. Princeton: Princeton University Press, 1978.

_____. 1921. *Psychological types.* In *Collected works,* vol. 6. Princeton: Princeton University Press, 1977.

_____. 1933. Brother Klaus. In *Collected works,* vol. 11, pp. 316–23. Princeton: Princeton University Press, 1975.

_____. 1947. On the nature of the psyche. In *Collected works,* vol. 8, pp. 159–234. Princeton: Princeton University Press, 1969.

_____. 1952. Synchronicity: An acausal connecting principle. In *Collected works,* vol. 8, pp. 419–519. Princeton: Princeton University Press, 1978.

—————. 1956. *Symbols of transformation.* In *Collected works*, vol. 5. Princeton: Princeton University Press, 1967.

—————. 1959a. *The archetypes and the collective unconscious.* In *Collected works*, vol. 9, i. Princeton: Princeton University Press, 1977.

—————. 1959b. *Aion: Researches into the phenomenology of the Self.* In *Collected works*, vol. 9, ii. Princeton: Princeton University Press, 1968.

—————. 1961. *Memories, dreams, reflections.* New York: Random House.

—————. 1963. *Mysterium coniunctionis.* In *Collected works*, vol. 14. Princeton: Princeton University Press, 1976.

—————. 1968. *Psychology and Alchemy.* In *Collected works*, vol. 12. Princeton: Princeton University Press, 1974.

Kalff, D. M. 1962. Archetypus Als Heilender Faktor. In *The archetype, proceedings of the second international congress of analytical psychology, Zurich.* pp. 182–200. Basel/New York: S. Karger, 1964.

Lynd, H. 1958. *On shame and the search for identity.* New York: Harcourt, Brace.

Neumann, E. 1973. *The child.* New York: G. P. Putnam's Sons.

Osterman, E. 1965. The tendency toward patterning and order in matter and in the psyche. In *The reality of the psyche.* Wheelwright, J. B., ed., pp. 14–27. New York: G. P. Putnam's Sons, 1968.

Otto, R. 1923. *The idea of the holy.* Oxford/New York: Oxford University Press, 1981.

Piaget, J. 1962. *Play, dreams and imitation in childhood.* New York: W. W. Norton & Co., Inc.

Stewart, L. H. and Stewart, C. T. 1979. Play, games and affects: A contribution toward a comprehensive theory of play. In *Play as context.* A. T. Cheska, ed., pp. 42–52. Proceedings of The Association for the Anthropological Study of Play. Westpoint, N.Y.: Leisure Press, 1981.

Stewart, L. H. 1976. Kinship libido: Toward an archetype of the family. In *Proceedings of the annual conference of Jungian analysts of the United States*, pp. 168–82. San Francisco: C. G. Jung Institute of San Francisco.

—————. 1977. Sand play therapy: Jungian technique. In *International encyclopedia of psychiatry, psychology, psychoanalysis and neurology*, Wolman, B., ed., pp. 9–11. New York: Aesculapius Publishers.

—————. 1981a. Play and sandplay. *Sandplay studies: Origins, theory and practice.* Hill, G., ed., pp. 21–37. San Francisco: C. G. Jung Institute of San Francisco.

—————. 1981b. The play-dream continuum and the categories of the imagination. Presented at the 7th annual conference of The Association for the Anthropological Study of Play. Fort Worth, Texas, April 1981.

—————. 1982. Sandplay and analysis. In *Jungian analysis*, M. Stein, ed., pp. 204–18. La Salle, Ill., and London: Open Court Publishing Co.

Tomkins, S. S. 1962. *Affect imagery consciousness, Volume I: The positive affects.* New York: Springer Publishing Company, Inc.

—————. 1963. *Affect imagery consciousness, Volume II: The negative affects.* New York: Springer Publishing Company, Inc.

Book Reviews

Psychotherapy in the Third Reich: The Göring Institute
Geoffrey Cocks. New York and Oxford: Oxford University Press, 1985. 326 pp.
$24.95.

Reviewed by Hans Dieckmann

Psychotherapy in the Third Reich is an unusually well-researched book. Not only
has the author carefully examined practically all the available documentary
sources concerning the Berlin Institute for Psychological Research and Psychotherapy and its branches in Munich, Stuttgart, Frankfurt am Main, Vienna, and
Düsseldorf, but he also spoke with a multitude of persons in Germany and
abroad who were knowledgeable concerning the history of and personalities in
the Institute. Likewise, he has conducted in-depth interviews with living mem-
bers of the "Reichsinstitut" (as the Berlin Institute was renamed toward the end of
the war) and with the relatives of those deceased (e.g., with the son of the former
president, Matthias Heinrich Göring, and Mrs. Lucie Heyer). As I read the book, I
experienced again and again a remarkable feeling to learn so many details concerning the people whom I had known personally during my training at the Berlin Institute for Psychotherapy in the years 1952–57, persons by whom I was
trained and with whom I had worked. Reading the book, I again recognized how
great had been the repressive silence during the early post-war years in Germany, even in psychoanalytic circles. Aside from a few allusions, anecdotes, ex-

Hans Dieckmann, M.D., president of the International Association for Analytical Psy-
chology, practices Jungian psychoanalysis in Berlin, West Germany. He is the author of
Methods of Analytical Psychology and *Twice-Told Tales: The Psychological Use of Fairy
Tales* (Chiron Publications 1986).

cuses, and accusations, we younger therapists were informed either not at all or only meagerly concerning the events and conditions that had obtained during the Nazi period in the field of psychotherapy and psychoanalysis. It is only within the last decade that Germany has begun to face and deal with these issues, and only very lately has our generation gotten a comprehensive picture of the Nazi period. I would like to emphasize here that I was particularly touched by the factual tone of this book, a tone informed by an obviously very deep human understanding, a tone which forgoes all wholesale moral condemnation while exercising the necessary criticism, and which repeatedly strives to understand the deeper interconnections.

The book has seven chapters. The author first gives an overview of National Socialist psychotherapy. The second chapter, "Psychotherapy and Medicine," discusses the development of psychoanalysis and psychotherapy in the years from 1926 to 1933. Chapter Three, "Psyche and Swastika," discusses primarily the histories of the various schools that were brought together in the "Göring Institute": the Adlerians, the Jungians, the Freudians, the independents, and the so-called "Voelkischen." Chapter Four deals with the integration of psychotherapy into the whole National Socialist system and with the confrontation and conflicts that took place in those years between psychotherapy and German psychiatry. Chapter Five examines the relationships of the Institute with the various party organizations, in particular the collaboration with and the financing of the Institute by the Deutsche Arbeitsfront and later also by the Luftwaffe. Here also the Rittmeister affair is discussed. Rittmeister was the sole resistance fighter who was active in the "rote Kapelle," who was sentenced to death during the Nazi period. Chapter Six is concerned above all with the scientific and clinical work of the Institute, the latter having a particularly broad scope. For example, in 1937, 259 patients were seen in the Out-Patient Clinic; in 1941, 464 were seen, 260 of whom were accepted for treatment. This chapter also discusses the training conditions, which for those times had attained a very good level. Last, but not least, in the seventh chapter the author discusses psychotherapy in the early post-war years in Germany. With one exception cited below (which the reviewer personally experienced) Cocks correctly and subtly examines how the various psychotherapeutic and psychoanalytic schools, which had been forcibly united in the Reichsinstitut, eventually sought their own separate paths and identities by demarcating their boundaries and forming their own institutes. Nonetheless, they also recognized the positive aspects of banding together. Continuing into the present day, the three great depth-psychology schools—Freud's psychoanalysis, Jung's analytical psychology, and Schultz-Henckes's neo-psychoanalysis—are united under a common German umbrella organization, the DGPT, or German Society for Psychotherapy and Depth Psychology, and cooperate both in scientific exchanges (annual joint congresses) and in professional policy. Here it should also be mentioned that this umbrella organization—previously called the DGPT—has always consisted of Freudians, Jungians, and neo-analysts. The Freudians, contrary to what appears in Chapter Seven, have never left this umbrella organization. The error probably arose because the Freudians left the joint Berlin Institute relatively early, following the restoration of their international recognition, and founded their own institute in Berlin.

The essential contribution of *Psychotherapy in the Third Reich*, beyond the description of the activities of the "Göring Institute" and the personalities who were active in it, is the articulation of the whole of German psychotherapy in the National Socialist Weltanschauung. Within the realm of the total health system —and this stands out with precise clarity in the book—was a decided confusion created by flirtations with holistic ideas, naturopathic tendencies, regressive mythologisms, and attempted objective science, all of which were brought out by the various "Führer" personalities and by the characteristics of the National Socialist organizations which they influenced. In part this book is very difficult reading in this area, even for a German who grew up in those years, since one can scarcely find one's way through the abundance of organizations and conflicting ideologies. We must grant, however, that these influences from outside, these very different ideologies, played a considerable role throughout this period and had a marked influence on German psychotherapy in the years 1933 to 1945. The author guides us through this labyrinth very carefully and very well.

Over against the previously mentioned general political trends that were advantageous to depth psychology, and even to psychoanalysis, and made possible their continued existence (which by no means is intended to gloss over the severe persecution under which Freud's "Jewish psychoanalysis" (p. 89) suffered during the Nazi period), it is important to consider the role of Matthias Heinrich Göring, the director of the Institute. To him alone the very survival of German psychotherapy in the Third Reich is attributed. His name and person shielded the institute from the outside because as a cousin of Hermann Göring, he was considered by the National Socialist government to be a confidential person. As a matter of fact, the Freudian positions continued to be taught with his knowledge at the institute where Freud's name was rarely spoken.

This book makes it very clear that the Berlin Institute, later renamed "Reichsinstitut," was a very active—one almost might say flourishing and great —institute. With its many connections to the National Socialist organizations, it had opportunities to exert influence on them while it also attempted to carry out, at the direction of those sorts of organizations, certain scientific and pseudo-scientific projects. However, measured against what transpired and was developed outside Germany in the scientific realm in psychoanalysis and in Jung's analytical psychology, the results and the scientific value of these activities are minimal. (It should be stressed here that the Institute never participated in projects of research incompatible with medical ethics.)

What certainly was not minimal and what the author emphasizes were the protective functions that the Institute fulfilled, not only in regard to colleagues but also on behalf of persecuted patient groups (such as homosexuals and so-called psychopaths threatened with sterilization). It is also obvious that no one in the entire circle of Institute colleagues made any malicious denunciations or committed any indiscretions by violating confidential case histories, a practice that the National Socialists always pressured for and valued.

Psychotherapy in the Third Reich is a good, instructive book, well worth reading, which can be recommended to anyone who is interested in that period and in psychotherapeutic and psychoanalytic material.

The Vertical Labyrinth: Individuation in Jungian Psychology
Aldo Carotenuto, translated by John Shepley. Toronto: Inner City Books, 1985.
140 pp. $12.00. Paper.

Reviewed by Julia M. Jewett

Analysands and others occasionally request the title of a single book that offers a basic Jungian perspective. *The Vertical Labyrinth* is the newest addition to my relatively short list of such books. Subtitled "Individuation in Jungian Psychology," it outlines the process of a single six-year analysis, progressing through a variety of stages. Taking the reader from the importance of the initial dream through termination, the author includes most areas basic to Jung's thought-in-practice, putting emphasis on the transformative aspect of analysis for both analyst and analysand. The book itself seems to be a post-analytic reflection by the analyst, which is no doubt a familiar state for the practitioner, but not one that is often discussed.

The Vertical Labyrinth is a book about creativity—or, rather, about the imperative of the creative necessity in the psyche. The protagonist of this near-novella is an artist who is outwardly successful in the world of ego and commerce but agonizingly out of touch with soul and the levels of animation which that implies: inner creative impetus, vocational devotion, and outer relationships with women. The name chosen for this hero: Arion. Two related mythical figures that carry that name: one, the offspring of Poseidon and Demeter, a wonder-horse that could speak; the other the originator of the dithyramb, a poet who taught his style to Corinthian choirs. In both instances the ability to communicate is remarkably creative.

That Carotenuto has given his character a mythical inheritance perhaps tells us of the analyst/author's general place among the currently diverse theoretical positions within the Jungian collective. While tipping his hat to Freud, and more recently to Melanie Klein and the school of object relations, Carotenuto seems clearly to be in the mythopoetic line among Jungians. Neumann is most heavily referenced (more than a quarter of the footnotes), with Jung only slightly lagging. James Hillman, while present in many actual quotes, is most noticeable in spirit. The author's style is imagistic; the reader is immersed in a dominantly perceptual rather than essentially rational field. Carotenuto believes that certain states of being cannot be remediated by medicine, but that one instead has recourse to the worlds of religion and psychology. If myth is basic to all religion and represents an attempt to penetrate and structure the mysteries of experience, and if psychology is an approach to the ways of soul, then we need to walk a path that is mythopoetic—a making of one's personal myth, stemming from the archetypal, toward the goal of soul-making.

Julia M. Jewett, D. Min., is an ordained minister of the United Church of Christ and a pastoral therapist, First Presbyterian Church, Evanston, Ill. She maintains a private practice in Wilmette, Ill., and is a candidate in the Analyst Training Program of the C. G. Jung Institute of Chicago.

Following Jung, Carotenuto disclaims the strictly religious as being outside the analyst's sphere, yet he uses specifically religious textual material to describe his view of psychological process. For instance:

> Myths were developed during the course of history, and an examination of them permits us to see the development of consciousness in all its stages. Thus one can rightly say that at least a portion of myth is the unconscious self-representation of the development of consciousness. (p. 10)

Carotenuto then discusses the early dreams in the initial stage of the artist's analysis and makes suggestive analogies, but he frustrates the reader by not developing his ideas. Initial stages of analysis are paralleled with biblical themes of chaos, the infantile bliss of the garden of Eden, and the out-of-the-garden reality with its attendant dualities and ambivalences.

The fragmentation of the original Oneness is seen as an ongoing process throughout life, to be dealt with repeatedly whenever new difficulties emerge. Carotenuto subtly carries the religious theme through his exposition, as reflected in his chapter headings such as "The Mythical Unconscious," "Death and Rebirth," "Immense Light," and "Human Dignity." The book's central chapter is titled "The Destiny of Great Souls," and it is here that he dwells most deeply on the difficulty of living out one's portion of creative life. He says of analysis, "It does not create illusions, but rather activates intrinsic pessimism in the understanding of life, while simultaneously nourishing and providing support and foundation for the optimism of the will" (p. 59).

For Carotenuto, it is the erosion of the will, the giving way to pessimism or regression to primal inertia, that forestalls creative life. Acknowledging the tenacity of early conditioning, Carotenuto makes an observation that I find particularly true of *women's* experience, although he actually refers to persons from lower socio-economic levels:

> [They] must make an enormous effort to bridge the gap and actually travel much farther than those who had been close to the goal since birth. Those who are born where no paths have been laid out go to immense difficulties to find their own. Unimaginable tears are shed in the course of their psychological journey by those who, lacking any support, have to create everything for themselves. It is like having to force one's way through a forest with one's bare hands. . . . Unless one has a solid social and cultural background, one always feels in danger and even in debt in the presence of life: it is as though everything we have, despite the effort it has cost us, has been in some way given to us and could therefore be taken away at a moment's notice. One is then obliged to thank the good Lord daily for the very fact of survival, and if we also have success, there is an extremely acute feeling of not deserving it. This attitude of renunciation is imparted to us almost with our mother's milk, and remains within us like a negative imprinting that keeps us from enjoying our achievements. (p. 60)

The soul confronting the necessity to live its own creative life is at once occupied with the struggle against the persistence of the old order and the urge to flee from the potential envy of others.

A possible explanation of the inability to demonstrate one's own values and richness . . . lies, in my opinion, in a fundamental and structural fear of other people's envy. . . . To be creative, to carry the world forward by one's thought or by one's works, means to risk drawing down hatred on oneself, and only someone who is capable of withstanding it is able to say the right words. What prevents us from discovering ourselves, and from expressing our truth, is always the fear of losing other people's love. But if the purpose of life becomes that of gaining the love of others rather than seeking truth, our existence is reduced to a psychological conformism that does not allow us to express anything new.

Any man who thinks for himself and travels unbeaten paths provokes consternation and aggression, and becomes the target of abuse. In others he evokes desperate ghosts of ruin and transgression. In other words, his example bears witness to and inevitably signals the lack of soul in others. (pp. 61–62)

This notion of exploring the lack of soul in others seems to me to be a new and useful twist on the theme of envy. It is not only that the creative soul comes forth with what another has not, but in so doing it exposes the other's lodging in some realm *not of soul*. If humans are by nature religious (*homo religioso*) and our souls are naturally creative, then to live out of that religious and creative dimension is to risk casting the one who is not so disposed as not fully human; while this may be true, at some level it feels an inhuman thing to do . . . yet psychologically it is more monstrous not to.

The above is a basic intrapsychic double-bind that the analysand brings to the analysis. It is reflected (or repeated) in the analytic relationship. Although it is appealing imagery, the vertical descent to the labyrinth of possible passages in the psyche is not particularly new imagery, and a seasoned reader will come upon other familiar motifs. The new element in *this* telling is Carotenuto's insistence on the relationship between analyst and analysand, his open engagement with his analysand, the mutual willingness of both to enter territory that is little known and most sensitive to both. I doubt that such willingness and courage would be activated in the analysand if either attachment to an old order or unconscious envy were much present in the analyst. The necessity of the analyst's original personal analysis, as well as ongoing work-on-self, is clear, particularly since the analyst can say, "I leave myself open to him completely to allow him to fill my unconscious with his illness, but I too will fill him with my own contents" (p. 9). This mutual meeting at the unconscious level is the vehicle of transformation for both, and must be part of every thoroughgoing analysis. Carotenuto says of hearing the other:

And so the fact is that my understanding has passed through my own suffering and been filtered by the comparison with my personal situation. Every true analysis has this characteristic, and if it is missing it is not an analysis but a benevolent relationship in the course of which, if things go well, a modest strengthening of the conscious situation is achieved. And if there are analysts who state the contrary, they are lying and know they are lying: this is actually a defensive attitude taken against the direct impact of the other, an impact involving deep and serious problems since sooner or later the most scabrous and painful things in our experience come to light. But this path is necessary for psychological rebirth. (p. 9)

In Carotenuto's view, the analyst's capacity to maintain a position of informed vulnerability is an essential component of the required level of mutuality.

For one reader, the particular strength of this book will be its readability, which fosters a beginning grasp of theory by way of telling a particular story; for another, it will be the especially lucid exposition of a mythopoetic approach; and for a third, the treatment of issues of countertransference and therapeutic style will make it a stand-out. Whatever the reader's interests, the variety of aspects and perspectives included here makes reading the book a labyrinthine experience.

The Unconscious in its Empirical Manifestations
C. A. Meier. Boston: Sigo Press, 1984. 236 pp. $25.50.

Reviewed by Thomas B. Kirsch

This volume, the first in a series of four, has had a long and circuitous incubation period prior to its translation and publication in English. When first published in German, the series was intended for use as textbooks in the study of psychiatry. The author, C. A. Meier, is Professor Emeritus at the Federal Technical Institute (ETH) in Zurich and a successor to Jung in that post. This book, along with the other three in the series, has its origins in a series of lectures that Professor Meier gave over the years to the students at the ETH. For many years Jung's close and trusted colleague, Meier is preeminent among the first generation of analysts, having served as the first president of the Jung Institute in Zurich and the first president of the International Association for Analytical Psychology. For the past twenty years, he has been Director of the Clinic Am Zurichberg, where he has been actively engaged in basic scientific research on the nature of sleep and dreams. This long-awaited volume comes out of an intimate knowledge of Jung and his work over several decades. It was first scheduled for publication by the Jung Foundation in New York in the early '60s, but entered a liminal state when the Jung Foundation decided to get out of the book-publishing business. After many abortive attempts, it has been published by the Sigo Press, and we can be grateful to them for having finally made this book available in English.

Meier's focus of interest is the empirical foundations of the unconscious, with special reference to the word-association test. The book begins by demonstrating the creative aspect of the unconscious through commentary on excerpts

Thomas B. Kirsch, M.D., is an analyst in private practice in Palo Alto, California. He is first vice-president of the International Association for Analytical Psychology, and clinical associate professor of psychiatry at Stanford Medical School.

from the diaries of famous writers, philosophers, and scientists. Meier then goes on to review Freud's work with parapraxis, etc., to show the disturbing features of the unconscious. So far the author is going over familiar ground, although even here he does it in a clear and lively fashion.

For me the most exciting part of the book is the section on the word-association experiment. Usually this part of Jung's work is treated as important historically, but its relevance to the more mature Jung is accorded little significance. Meier's all-inclusive knowledge of the history and significance of the word-association test makes this long and central chapter of the book "must" reading for all students of analytical psychology. I had never before realized the scientific rigor that Jung and his assistants had used in developing the word-association test. Jung's results with the test provided the first truly scientific foundation for *any* kind of psychoanalytic approach. The discovery, the naming and clinical evaluation of complexes, in association with quantitative measuring techniques, was Jung's first great contribution to psychoanalysis. The psychoanalytic nature of this work emerges especially when we consider where the association experiments had been.

Prior to Jung, association experiments had been developed to find out what happened within the psyche between sensory perception and apperception (or comprehension). The aim was to gain insight into the process of the succession of ideas in the psyche. In contrast, as we all know, Jung was interested in the serious analysis of the disturbance of the normal (discontinuity), the prolonged reaction time. As Jung continued his experiments, he became aware of a whole series of other signs that could be understood as additional features of the disturbance. He realized that the nature of these disturbances could only be understood as the effects of an already existing complex. Jung identified eighteen different forms of disturbed reaction that are all "complex indicators." He painstakingly demonstrated how each of the eighteen categories fits into the overall expression of the pathological complex, a testimony to his scientific rigor. By focusing on these areas of sensitivity, Jung was able to penetrate the nature of the subjects' unconscious complexes. Time and space does not permit a discussion of all the ramifications. Suffice it to say there were important theoretical and clinical implications for such diverse areas as schizophrenia, neurosis, family psychotherapy, criminal evidence, and several others. Meier has summarized these findings elegantly.

Another crucial area of development in the association experiment was the examination of physical reactions to the stimulus words. It was a natural step to investigate both galvanic skin response and respiration rates as measures of complex indication. The demonstrated relationship between the two was the beginning of a psychosomatic theory in medicine, and Meier goes on to trace the history of psychosomatic medicine from those early days. Much of psychosomatic medicine adopted a causalistic approach, that is, it focused on the psychogenesis of the ensuing physical symptom. Meier makes a strong argument for an acausal —i.e., synchronistic—approach. He suggests that this is a more fruitful way to interpret psychosomatic phenomena.

At a time when Jungian analysts are looking to psychoanalytic writers for clinical and empirical data, it is ironic that Meier's book should bring us back to the clinical and scientific origins of Jung's own work. This book reinforces the sound clinical and scientific bases for the analysis of complexes. I find that in my own analytical practice, the analysis of affective states and their concomitant underlying complexes is a most fruitful approach. As I have already said, I recommend this book most highly.

Jung and the Post-Jungians
Andrew Samuels. London, Boston, Melbourne, and Henley: Routledge and Kegan Paul, 1985. 293 pp. $25.00.

Reviewed by John E. Talley

Informing Andrew Samuels's broad and generous viewpoint in this praiseworthy book is Poincaré's statement about the development of science: "at one and the same time we are advancing 'towards variety and complexity' and also 'towards unity and simplicity.' Poincaré wondered if this apparent contradiction might be a necessary condition of knowledge" (p. 269). In describing developments within analytical psychology during Jung's life and since his death, the author delineates both movements at work.

His aims are explicit. Besides relating post-Jungian thought to a critical evaluation of Jung's writing and the two to similar processes within psychoanalysis, Samuels makes a credible case for Jung's generally unacknowledged but real impact on the present-day practice of analysis, psychotherapy, counselling, and casework of all schools. At one point, he quotes the psychoanalyst Roazen: "Few responsible figures in psychoanalysis would be disturbed today if an analyst were to present views identical to Jung's in 1913" (p. 9). Samuels refers to them as the "unknowing Jungians."

While wishing to inform these unknowing Jungians about analytical psychology, he is primarily addressing analytical psychologists and those in Jungian training. Cozily, he says, "I suppose that in this book I am charting the course of Jungian family life with its healthy differences" (p. 3). More passionately and urgently, he says:

> [I]n analytical psychology . . . a tension exists between working with the person and with the image. This tension has sometimes been expressed in terms of a split between "clinical" and "symbolic" approaches. . . . Even though there may be immense methodological and expository differences, such a divide can be bridged. Otherwise analytical psychology would cease to exist as a discipline.
>
> We need to envision our field of reference as seamless and continuous so that ostensible "images" and ostensible "interpersonal communications"

John E. Talley, M.D., is a clinical professor of psychiatry, University of New Mexico, Albuquerque, and past president of the Inter-Regional Soceity of Jungian Analysts.

do not get separated, nor one gain ascendency over the other on the basis of a preconceived hierarchy of importance. (p.265)

To this end Samuels delineates three schools within analytical psychology, each emphasizing and professing to address various weaknesses and strengths of Jung's original theoretical and clinical formulations. In common, and therefore part of the seamless field of analytical psychology are:

Three *theoretical* areas:
1) The definition of archetypal,
2) The concept of self,
3) The development of personality, and
Three *clinical* aspects:
1) The analysis of transference-countertransference,
2) Emphasis upon symbolic experience of the self,
3) Examination of highly differentiated imagery. (p.15)

It is the different emphases placed on each of these categories that form the bases for Samuel's classification of the three schools. The Classical School, that closest to Jung's original "ordering of priorities," would weight the theoretical possibilities in the order of 2, 1, 3, and the clinical aspects 2, 3, 1, or perhaps 2, 1, 3. The Developmental School, in addressing early childhood phenomena and their transference-countertransference implications, would weight the theoretical possibilities 3, 2, 1, and the clinical 1, 2, 3, or 1, 3, 2. The Archetypal School, in emphasizing the immediacy of the image, would weight the theoretical possibilities 1, 2, 3, and the clinical aspects 3, 2, 1.

From this simple schema, Samuels is able to describe, based on their writings, a number of analytical psychologists as Classical (Adler, Henderson, Von Franz, Wheelwright, *et al.*), Developmental (Fordham, Gordon, Dieckmann, Goodheart, *et al.*) or Archetypal (Hillman, Berry, Güggenbuhl, *et al.*), and from these categorizations based on the theoretical and clinical emphases, one can locate oneself.

Samuels does not attempt to blur the differences and controversies that are part of analytical psychology. While he wants to build bridges between the factions, he explicitly wants to do it through dispute and dialogue. Calling on Popper and William James, Samuels urges:

[the] beginning seeker after knowledge to go . . . *where the disagreements are*. . . . [T]he point where current practitioners disagree reflects the state of the art. Here you can be sure of being in the presence of the best minds and talents and the most contemporary viewpoints or syntheses of what has gone before and predictions of what might happen next. (pp. 21–22)

An interesting point that Samuels gleans from the psychoanalyst Sandler describes the gap between "'standard,' 'official,' 'public' formulations of theory, and something described as 'private,' and 'implicit' theory" (p. 267). Over time, with experience, "original concepts are stretched, or new concepts emerge, which conflict with standard, official and public formulations" (ibid.) and what is *actually* being practiced by various individuals is often quite different from original concepts still quoted as standard and official. Samuels makes us acutely aware of this discrepancy. Critics of psychoanalysis often quote what Freud was writing in 1898 or 1910, and critics of analytical psychology quote early Jung.

One could say that a principal aim of *Jung and the Post-Jungians* is to present what is really going on in analytical psychology today, as distinct from the official, standard handbook of what Jung was doing between 1907 and 1961, when he died. Of course, this is not to say that the monumental contribution of Jung as the founder of analytical psychology does not inform this book at every point. Samuels makes very clear analytical psychology's debt to Jung. Yet he does not hesitate to disagree or to give serious voice to those who have disagreed. He makes it clear that psychology is a body of ideas, not a doctrine or series of immutable laws, and that analytical psychology, to remain vital, must be flexible and open to new discoveries and viewpoints.

Using his classification of the three schools within analytical psychology as the basis for comparison of different attitudes possible within Jungian theory, and with psychoanalysis, Samuels devotes chapters to archetype and complex; the ego (with an appendix on developments in typology); the self and individuation; the development of personality; the analytic process; gender, sex, and marriage; dreams; archetypal psychology; and theory in practice: an illustration. These chapters provide excellent reviews of classical Jungian theory and rich embellishments and amplifications from fields outside psychology, as well as critiques from those, notably classical Freudians, who have been unsympathetic to Jung. Glover makes some particularly amusing, if venomous remarks. For example, in attacking any notion of compromise (with another viewpoint), he said in 1950:

> At the bottom of the advocacy of a dual doctrine slumbers the idea that there is not harm in men being mistaken, or at least only so little harm as is more than compensated for by the marked tranquility in which their mistake wraps them. (p. 20)

In Chapter 2, "Archetype and Complex," there are contributions from the literature of ethology, biology, neurology, and structuralism, as well as comparisons with Lacan, Bion, Klein, and Kohut, and lively, timely personal comments by Samuels suggesting the need for some revision of archetypal and complex theory. In discussing the role of archetypes in the self-regulatory nature of the psyche, Samuels uses as an example the development of a sexual perversion as a protection from Oedipal punishment. The perversion is seen as holding the individual's sexual conflict in momentary balance. He goes on to say (in what is characteristic of his felicitous style):

> I give this example because it is important to protect the idea of the self-regulatory psyche from panglossian excesses, in which everything is seen as being the best or as part of some giant benevolent plan. Talking to some Jungians, it is often hard to see how anything bad could ever have happened; everything is given a purposive colouring and tragedy is denied. (pp. 28–29)

In subsequent chapters, a similar format is observed: the presentation of classical theory and practice, contributions from other fields and from other schools of psychology, critiques, discussion, and review of the current situation, and suggestions for revisions and/or for syntheses. The differences between the

Developmental and Archetypal Schools are prominent, as well as Samuels's serious efforts to suggest their similarities, especially in *process*, if not in what each chooses to emphasize.

In Chapter 5, "The Development of Personality," I especially appreciated the explicit comparison, in parallel columns, of Fordham's and Neumann's developmental models (pp. 155–59). This is an excellent example of Samuels's style throughout the book. He compares, contrasts, and, where he feels it appropriate, synthesizes in a simple, direct way that brings clarity as well as appreciation and respect for the complexity of the issues addressed.

As a metapyschological concept encompassing his view of what analytical psychology can be, Samuels proposes the idea of a shared, two-person *mundus imaginalis* in which "we can place the interaction of patient and analyst firmly within the imaginal realm without forgetting that there are two people present" (p. 264). What makes this possible is *countertransference*. "If the idea of a two-person 'mundus imaginalis' is taken seriously then we must regard the interpersonal in terms of psyche speaking, and the imaginal in terms of an avenue of communication between two people" (ibid.).

It should be stated that except for mention of Dieckmann and Humbert, this book includes only those analytical psychologists writing in or translated into English. One cannot help wondering about post-Jungian developments in Italy, France, Germany, Brazil, and those other centers whose literature is less familiar to English-speaking analytical psychologists. While one would expect to find similar developments there, I look forward to hearing their commentaries on Samuels's observations.

I cannot praise *Jung and the Post-Jungians* enough. First, it is beautifully written in the Queen's English. It is scholarly, thorough, serious-minded, yet deliciously humorous and satisfyingly irreverent in appropriate places.

The book brings into relief the importance of the analysis of countertransference, of the necessity for relationship and dialogue with the other individual person, and of the inestimable value of the life of the imagination and of the image. In his visioning of a post-Jungian ethos, Samuels makes clear that the real child whom each of us was, and the imaginal child who is our own creativity, form the foundation for the future of analytical psychology.

Living in Two Worlds: Communication Between a White Healer and Her Black Counterparts.
M. Vera Bührmann. Cape Town and Pretoria: Human & Rousseau, 1984. 108 pp. [Forthcoming from Chiron Publication, 1986]

Reviewed by Lee Zahner-Roloff

The word of greatest subtlety that haunts this moving testimony is the two-letter word in the title: *in*. Precisely what this suggests must be carefully noted, for not only is it an important word, but one of the greatest consequence for the author, M. Vera Bührmann. That small preposition points to being contained within, of having entered, of going inside, and the word, moreover, is incontrovertible. It is the opposite of *outside of*, or *beside*, or *alongside of*. In the work of Dr. Bührmann, it is nothing less than immersion, of being inside, of a knowing of the parts. It is true, in the largest sense, that we all live in two worlds, conscious and unconscious, public and private, but few of us live in the outer reality of a two-world *gnosis*. To live in two worlds, and to establish a dialectical relationship with the two worlds, and to translate the values and imperatives of two worlds is not a common fate. Hence, the uncommonness of the premise. Dr. Bührmann not only has entitled her book out of her personal imperatives, but also for those of the culture in which she resides and to which she addressed her work: the Republic of South Africa. For within her country, the fact of living amongst the plurality of cultures, both black and white, is a daily confrontation that those of us who live in a more heterogenous culture (as opposed to South Africa with multiple cultures within a single hegemony) cannot so easily understand.

Consider the magnitude of the situation. Dr. Bührmann, an Afrikaner of a long-established and distinguished family of Dutch tradition, a child psychiatrist and Jungian analyst practicing in South Africa, dedicates her book, "To my parents and Mongezi Tisu who taught me the meaning of respect" (p. v). This dedicatory statement, which can go all but unnoticed outside South Africa, is an astonishing cultural announcement. It states that she has two "parental" sources of nourishment, white and black, and she underscores this dedication with a statement of Jung, "We fear and reject with horror any sign of living sympathy, partly because a sympathetic understanding might permit contact with an alien spirit to become a serious experience (Jung 1958, par. 1). One must ponder this. A woman physician of the soul pays homage to the love and nourishings of her white parents as well as to the nourishing that a black physician of the soul gave to her in her quest for an understanding of native healing. The dedication, aside from being a most courageous utterance to a most troubled culture, is the mark of the woman herself. If readers of this book outside her culture do not reflect upon the dedication, the *ethos* of this exercise in psychological anthropology cannot be sympathetically understood.

Lee Zahner-Roloff, Ph.D., Professor, Department of Performance Studies, Northwestern University, is the author of *Perception and Evocation in Literature* (1973) and is a practicing Jungian analyst in Evanston, Illinois.

Living in Two Worlds is an account of Dr. Bührmann's journey into the nature of preliterate healing practices, and is, notably, the encounter with her black counterpart Mongezi Tisu, a Xhosa living in the Ciskei, a geographical area west of the Transkei and northeast of Cape Town province, where Dr. Bührmann resides. Her work among the Xhosa, and particularly her accounts of Mr. Tisu's practice, has been chronicled in over twenty scholarly articles that have appeared in a variety of psychiatric and psychological journals. This book, in contrast to her scholarly essays, might more appropriately be called a professional autobiography, and though the modesty of the first-person presence is evident in her style, the scientific and emotional commitment to the cause of understanding an alternate mode of healing by Western standards is not. To her South African readership she writes:

> My concern in writing this book was to convey . . . understanding and to give the reader a glimpse of the inner world of another culture. The book is largely, but not exclusively, directed at the people of the Western world, and it aims at giving those of us living in a multiracial country a deeper knowledge, respect and acceptance of one another. . . . My hope is that through this knowledge we will complement and enrich one another and be stimulated to growth and development of greater awareness and increased consciousness. This should in turn enable us to live in two worlds with a greater degree of comfort. (pp. 99–100)

The vehicle that can assist in this understanding, the realm of psychological discourse that can amplify and provide a conceptual base for enlightening a culture and its healing practices, is the psychology of C. G. Jung. The healer, after all, is an archetypal presence in all cultures, though what is different between cultures are the forms of knowledge and the bases for this knowledge. As Bührmann stresses, the Western medical and scientific model has stressed a particular form of ego development and consciousness, a stress upon individuality and personal achievement, and preeminently, a rational discourse and methodology that articulates the nature of man and his presence in his created world. While prevalent in the West, this mode of consciousness is not universal, and it is from the differences in the mode of consciousness present among certain black peoples that the Western world can learn much. For while the West might enshrine rationality, for Bührmann's black counterpart the precise opposite is valued. This might be called an *umbelini* consciousness, a knowledge that originates within the body from the *solar plexus*, a knowledge "of the intestines," if you will. She writes:

> From my first contact with the healers and their ceremonies . . . I was so strongly influenced by the way in which preliterate people in therapy *act out* what the Western people *talk about* that I felt compelled to start a research programme, at considerable cost and discomfort to me. I felt the need to experience and understand the meaning of the methods of the healers, their rituals, ceremonies and symbols, so as to satisfy myself about the effectiveness of their healing procedures and the effect these had on me. (p. 13; italics in original)

Living in Two Worlds is an essay in the therapeutic methods that are *acted out* rather than *talked about*, an ancient form of healing that the West has developed into a host of "ancillary therapies" that are known by various names: active imagination, dance and movement therapy, poetry therapy, art therapy, and the like. But in contrast to the Xhosa culture of Dr. Bührmann (and all cultures in which "acting out" is valued) our western ancillary therapies do not function centrally to the therapeutic process, and they are bereft of a cultural imprimatur that places them at the heart of healing. Western healing does not have the cultural forms and traditions that would allow either an *intlombe* or a *xhentsa*, performed rituals in which altered states of consciousness are obtained through dance and movement. It is the particular genius of Jung to have understood that the making of images is an additional "royal road" to the unconscious, but even Jung could not cross cultural boundaries for the ecstasies of healing. Bührmann leads us across this boundary.

To give the book focus, Bührmann centers her attention upon the *amagqira* and the *igqira* (the indigenous healers), the nature of the condition (*thwasa*) by which one is called to be a healer, and the processes and ceremonies that lead to the healing from the states of *thwasa*, culminating in the cultural investiture of becoming an *igqira*. The Western equivalent for this would be in the identification of those talented to become analysts, the necessity of prolonged personal analysis (or analyses), and the conferring of suitable professional recognitions for the training process. Though Bührmann does not explicitly draw the parallels of these two processes in Western and black cultures, it is an implicit comparison, for after all it is a Western psychiatrist and analyst who is writing about the nature of training that she observed in her black counterpart, Mr. Tisu. The quest is "wholemaking" (her term), and from the diagnosis to the final ceremony of investiture, from *thwasa* to *amagqira*, the reader is led into the other world from Western medicine and psychoanalysis.

The process that Bührmann stresses and elaborates is something like this: Among the Xhosa there must be a persistent and prevailing awareness of what the continuity of relatedness demands, and by this is meant that a person who "falls away" from the ancestors and their wishes, their promptings, their prerogatives and wisdom falls, or is capable of falling, into *thwasa*. This state is a disorientation for the person, a state in which physical (somatic) and spiritual (psychological) malaise reigns. Only by a reorientation to the ancestors through dream consciousness (the "callings" of the ancestors), proper healing rituals and realignments to the cultural base of body and spirit, and the meticulous observances of healing rituals (*intlombe* and *xhentsa*) can the inner and outer world be put right. Here, the person is reunited with the collectivity of the truer identity. The base is culture not person (as contrasted with the Western psychological emphasis upon the person and not culture, an enantiodromian difference of some consequence). Yet, there is one condition that persists among the blacks that is greatly misunderstood by the white and Western consciousness, and for Bührmann this misunderstanding is because there is no real Western counterpart. And this is bewitchment. While the causes for this are complex, the effects are all too evident: a complete loss of personal responsibility, and, worse, the presence of a psychological futility that can lead to death. In a rigorous personal psychology, this may appear as irrational, but among blacks it is a reality of stunning and tragic consequences. In a culture that would fail to understand bewitchment, responsibility would be laid to personal actions alone and not to the collective agony by which soul is lost to another. By understanding bewitchment and its causes, by employing the proper healing procedures for the elimination of bewitchment, and by empathetically understanding the cultural phenomenon, the treatment of African blacks can be not only understood but also can be adapted to Western humankind. It is precisely this level of understanding that marks *Living in Two Worlds* as a psychological treatise of great importance for Western analysts.

Bührmann concludes her work:

> When I started on my unconsciously prompted voyage into the inner world of Black people I did not know that I was setting out on a quest for the numinous and the non-rational. The measure of success which I seem to have achieved can largely be attributed to the personalities and attitudes of my Black mentors. They made it possible for me to fathom some of their ideas about the causes underlying illness and their therapeutic procedures and thus illustrated that what appears to be irrational is really symbolic and mythical and portrays the lawfulness of the collective psyche. (pp. 103–104)

What she accomplished for herself has been translated into a model for all analysts and professionals in the psychiatric and psychological professions. Is it possible to bridge two vastly different realms of consciousness, knowing and living? Is it possible to translate black modes of healing into the correlative language of Western psychological discourse? The answer is yes, and it is an answer to the crippling and limiting projection of Western ego psychology upon all peoples. And Bührmann concurs with Jung's belief that "psychic reality still exists in its original oneness and awaits man's advance to a level of consciousness where he no longer believes in the one part and denies the other but recognizes both as constituent elements of one psyche" (Jung 1954, par. 682). *Living in Two Worlds* is a metaphor that is easily recognized, and from South Africa has come a voice of compassion, tolerance, generosity, and psychological understanding uncommon in our time.

References

Jung, C. G. 1954. *The practice of psychotherapy.* In *Collected works*, vol. 16. Princeton: Princeton University Press, 1966.
————. 1958. *Psychology and religion: West and east.* In *Collected works*, vol. 11. Princeton: Princeton University Press, 1969.